COMMITTED

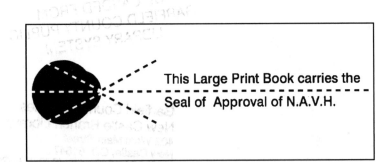

This Large Print Book carries the
Seal of Approval of N.A.V.H.

COMMITTED

A SKEPTIC MAKES PEACE WITH MARRIAGE

ELIZABETH GILBERT

LARGE PRINT PRESS
A part of Gale, Cengage Learning

GALE
CENGAGE Learning

Detroit • New York • San Francisco • New Haven, Conn • Waterville, Maine • London

Copyright © Elizabeth Gilbert, 2010.
Large Print Press, a part of Gale, Cengage Learning.

ALL RIGHTS RESERVED
The text of this Large Print edition is unabridged.
Other aspects of the book may vary from the original edition.
Set in 16 pt. Plantin.

LIBRARY OF CONGRESS CATALOGING-IN-PUBLICATION DATA

Gilbert, Elizabeth, 1969–
    Committed : a skeptic makes peace with marriage / by Elizabeth Gilbert.
        p. cm.
    ISBN-13: 978-1-4104-2276-7 (hardcover : alk. paper)
    ISBN-10: 1-4104-2276-3 (hardcover : alk. paper)
        1. Gilbert, Elizabeth, 1969– 2. Divorced women—United States—Biography. 3. Wives—United States—Biography. 4. Marriage. 5. Large type books. I. Title.
    HQ834.G48 2010b
    306.81—dc22   2009039043

ISBN 13: 978-1-59413-453-1 (pbk. : alk. paper)
ISBN 10: 1-59413-453-7 (pbk. : alk. paper)

Published in 2011 by arrangement with Viking, a member of Penguin Group (USA) Inc.

Printed in the United States of America
1 2 3 4 5 6 7 15 14 13 12 11

Para J.L.N. — o meu coroa

There is no greater risk
than matrimony.
But there is nothing happier than a
happy marriage.
BENJAMIN DISRAELI, 1870,
IN A LETTER TO QUEEN VICTORIA'S
DAUGHTER LOUISE, CONGRATULATING
HER ON HER ENGAGEMENT

CONTENTS

A NOTE TO THE READER

A few years ago, I wrote a book called *Eat, Pray, Love,* which told the story of a journey I had taken around the world, alone, after a bad divorce. I was in my midthirties when I wrote that book, and everything about it represented a huge departure for me as a writer. Before *Eat, Pray, Love,* I had been known in literary circles (if I was known at all) as a woman who wrote predominantly for, and about, men. I'd been working for years as a journalist for such male-focused magazines as *GQ* and *Spin,* and I had used those pages to explore masculinity from every possible angle. Similarly, the subjects of my first three books (both fiction and nonfiction) were all supermacho characters: cowboys, lobster fishermen, hunters, truckers, Teamsters, woodsmen . . .

Back then, I was often told that I wrote like a man. Now, I'm not entirely sure what writing "like a man" even means, but I do believe it is generally intended as a compliment. I certainly took it as a compliment at the time. For one *GQ* article, I even went so far as to impersonate a man for a week. I cropped my hair, flattened my breasts, stuffed a birdseed-filled condom down my pants, and affixed a soul patch beneath my lower lip — all in an effort to somehow inhabit and comprehend the alluring mysteries of manhood.

I should add here that my fixation with men also extended into my private life. Often this brought complications.

No — *always* this brought complications.

Between my romantic entanglements and my professional obsessions, I was so absorbed by the subject of maleness that I never spent any time whatsoever contemplating the subject of femaleness. I certainly never spent any time contemplating my *own* femaleness. For that reason, as well as a general indifference toward my own well-being, I never became very familiar to myself. So when a massive wave of depression finally struck me down around the age of thirty, I had no way of understanding or articulating what was happening to me. My body fell apart first, then my marriage, and then — for a terrible and frightening interval — my mind. Masculine flint offered no solace in this situation; the only way out of the emotional tangle was to feel my way through it. Divorced, heartbroken, and lonely, I left everything behind and took off for a year of travel and introspection, intent on scrutinizing myself as closely as I'd once studied the elusive American cowboy.

Then, because I am a writer, I wrote a book about it.

Then, because life is really strange sometimes, that book became a megajumbo international best seller, and I suddenly found myself — after a decade spent writing exclusively about men and maleness — being referred to as a chick-lit author. Again, I'm not entirely sure what "chick-lit" even means, but I'm pretty certain it's never intended as a compliment.

In any case, people ask me all the time now whether I saw any of this coming. They want to know if, as I was writing *Eat, Pray, Love,* I had somehow anticipated how big it would become. No. There was no way in the world I could possibly have predicted or planned for such an overwhelming response. If anything, I'd been hoping as I wrote the book that I'd be forgiven for writing a memoir at all. I had only a handful of readers, it was true, but they were loyal readers, and they had always liked the stalwart young lady who wrote tough-minded stories about manly men doing manly things. I did not anticipate that those readers would enjoy a rather emotional first-person chronicle about a divorced woman's quest for psychospiritual healing. I hoped they would be generous enough, though, to understand that I had needed to write that book for my own personal reasons, and maybe everyone would let it slide, and then we could all move on.

That was not how things turned out.

(And just to be clear: The book that you are now holding is not a tough-minded story about manly men doing manly things either. Never let it be said that you were not warned!)

Another question people ask me all the time these days is how *Eat, Pray, Love* has changed my life. That one is difficult to answer because the scope has been so massive. A useful analogy from my childhood: When I was little, my parents once took me to the American Museum of Natural History in New York City. We stood there together in the Hall of Oceans. My dad pointed up toward the ceiling at the life-sized model of the great blue whale that hung suspended over our heads. He tried to impress upon me the size of this gargantuan creature, but I could not see the whale. I was standing right underneath the whale, mind you, and I was staring directly up at the whale, but I could not absorb the whale. My mind had no mechanism for comprehending something so large. All I could see was the blue ceiling and the wonderment on everyone else's faces (obviously something exciting was happening here!), but I could not grasp the whale itself.

That's how I feel sometimes about *Eat, Pray, Love*. There came a point in that book's trajectory when I could no longer sanely absorb its dimensions, so I gave up trying and turned my attention to other pursuits. Planting a garden helped; there's nothing like picking slugs off your tomato plants to keep things in perspective.

That said, it has been a bit of a perplexity for me to figure out how, after that phenomenon, I would ever write unself-consciously again. Not to act all falsely nostalgic for literary obscurity, but in the past I had always written my books in the belief that very few people would read them. For the most part, of course, that knowledge had always been depressing. In one critical way, though, it was comforting: If I humiliated myself too atrociously, at least there wouldn't be many witnesses. Either way, the question was now academic: I suddenly had millions of readers awaiting my next project. How in the world does one go about writing a book that will satisfy millions? I didn't want to blatantly pander, but I also didn't want to dismiss out of hand all those bright, passionate, and predominantly female readers — not after everything we'd been through together.

Uncertain of how to proceed, I proceeded anyhow. Over the course of a year, I wrote an entire first draft of this very book — five hundred pages — but I realized immediately upon completion that it was somehow wrong. The voice didn't sound like me. The voice didn't sound like anybody. The voice sounded like something coming through a megaphone, mistranslated. I put that manuscript away, never to be looked at again, and headed back out to the garden for some more contemplative digging, poking, and pondering.

I want to make it clear here that this was not exactly a *crisis,* that period when I could not figure out how to write — or, at least, when I could not figure out how to write naturally. Life was really nice otherwise, and I was grateful enough for personal contentment and professional success that I wasn't about to manufacture a calamity from this particular puzzle. But it certainly was a puzzle. I even started wondering if maybe I was finished as a writer. Not being a writer anymore didn't seem like the worst fate in the world, if indeed that was to be my fate, but I honestly couldn't tell yet. I had to spend a lot more hours in the tomato patch, is all I'm saying, before I could sort this thing out.

In the end, I found a certain comfort in recognizing that I could not — *cannot* — write a book that would satisfy millions of readers. Not deliberately, anyhow. The fact is, I do not know how to write a beloved best seller on demand. If I knew how to write beloved best sellers on demand, I can assure you that I would have been writing them all along, because it would have made my life a lot easier and more comfortable ages ago. But it doesn't work that way — or at least not for writers like me. We write only the books that we need to write, or are able to write, and then we must release them, recognizing that whatever happens to them next is somehow none of our business.

For a multitude of personal reasons, then, the book that I needed to write was exactly *this* book — another memoir (with extra socio-historical bonus sections!) about my

17

efforts to make peace with the complicated institution of marriage. The subject matter was never in doubt; it's just that I had trouble there for a while finding my voice. Ultimately I discovered that the only way I could write again at all was to vastly limit — at least in my own imagination — the number of people I was writing *for.* So I started completely over. And I did not write this version of *Committed* for millions of readers. Instead, I wrote it for exactly twenty-seven readers. To be precise, the names of those twenty-seven readers are: Maude, Carole, Catherine, Ann, Darcey, Deborah, Susan, Sofie, Cree, Cat, Abby, Linda, Bernadette, Jen, Jana, Sheryl, Rayya, Iva, Erica, Nichelle, Sandy, Anne, Patricia, Tara, Laura, Sarah, and Margaret.

Those twenty-seven women constitute my small but critically important circle of female friends, relatives, and neighbors. They range in age from their early twenties to their midnineties. One of them happens to be my grandmother; another is my step-daughter. One is my oldest friend; another is my newest friend. One is freshly married; another two or so sorely wish to be married; a few have recently remarried; one in particular is unspeakably grateful never to have married at all; another just ended a nearly decade-long relationship with a woman. Seven are mothers; two (as of this writing) are pregnant; the rest — for a variety of reasons and with a wide range of feelings about it — are childless. Some are homemakers; others are professionals; a couple of them, bless their hearts, are homemakers *and* professionals. Most are white; a few are black; two were born in the Middle East; one is Scandinavian; two are Australian; one is South American; another is Cajun. Three are devoutly religious; five are utterly uninterested in all questions of divinity; most are somewhat spiritually perplexed; the others have somehow, over the years, brokered their own private agreements with God. All these women have an above-average sense of humor. All of them, at some point in their lives, have experienced heartbreaking loss.

Over many years, over many cups of tea and booze, I have sat with one or another of these dear souls and wondered aloud over questions of marriage, intimacy, sexuality, divorce, fidelity, family, responsibility, and autonomy. This book was built on the bones of those conversations. While I pieced together various pages of this story, I would find myself literally speaking aloud to these friends, relatives, and neighbors — responding to questions that sometimes dated back decades, or posing new questions of my own. This book could never have come into existence without the influence of those twenty-seven extraordinary women and I am enormously grateful for their collective presence. As ever, it has been an education and a comfort just to have them in the room.

ELIZABETH GILBERT
New Jersey, 2009

CHAPTER ONE: MARRIAGE AND SURPRISES

MARRIAGE IS A FRIENDSHIP
RECOGNIZED BY THE POLICE.
— *Robert Louis Stevenson*

Late one afternoon in the summer of 2006, I found myself in a small village in northern Vietnam, sitting around a sooty kitchen fire with a number of local women whose language I did not speak, trying to ask them questions about marriage.

For several months already, I had been traveling across Southeast Asia with a man who was soon to become my husband. I suppose the conventional term for such an individual would be "fiancé," but neither one of us was very comfortable with that word, so we weren't using it. In fact, neither one of us was very comfortable with this whole idea of matrimony at all. Marriage was not something we had ever planned with each other, nor was it something either of us wanted. Yet providence had interfered with our plans, which was why we were now wandering haphazardly across Vietnam, Thailand, Laos, Cambodia, and

Indonesia, all the while making urgent — even desperate — efforts to return to America and wed.

The man in question had been my lover, my sweetheart, for over two years by then, and in these pages I shall call him Felipe. Felipe is a kind, affectionate Brazilian gentleman, seventeen years my senior, whom I'd met on another journey (an actual planned journey) that I'd taken around the world a few years earlier in an effort to mend a severely broken heart. Near the end of those travels, I'd encountered Felipe, who had been living quietly and alone in Bali for years, nursing his own broken heart. What had followed was attraction, then a slow courtship, and then, much to our mutual wonderment, love.

Our resistance to marriage, then, had nothing to do with an absence of love. On the contrary, Felipe and I loved each other unreservedly. We were happy to make all sorts of promises to stay together faithfully forever. We had even sworn lifelong fidelity to each other already, although quite privately. The problem was that the two of us were both survivors of bad divorces, and we'd been so badly gutted by our experiences that the very idea of legal marriage — with *anyone,* even with such nice people as each other — filled us with a heavy sense of dread.

As a rule, of course, most divorces are pretty bad (Rebecca West observed that "getting a divorce is nearly always as cheerful and useful an occupation as breaking very valuable china"), and our divorces had been no exception. On the mighty cosmic one-to-ten Scale of Divorce Badness (where one equals an amicably executed separation, and ten equals . . . well, an actual execution), I would probably rate my own divorce as something like a 7.5. No suicides or homicides had resulted, but aside from that, the rupture had been about as ugly a proceeding as two otherwise well-mannered people could have possibly manifested. And it had dragged on for more than two years.

As for Felipe, his first marriage (to an intelligent, professional Australian woman) had ended almost a decade before we'd met in Bali. His divorce had unfolded graciously enough at the time, but losing his wife (and access to the house and kids and almost two decades of history that came along with her) had inflicted on this good man a lingering legacy of sadness, with special emphases on regret, isolation, and economic anxiety.

Our experiences, then, had left the two of us taxed, troubled, and decidedly suspicious of the joys of holy wedded matrimony. Like anyone who has ever walked through the valley of the shadow of divorce, Felipe and I had each learned firsthand this distressing truth: that every intimacy carries, secreted somewhere below its initial lovely surfaces, the ever-coiled makings of complete catastrophe. We had also learned that marriage is an estate that is very much easier to enter than it is to exit. Unfenced by law, the unmarried lover can quit a bad relationship at any time. But you — the legally married person who wants to escape doomed love — may soon discover that a significant portion of your marriage contract belongs to the State, and that it sometimes takes a very long while for the State to grant you your leave. Thus, you can feasibly find yourself trapped for months or even years in a loveless legal bond that has come to feel rather like a burning building. A burning building in which you, my friend, are handcuffed to a radiator somewhere down in the basement, unable to wrench yourself free, while the smoke billows forth and the rafters are collapsing . . .

I'm sorry — does all this sound unenthusiastic?

I share these unpleasant thoughts only to explain why Felipe and I had made a rather unusual pact with each other, right from the beginning of our love story. We had sworn with all our hearts to never, ever, under any circumstances, marry. We had even promised never to blend together our finances or our worldly assets, in order to avoid the potential nightmare of ever again having to divvy up an explosive personal munitions dump of shared mortgages, deeds, property, bank accounts, kitchen appliances, and favorite books. These promises having been duly pledged, the two of us proceeded forth into our carefully partitioned companionship with a real sense of calmness. For just as a sworn engagement can bring to so many other couples a sensation of encircling protection, our vow *never* to marry had cloaked the two of us in all the emotional security we required in order to try once more at love. And this commitment of ours — consciously devoid of official commitment — felt miraculous in its liberation. It felt as though we had found the Northwest Passage of Perfect Intimacy — something that, as García Márquez wrote, "resembled love, but without the problems of love."

So that's what we'd been doing up until the spring of 2006: minding our own business, building a delicately divided life together in unfettered contentment. And that is very well how we might have gone on living happily ever after, except for one terribly inconvenient interference.

The United States Department of Homeland Security got involved.

The trouble was that Felipe and I — while we shared many similarities and blessings — did not happen to share a nationality. He was a Brazilian-born man with Australian citizenship who, when we met, had been living mostly in Indonesia. I was an American woman who, my travels aside, had been living mostly on the East Coast of the United States. We didn't initially foresee any problems with our countryless love story, although in retrospect perhaps we should have anticipated complications. As the old adage goes: A fish and a bird may indeed fall in love, but where shall they live? The solution to this dilemma, we believed, was that we were both nimble travelers (I was a bird who could dive and Felipe was a fish who could fly), so for our first year together, at least, we basically lived in midair — diving and flying across oceans and continents in order to be together.

Our work lives, fortunately enough, facilitated such footloose arrangements. As a writer, I could carry my job with me any-place. As a jewelry and gemstone importer who sold his goods in the United States, Felipe always needed to be traveling anyhow. All we had to do was coordinate our loco-motion. So I would fly to Bali; he would come to America; we would both go to Brazil; we would meet up again in Sydney. I took a temporary job teaching writing at the University of Tennessee, and for a few curious months we lived together in a decaying old hotel room in Knoxville. (I can recommend *that* living arrangement, by the way, to anyone who wants to test out the actual compatibility levels of a new relationship.)

We lived at a staccato rhythm, on the hoof, mostly together but ever on the move, like witnesses in some odd international protec-tion program. Our relationship — though steadying and calm at the personal level — was a constant logistical challenge, and what with all that international air travel, it was bloody expensive. It was also psychologi-cally jarring. With each reunion, Felipe and I had to learn each other all over again. There was always that nervous moment at the airport when I would stand there wait-ing for him to arrive, wondering, *Will I still know him? Will he still know me?* After the first year, then, we both began to long for something more stable, and Felipe was the one who made the big move. Giving up his modest but lovely cottage in Bali, he moved with me to a tiny house I had recently rented on the outskirts of Philadelphia.

While trading Bali for the suburbs of Philly may seem a peculiar choice, Felipe swore that he had long ago grown tired of life in the tropics. Living in Bali was too easy, he complained, with each day a pleasant, boring replica of the day before. He had been longing to leave for some time already, he insisted, even before he'd met me. Now, growing bored with paradise might be impossible to understand for someone who has never actually lived in paradise (I certainly found the notion a bit crazy), yet Bali's dreamland setting honestly had come to feel oppressively dull to Felipe over the years. I will never forget one of the last enchanting evenings that he and I spent together at his cottage there — sitting outside, barefoot and dewy-skinned from the warm November air, drinking wine and watching a sea of constellations flicker above the rice fields. As the perfumed winds rustled the palm trees and as faint music from a distant temple ceremony floated on the breeze, Felipe looked at me, sighed, and said flatly, "I'm so sick of this shit. I can't wait to go back to Philly."

So — to Philadelphia (city of brotherly potholes) we duly decamped! The fact is we both liked the area a lot. Our little rental was near my sister and her family, whose proximity had become vital to my happiness over the years, so that brought familiarity. Moreover, after all our collective years of travel to far-flung places, it felt good and even revitalizing to be living in America, a country which, for all its flaws, was still *interesting* to both of us: a fast-moving, multicultural, ever-evolving, maddeningly contradictory, creatively challenging, and fundamentally alive sort of place.

There in Philadelphia, then, Felipe and I set up headquarters and practiced, with encouraging success, our first real sessions of shared domesticity. He sold his jewelry; I worked on writing projects that required me to stay in one place and conduct research. He cooked; I took care of the lawn; every once in a while one of us would fire up the vacuum cleaner. We worked well together in a home, dividing our daily chores without strife. We felt ambitious and productive and optimistic. Life was nice.

But such intervals of stability could never last long. Because of Felipe's visa restrictions, three months was the maximum amount of time that he could legally stay in America before he would have to excuse himself to another country for a spell. So off he would fly, and I would be alone with my books and my neighbors while he was gone. Then, after a few weeks, he'd return to the United States on another ninety-day visa and we'd recommence our domestic life together. It is a testament to how warily we both regarded long-term commitment that these ninety-day chunks of togetherness felt just about perfect for us: the exact amount of future planning that two tremulous divorce survivors could manage without feeling too threatened. And sometimes, when my schedule allowed, I would join him on his visa runs out of the country.

This explains why one day we were returning to the States together from a business trip overseas and we landed — due to the peculiarity of our cheap tickets and our connecting flight — at the Dallas/Fort Worth International Airport. I passed through Immigration first, moving easily through the line of my fellow repatriating American citizens. Once on the other side, I waited for Felipe, who was in the middle of a long line of foreigners. I watched as he approached the immigration official, who carefully studied Felipe's bible-thick Australian passport, scrutinizing every page, every mark, every hologram. Normally they were not so vigilant, and I grew nervous at how long this was taking. I watched and waited, listening for the all-important sound of any successful border crossing: that thick, solid, librarian-like *thunk* of a welcoming visa-entry stamp. But it never came.

Instead, the immigration official picked up his phone and made a quiet call. Moments later, an officer wearing the uniform of the United States Department of Homeland Security came and took my baby away.

The uniformed men at the Dallas airport held Felipe in interrogation for six hours. For six hours, forbidden to see him or ask questions, I sat there in a Homeland Security waiting room — a bland, fluorescent-lit space filled with apprehensive people from all over the world, all of us equally rigid with fear. I had no idea what they were doing to Felipe back there or what they were asking from him. I knew that he had not broken any laws, but this was not as comforting a thought as you might imagine. These were the late years of George W. Bush's presidential administration: not a relaxing moment in history to have your foreign-born sweetheart held in government custody. I kept trying to calm myself with the famous prayer of the fourteenth-century mystic Juliana of Norwich ("All shall be well, and all shall be well, and all manner of thing shall be well"), but I didn't believe a word of it. Nothing was well. Not one single manner of thing whatsoever was well.

Every once in a while I would stand up from my plastic chair and try to elicit more information from the immigration officer behind the bulletproof glass. But he ignored my pleas, each time reciting the same response: "When we have something to tell you about your boyfriend, miss, we'll let you know."

In a situation like this, may I just say, there is perhaps no more feeble-sounding word in the English language than *boyfriend.* The dismissive manner in which the officer uttered that word indicated how unimpressed he was with my relationship. Why on earth should a government employee ever release information about a mere *boyfriend?* I longed to explain myself to the immigration officer, to say, "Listen, the man you are detaining back there is far more important to me than you could ever begin to imagine." But even in my anxious state, I doubted this would do any good. If anything, I feared that pushing things too far might bring unpleasant repercussions on Felipe's end, so I backed off, helpless. It occurs to me only now that I probably should have made an effort to call a lawyer. But I didn't have a telephone with me, and I didn't want to abandon my post in the waiting room, and I didn't know any lawyers in Dallas, and it was a Sunday afternoon, anyhow, so who could I have reached?

Finally, after six hours, an officer came and led me through some hallways, through a rabbit warren of bureaucratic mysteries, to a small, dimly lit room where Felipe was sitting with the Homeland Security officer who had been interrogating him. Both men looked equally tired, but only one of those men was *mine* — my beloved, the most familiar face in the world to me. Seeing him in such a state made my chest hurt with longing. I wanted to touch him, but I sensed this was not allowed, so I remained standing.

Felipe smiled at me wearily and said, "Darling, our lives are about to get a lot more interesting."

Before I could respond, the interrogating officer quickly took charge of the situation and all its explanations.

"Ma'am," he said, "we've brought you

back here to explain that we will not be allowing your boyfriend to enter the United States anymore. We'll be detaining him in jail until we can get him on a flight out of the country, back to Australia, since he does have an Australian passport. After that, he won't be able to come back to America again."

My first reaction was physical. I felt as if all the blood in my body had instantly evaporated, and my eyes refused to focus for a moment. Then, in the next instant, my mind kicked into action. I revved through a fast summation of this sudden, grave crisis. Starting long before we had met, Felipe had made his living in the United States, visiting several times a year for short stays, legally importing gemstones and jewelry from Brazil and Indonesia for sale in American markets. America has always welcomed international businessmen like him; they bring merchandise and money and commerce into the country. In return, Felipe had prospered in America. He'd put his kids (who were now adults) through the finest private schools in Australia with income that he'd made in America over the decades. America was the center of his professional life, even though he'd never lived here until very recently. But his inventory was here and all his contacts were here. If he could never come back to America again, his livelihood was effectively destroyed. Not to mention the fact that I lived here in the United States, and that Felipe wanted to be with me, and that — because of my family and my work — I would always want to remain based in America. And Felipe had become part of my family, too. He'd been fully embraced by my parents, my sister, my friends, my world. So how would we continue our life together if he were forever banned? What would we do? (*"Where will you and I sleep?"* go the lyrics to a mournful Wintu love song. *"At the down-turned jagged rim of the sky? Where will you and I sleep?"*)

"On what grounds are you deporting him?" I asked the Homeland Security officer, trying to sound authoritative.

"Strictly speaking, ma'am, it's not a deportation." Unlike me, the officer didn't have to try sounding authoritative; it came naturally. "We're just refusing him entrance to the United States on the grounds that he's been visiting America too frequently in the last year. He's never overstayed his visa limits, but it does appear from all his comings and goings that he's been living with you in Philadelphia for three-month periods and then leaving the country, only to return

37

to the United States again immediately after."

This was difficult to argue, since that was precisely what Felipe had been doing.

"Is that a crime?" I asked.

"Not exactly."

"Not exactly, or no?"

"No, ma'am, it's not a crime. That's why we won't be arresting him. But the three-month visa waiver that the United States government offers to citizens of friendly countries is not intended for indefinite consecutive visits."

"But we didn't know that," I said.

Felipe stepped in now. "In fact, sir, we were once told by an immigration officer in New York that I could visit the United States as often as I liked, as long as I never overstayed my ninety-day visa."

"I don't know who told you that, but it isn't true."

Hearing the officer say this reminded me of a warning Felipe had given me once about international border crossings: "Never take it lightly, darling. Always remember that on any given day, for any given reason whatsoever, any given border guard in the world can decide that he does not want to let you in."

"What would you do now, if you were in

our situation?" I asked. This is a technique I've learned to use over the years whenever I find myself at an impasse with a dispassionate customer service operator or an apathetic bureaucrat. Phrasing the sentence in such a manner invites the person who has all the power to pause for a moment and put himself in the shoes of the person who is powerless. It's a subtle appeal to empathy. Sometimes it helps. Most of the time, to be honest, it doesn't help at all. But I was willing to try anything here.

"Well, if your boyfriend ever wants to come back into the United States again, he's going to need to secure himself a better, more permanent visa. If I were you, I would go about securing him one."

"Okay, then," I said. "What's the fastest way for us to secure him a better, more permanent visa?"

The Homeland Security officer looked at Felipe, then at me, then back at Felipe. "Honestly?" he said. "The two of you need to get married."

My heart sank, almost audibly. Across the tiny room, I could sense Felipe's heart sinking along with mine, in complete hollow tandem.

In retrospect, it does seem unbelievable

that this proposition could possibly have taken me by surprise. Had I never heard of a green card marriage before, for heaven's sake? Maybe it also seems unbelievable that — given the urgent nature of our circumstances — the suggestion of matrimony brought me distress instead of relief. I mean, at least we'd been given an option, right? Yet the proposition did take me by surprise. And it did hurt. So thoroughly had I barred the very notion of marriage from my psyche that hearing the idea spoken aloud now felt shocking. I felt mournful and sucker punched and heavy and banished from some fundamental aspect of my being, but most of all I felt *caught.* I felt we had both been caught. The flying fish and the diving bird had been netted. And my naïveté, not for the first time in my life, I'm afraid, struck me across the face like a wet slap: *Why had I been so foolish as to imagine that we could get away with living our lives as we pleased forever?*

Nobody spoke for a while, until the Homeland Security interrogation officer, regarding our silent faces of doom, asked, "Sorry, folks. What seems to be the problem with this idea?"

Felipe took off his glasses and rubbed his eyes — a sign, I knew from long experience, of utter exhaustion. He sighed, and said, "Oh, Tom, Tom, Tom . . ."

I had not yet realized that these two were on a first-name basis, though I suppose that's bound to happen during a six-hour interrogation session. Especially when the interrogatee is Felipe.

"No, seriously — what's the problem?" asked Officer Tom. "You two have obviously been cohabiting already. You obviously care about each other, you're not married to anyone else . . ."

"What you have to understand, Tom," explained Felipe, leaning forward and speaking with an intimacy which belied our institutional surroundings, "is that Liz and I have both been through really, really bad divorces in the past."

Officer Tom made a small noise — a sort of soft, sympathetic *"Oh . . ."* Then he took off his own glasses and rubbed his own eyes. Instinctively, I glanced at the third finger of his left hand. No wedding ring. From that bare left hand and from his reflexive re-action of tired commiseration I made a quick diagnosis: divorced.

It was here that our interview turned sur-real.

"Well, you could always sign a prenuptial agreement," Officer Tom suggested. "I mean, if you're worried about going through all the financial mess of a divorce again. Or if it's the relationship issues that scare you, maybe some counseling would be a good idea."

I listened in wonder. *Was a deputy of the United States Department of Homeland Security giving us* marital advice? *In an interrogation room? In the bowels of the Dallas/Fort Worth International Airport?*

Finding my voice, I offered this brilliant solution: "Officer Tom, what if I just found a way to somehow *hire* Felipe, instead of marrying him? Couldn't I bring him to America as my employee, instead of my husband?"

Felipe sat up straight and exclaimed, "Darling! What a terrific idea!"

Officer Tom gave us each an odd look. He asked Felipe, "You would honestly rather have this woman as your boss than your wife?"

"Dear God, yes!"

I could sense Officer Tom almost physically restraining himself from asking, "What the hell kind of people *are* you?" But he was far too professional for anything like that. Instead, he cleared his throat and said, "Unfortunately, what you have just proposed here is not legal in this country."

Felipe and I both slumped again, once more in complete tandem, into a depressed silence.

After a long spell of this, I spoke again. "All right," I said, defeated. "Let's get this over with. If I marry Felipe right now, right here in your office, will you let him into the country today? Maybe you have a chaplain here at the airport who could do that?"

There are moments in life when the face of an ordinary man can take on a quality of near-divinity, and this is just what happened now. Tom — a weary, badge-wearing, Texan Homeland Security officer with a paunch — smiled at me with a sadness, a kindness, a luminous compassion that was utterly out of place in this stale, dehumanizing room. Suddenly, he looked like a chaplain himself.

"Oh no-o-o . . . ," he said gently. "I'm afraid things don't work that way."

Looking back on it all now, of course I realize that Officer Tom already knew what was facing Felipe and me, far better than we ourselves could have known. He well knew that securing an official United States fiancé visa, particularly after a "border incident" such as this one, would be no small feat. Officer Tom could foresee all the trouble that was now coming to us: from the lawyers in three countries — on three continents, no less — who would have to secure all the necessary legal documents; to the federal police reports that would be required from every country in which Felipe had ever lived; to the stacks of personal letters, photos, and other intimate ephemera which we would now have to compile to prove that our relationship was real (including, with maddening irony, such evidence as shared bank accounts — details we'd specifically gone through an awful lot of trouble in our lives to keep *separated*); to the fingerprinting; to the inoculations; to the requisite tuberculosis-screening chest X-rays; to the interviews at the American embassies abroad; to the military records that we would somehow have to recover of Felipe's Brazilian army service thirty-five years earlier; to the sheer expanse and expense of time that Felipe now would have to spend out of the country while this process played itself out; to — worst of all — the horrible uncertainty of not knowing whether any of this effort would be enough, which is to say, not knowing whether the United States government (behaving, in this regard, rather much like a stern, old-fashioned father) would ever even accept this man as a husband for me, its jealously guarded natural-born daughter.

So Officer Tom already knew all that, and the fact that he expressed sympathy toward us for what we were about to undergo was an unexpected turn of kindness in an otherwise devastating situation. That I never, prior to this moment, imagined myself praising a member of the Department of Homeland Security in print for his personal tenderness only highlights how bizarre this whole situation had become. But I should say here that Officer Tom did us one other kind deed, as well. (That is, before he handcuffed Felipe and led him off to the Dallas county jail, depositing him for the night in a cell filled with actual criminals.) The gesture that Officer Tom made was this: He left me and Felipe alone together in the interrogation room for two whole minutes, so that we could say our good-byes to each other in privacy.

When you have only two minutes to say good-bye to the person you love most in the world, and you don't know when you'll see each other again, you can become log-jammed with the effort to say and do and settle everything at once. In our two minutes alone in the interrogation room, then, we made a hasty, breathless plan. I would go home to Philadelphia, move out of our rented house, put everything into storage, secure an immigration lawyer and start this legal process moving. Felipe, of course, would go to jail. Then he would be deported back to Australia — even if, strictly speaking, he wasn't being legally "deported." (Please forgive me for using the word "deported" throughout the pages of this book, but I'm still not sure what else to call it when a person gets thrown out of a country.) Since Felipe had no life in Australia anymore, no home or financial prospects, he would make arrangements as quickly as possible to go somewhere cheaper to live — Southeast Asia, probably — and I would join him on that side of the world once I got things rolling on my end. There, we would wait out this indefinite period of uncertainty together.

While Felipe jotted down the phone numbers of his lawyer, his grown children, and his business partners so that I could alert everyone to his situation, I emptied out my handbag, frantically looking for things I could give him to keep him more comfortable in jail: chewing gum, all my cash, a bottle of water, a photograph of us together, and a novel I had been reading on the airplane titled, aptly enough, *The People's Act of Love*.

Then Felipe's eyes filled with tears and he

said, "Thank you for coming into my life. No matter what happens now, no matter what you decide to do next, just know that you've given me the two most joyful years I've ever known and I will never forget you."

I realized in a flash: *Dear God, the man thinks I might leave him now.* His reaction surprised me and touched me, but more than anything it shamed me. It had not crossed my mind, since Officer Tom had laid out the option, that I would *not* now marry Felipe and save him from exile — but apparently it had crossed *his* mind that he might now be ditched. He genuinely feared that I might abandon him, leaving him high and dry, broke and busted. Had I earned such a reputation? Was I really known, even within the boundaries of our small love story, as somebody who jumps ship at the first obstacle? But were Felipe's fears entirely unjustified, given my history? If our situations had been reversed, I would never have doubted for a moment the solidity of his loyalties, or his willingness to sacrifice virtually anything on my account. Could he be certain of the same steadfastness from me?

I had to admit that if this state of affairs had taken place ten or fifteen years earlier, I almost certainly would have bailed out on my endangered partner. I am sorry to confess that I possessed a scant amount of honor in my youth, if any, and behaving in a flighty and thoughtless manner was a bit of a specialty of mine. But being a person of character matters to me now, and matters only more as I grow older. At that moment, then — and I had only one moment left alone with Felipe — I did the only right thing by this man whom I adored. I vowed to him — drilling the words into his ear so he would grasp my earnestness — that I would not leave him, that I would do whatever it took to fix things, and that even if things could not somehow be fixed in America, we would always stay together anyhow, somewhere, wherever in the world that had to be.

Officer Tom came back into the room.

At the last instant, Felipe whispered to me, "I love you so much, I will even marry you."

"And I love *you* so much," I promised, "that I will even marry you."

Then the nice Homeland Security people separated us and handcuffed Felipe and led him away — first to jail and then off to exile.

As I flew home alone that night to our now-obsolete little existence in Philadelphia, I considered more soberly what I had just promised. I was surprised to find that I was not feeling weepy or panicky; somehow the situation seemed too grave for any of that. What I felt, instead, was a ferocious sense of focus — a sense that this situation must be addressed with the utmost seriousness. In the space of only a few hours, my life with Felipe had been neatly flipped upside down, as though by some great cosmic spatula. And now, it seemed, we were engaged to be married. This had certainly been a strange and rushed engagement ceremony. It felt more like something out of Kafka than out of Austen. Yet the engagement was nonetheless official because it needed to be.

Fine, then. So be it. I would certainly not be the first woman in my family's history who ever had to get married because of a serious situation — although my situation, at least, did not involve accidental pregnancy. Still, the prescription was the same: Tie the knot, and do it quickly. So that's what we would do. But here was the real problem, which I identified that night all alone on the plane back home to Philadelphia: I had no idea what marriage *was*.

I had already made this mistake — entering into marriage without understanding anything whatsoever about the institution — once before in my life. In fact, I had jumped into my first marriage, at the totally unfinished age of twenty-five, much the same way that a Labrador jumps into a swimming pool — with exactly that much preparation and foresight. Back when I was twenty-five, I was so irresponsible that I probably should not have been allowed to choose my own toothpaste, much less my own future, and so this carelessness, as you can imagine, came at a dear cost. I reaped the consequences in spades, six years later, in the grim setting of a divorce court.

Looking back on the occasion of my first wedding day, I'm reminded of Richard Aldington's novel *Death of a Hero,* in which he ponders his two young lovers on *their* ill-fated wedding day: "Can one tabulate the ignorances, the relevant ignorances, of George Augustus and Isabel when they pledged themselves together until death do us part?" I, too, was once a giddy young bride very much like Aldington's Isabel, about whom he wrote: "What she *didn't* know included almost the whole range of human knowledge. The puzzle is to find out what she *did* know."

Now, though — at the considerably less giddy age of thirty-seven — I was not convinced that I knew very much more than ever about the realities of institutionalized companionship. I had failed at marriage and thus I was terrified of marriage, but I'm not sure this made me an expert on marriage; this only made me an expert on failure and terror, and those particular fields are already crowded with experts. Yet destiny had intervened and was demanding marriage from me, and I'd learned enough from life's experiences to understand that destiny's interventions can sometimes be read as invitations for us to address and even surmount our biggest fears. It doesn't take a great genius to recognize that when you are pushed by circumstance to do the one thing you have always most specifically loathed and feared, this can be, at the very least, *an interesting growth opportunity.*

So it slowly dawned on me on the airplane out of Dallas — my world now turned back-to-front, my lover exiled, the two of us having effectively been sentenced to marry — that perhaps I should use this time to somehow make peace with the idea of matrimony before I jumped into it once again. Perhaps it would be wise to put a little effort into unraveling the mystery of what in the name of God and human history this befuddling, vexing, contradictory, and yet stubbornly enduring institution of marriage actually is.

So that is what I did. For the next ten months — while traveling with Felipe in a state of rootless exile and while working like a dog to get him back into America so we could safely wed (getting married in Australia or anywhere else in the world, Officer Tom had warned us, would merely irritate the Homeland Security Department and slow down our immigration process even more) — the only thing I thought about, the only thing I read about, and pretty much the only thing I talked about with anybody was the perplexing subject of matrimony.

I enlisted my sister back home in Philadelphia (who, conveniently, is an actual historian) to send me boxes of books about marriage. Wherever Felipe and I happened to be staying, I would lock myself up in our hotel room to study the books, passing untold hours in the company of such eminent matrimonial scholars as Stephanie Coontz and Nancy Cott — writers whose names I had never heard before but who now became my heroes and teachers. To be honest, all this studying made me a lousy tourist. During those months of travel, Felipe and I fetched up in many beautiful and fascinating places, but I'm afraid I didn't always pay close attention to our surroundings. This stretch of traveling never had the feeling of a carefree adventure anyhow. It felt more like an expulsion, a hegira. Traveling because you cannot go back home again, because one of you is not legally allowed to go home again, can never be an enjoyable endeavor.

Moreover, our financial situation was worrisome. *Eat, Pray, Love* was less than a year away from becoming a lucrative best seller, but that welcome development had not yet occurred, nor did we anticipate its ever occurring. Felipe was now completely cut off from his income source, so we were both living off the fumes of my last book contract, and I wasn't sure how long that would hold out. A while, yes — but not forever. I had recently begun working on a new novel, but my research and writing had now been interrupted by Felipe's deportation. So this is how we ended up going to Southeast Asia, where two frugal people can feasibly live on about thirty dollars a day. While I won't say that we exactly suffered during this period of exile (we were hardly starving political refugees, for heaven's sake), I will say that it was an extremely odd and tense way to live, with the oddness and tension only heightened by the uncertainty of the outcome.

We wandered for close to a year, waiting for the day when Felipe would be called to his interview at the American Consulate in Sydney, Australia. Flopping in the meantime from country to country, we came to resemble nothing more than an insomniac couple trying to find a restful sleeping position in a strange and uncomfortable bed. For many anxious nights, in many strange and uncomfortable beds indeed, I would lie there in the dark, working through my conflicts and prejudices about marriage, filtering through all the information I was reading, mining history for comforting conclusions.

I should clarify right away here that I limited my studies largely to an examination of marriage in Western history, and that this book will therefore reflect that cultural limitation. Any proper matrimonial historian or anthropologist will find huge gaps in my narrative, as I have left unexplored entire continents and centuries of human history, not to mention skipping over some pretty vital nuptial concepts (polygamy, as just one example). It would have been pleasurable for me, and certainly educational, to have delved more deeply into an examination of every possible marital custom on earth, but

I didn't have that kind of time. Trying to get a handle on the complex nature of matrimony in Islamic societies alone, for instance, would have taken me years of study, and my urgency had a deadline that precluded such extended contemplation. A very real clock was ticking in my life: Within one year — like it or not, ready or not — I had to get married. That being the case, it seemed imperative that I focus my attention on unraveling the history of monogamous Western marriage in order to better understand my inherited assumptions, the shape of my family's narrative, and my culturally specific catalogue of anxieties.

I hoped that all this studying might somehow mitigate my deep aversion to marriage. I wasn't sure how that would happen, but it had always been my experience in the past, anyhow, that the more I learned about something, the less it frightened me. (Some fears can be vanquished, Rumpelstiltskin-like, only by uncovering their hidden, secret names.) What I really wanted, more than anything, was to find a way to somehow embrace marriage to Felipe when the big day came rather than merely swallowing my fate like a hard and awful pill. Call me old-fashioned, but I thought it might be a nice touch to be happy on my wedding day.

Happy *and* conscious, that is.

This book is the story of how I got there.

And it all begins — because every story must begin somewhere — in the mountains of northern Vietnam.

CHAPTER TWO:
MARRIAGE
AND EXPECTATION

A MAN CAN BE HAPPY WITH ANY WOMAN AS
LONG AS HE DOES NOT LOVE HER.

— Oscar Wilde

A little girl found me that day.

Felipe and I had arrived in this particular village after an overnight journey from Hanoi on a loud, dirty, Soviet-era train. I can't rightly remember now why we went to this specific town, but I think some young Danish backpackers had recommended it to us. In any case, after the loud, dirty train journey, there had been a long, loud, dirty bus ride. The bus had finally dropped us off in a staggeringly beautiful place that teetered on the border with China — remote and verdant and wild. We found a hotel and when I stepped out alone to explore the town, to try to shake the stiffness of travel out of my legs, the little girl approached me.

She was twelve years old, I would learn later, but tinier than any American twelve-year-old I'd ever met. She was exceptionally beautiful. Her skin was dark and healthy, her hair glossy and braided, her compact body all sturdy and confident in a short woolen tunic. Though it was summertime and the days were sultry, her calves were wrapped in brightly colored wool leggings. Her feet tapped restlessly in plastic Chinese sandals. She had been hanging around our hotel for some time — I had spotted her when we were checking in — and now, when I stepped out of the place alone, she approached me full-on.

"What's your name?" she asked.

"I'm Liz. What's your name?"

"I'm Mai," she said, "and I can write it down for you so you can learn how to spell it properly."

"You certainly speak good English," I complimented her.

She shrugged. "Of course. I practice often with tourists. Also, I speak Vietnamese, Chinese, and some Japanese."

"What?" I joked. "No French?"

"*Un peu,*" she replied with a sly glance. Then she demanded, "Where are you from, Liz?"

"I'm from America," I said. Then, trying to be funny, since obviously she was from right there, I asked, "And where are *you* from, Mai?"

She immediately saw my funny and raised

it. "I am from my mother's belly," she replied, instantly causing me to fall in love with her.

Indeed, Mai was from Vietnam, but I realized later she would never have called herself Vietnamese. She was Hmong — a member of a small, proud, isolated ethnic minority (what anthropologists call "an original people") who inhabit the highest mountain peaks of Vietnam, Thailand, Laos, and China. Kurdish-like, the Hmong have never really belonged to any of the countries in which they live. They remain some of the world's most spectacularly independent people — nomads, storytellers, warriors, natural-born anticonformists, and a terrible bane to any nation that has ever tried to control them.

To understand the unlikelihood of the Hmong's continued existence on this planet you have to imagine what it would be like if, for instance, the Mohawk were still living in upstate New York exactly as they had for centuries, dressing in traditional clothing, speaking their own language, and absolutely refusing to assimilate. Stumbling on a Hmong village like this one, then, in the early years of the twenty-first century is an anachronistic wonder. Their culture provides a vanishingly rare window into an older version of the human experience. All of which is to say, if you want to know what your family was like four thousand years ago, they were probably something like the Hmong.

"Hey, Mai," I said. "Would you like to be my translator today?"

"Why?" she asked.

The Hmong are a famously direct people, so I laid it out directly: "I need to talk to some of the women in your village about their marriages."

"Why?" she demanded again.

"Because I'm getting married soon, and I would like some advice."

"You're too old to be getting married," Mai observed, kindly.

"Well, my boyfriend is old, too," I replied. "He's fifty-five years old."

She looked at me closely, let out a low whistle, and said, "Well. Lucky him."

I'm not sure why Mai decided to help me that day. Curiosity? Boredom? The hope that I would pass her some cash? (Which, of course, I did.) But regardless of her motive, she did agree. Soon enough, after a steep march over a nearby hillside, we arrived at Mai's stone house, which was tiny, soot-darkened, lit only by a few small windows, and nestled in one of the prettiest river valleys you could ever imagine. Mai led me inside and introduced me around to a group of women, all of them weaving, cooking, or cleaning. Of all the women, it was Mai's grandmother whom I found most immediately intriguing. She was the laughingest, happiest, four-foot-tall toothless granny I'd ever seen in my life. What's more, she thought me hilarious. Every single thing about me seemed to crack her up beyond measure. She put a tall Hmong hat on my head, pointed at me, and laughed. She stuck a tiny Hmong baby into my arms, pointed at me, and laughed. She draped me in a gorgeous Hmong textile, pointed at me, and laughed.

I had no problem with any of this, by the way. I had long ago learned that when you are the giant, alien visitor to a remote and foreign culture it is sort of your job to become an object of ridicule. It's the least you can do, really, as a polite guest. Soon more women — neighbors and relations — poured into the house. They also showed me their weavings, stuck their hats on my head, crammed my arms full of their babies, pointed at me, and laughed.

As Mai explained, her whole family — almost a dozen of them in total — lived in this one-room home. Everyone slept on the floor together. The kitchen was on one side and the wood stove for winter was on the other side. Rice and corn were stored in a loft above the kitchen, while pigs, chickens, and water buffalo were kept close by at all times. There was only one private space in the whole house and it wasn't much bigger than a broom closet. This, as I learned later in my reading, was where the newest bride and groom in any family were allowed to sleep alone together for the first few months of their marriage in order to get their sexual explorations out of the way in private. After that initial experience of privacy, though, the young couple joins the rest of the family again, sleeping with everyone else on the floor for the rest of their lives.

"Did I tell you that my father is dead?" Mai asked as she was showing me around.

"I'm sorry to hear that," I said. "When did it happen?"

"Four years ago."

"How did he die, Mai?"

"He died," she said coolly, and that settled it. Her father had died of death. The way people used to die, I suppose, before we knew very much about why or how. "When he died, we ate the water buffalo at his funeral." At this memory, her face flashed a complicated array of emotions: sadness at the loss of her father, pleasure at the remembrance of how good the water buffalo had tasted.

"Is your mother lonely?"

Mai shrugged.

It was hard to imagine loneliness here. Just as it was impossible to imagine where in this crowded domestic arrangement you might find the happier twin sister of loneliness: *privacy.* Mai and her mother lived in constant closeness with so many people. I was struck — not for the first time in my years of travel — by how isolating contemporary American society can seem by comparison. Where I come from, we have shriveled down the notion of what constitutes "a family unit" to such a tiny scale that it would probably be unrecognizable *as* a family to anybody in one of these big, loose, enveloping Hmong clans. You almost need an electron microscope to study the modern Western family these days. What you've got are two, possibly three, or maybe sometimes four people rattling around together in a giant space, each person with her own private physical and psychological domain, each person spending large amounts of the day completely separated from the others.

I don't want to suggest here that everything about the shrunken modern family unit is necessarily bad. Certainly women's lives and women's health improve whenever they reduce the number of babies they have, which is a resounding strike against the lure of bustling clan culture. Also, sociologists have long known that incidences of incest and child molestation increase whenever so many relatives of different ages live together in such close proximity. In a crowd so big, it can become difficult to keep track of or defend individuals — not to mention individuality.

But surely something has been lost, as well, in our modern and intensely private, closed-off homes. Watching the Hmong women interact with each other, I got to wondering whether the evolution of the ever smaller and ever more nuclear Western family has put a particular strain on modern marriages. In Hmong society, for instance, men and women don't spend all that much time together. Yes, you have a spouse. Yes, you have sex with that spouse. Yes, your fortunes are tied together. Yes, there might very well be love. But aside from that, men's and women's lives are quite firmly separated into the divided realms of their gender-specific tasks. Men work and socialize with other men; women work and socialize with other women. Case in point: there was not a single man to be found anywhere that day around Mai's house. Whatever the men were off doing (farming, drinking, talking, gambling) they were doing it somewhere else, alone together, separated from the universe of the women.

If you are a Hmong woman, then, you don't necessarily expect your husband to be your best friend, your most intimate confidant, your emotional advisor, your intellectual equal, your comfort in times of sorrow. Hmong women, instead, get a lot of that emotional nourishment and support from other women — from sisters, aunties, mothers, grandmothers. A Hmong woman has many voices in her life, many opinions and emotional buttresses surrounding her at all times. Kinship is to be found within arm's reach in any direction, and many female hands make light work, or at least lighter work, of the serious burdens of living.

At last, all the greetings having been exchanged and all the babies having been dandled and all the laughter having died down into politeness, we all sat. With Mai as our translator, I began by asking the grandmother if she would please tell me about Hmong wedding ceremonies.

It's all quite simple, the grandmother

explained patiently. Before a traditional Hmong wedding, it is required that the groom's family come and visit the bride's house, so the families work out a deal, a date, a plan. A chicken is always killed at this time in order to make the families' ghosts happy. Once the wedding date arrives, a good many pigs are killed. A feast is prepared and relatives come from every village to celebrate. Both the families chip in to cover expenses. There is a procession to the wedding table, and a relative of the groom will always carry an umbrella.

At this point, I interrupted to ask what the umbrella signified, but the question brought some confusion. Confusion, perhaps, over what the word "signifies" signifies. The umbrella is the umbrella, I was told, and it is carried because umbrellas are always carried at weddings. That is why, and that is that, and so it has always been.

Umbrella-related questions thereby resolved, the grandmother went on to explain the traditional Hmong marital custom of kidnapping. This is an ancient custom, she said, though it is much less in practice these days than it was in the past. Still, it does exist. Brides — who are sometimes consulted beforehand about their kidnapping and sometimes not — are abducted by their potential grooms, who carry them by pony to their own families' homes. This is all strictly organized and is permitted only on certain nights of the year, at celebrations after certain market days. (You can't just kidnap a bride any old time you want. There are *rules*.) The kidnapped girl is given three days to live in the home of her captor, with his family, in order to decide whether or not she would like to marry this fellow. Most of the time, the grandmother reported, the marriage proceeds with the girl's consent. On the rare occasion that the kidnapped potential bride doesn't embrace her captor, she is allowed to return home to her own family at the end of the three days, and the whole business is forgotten. Which sounded reasonable enough to me, as far as kidnappings go.

Where our conversation did turn peculiar for me — and for all of us in the room — was when I tried to get the grandmother to tell me the story of her own marriage, hoping to elicit from her any personal or emotional anecdotes about her own experience with matrimony. The confusion started immediately, when I asked the old woman, "What did you think of your husband, the first time you ever met him?"

Her entire wrinkled face arranged itself

into a look of puzzlement. Assuming that she — or perhaps Mai — had misunderstood the question, I tried again:

"When did you realize that your husband might be somebody you wanted to marry?"

Again, my question was met with what appeared to be polite bafflement.

"Did you know that he was special right away?" I tried once more. "Or did you learn to like him over time?"

Now some of the women in the room had started giggling nervously, the way you might giggle around a slightly crazy person — which was, apparently, what I had just become in their eyes.

I backed up and tried a different tack: "I mean, when did you first meet your husband?"

The grandmother sorted through her memory a bit on that one, but couldn't come up with a definitive answer aside from "long ago." It really didn't seem to be an important question for her.

"Okay, *where* did you first meet your husband?" I asked, trying to simplify the matter as much as possible.

Again, the very shape of my curiosity seemed a mystery to the grandmother. Politely, though, she gave it a try. She had never particularly *met* her husband before she married him, she tried to explain. She'd seen him around, of course. There are always a lot of people around, you know. She couldn't really remember. Anyway, she said, it is not an important question as to whether or not she knew him when she was a young girl. After all, as she concluded to the delight of the other women in the room, she certainly knows him now.

"But when did you fall in love with him?" I finally asked, point-blank.

The instant Mai translated this question, all the women in the room, except the grandmother, who was too polite, laughed aloud — a spontaneous outburst of mirth, which they then all tried to stifle politely behind their hands.

You might think this would have daunted me. Perhaps it should have daunted me. But I persisted, following up their peals of laughter with a question that struck them as even more ridiculous:

"And what do you believe is the secret to a happy marriage?" I asked earnestly.

Now they all really did lose it. Even the grandmother was openly howling with laughter. Which was fine, right? As has already been established, I am always perfectly willing to be mocked in a foreign country for somebody else's entertainment.

But in this case, I must confess, all the hilarity was a bit unsettling on account of the fact that I really did not get the joke. All I could understand was that these Hmong ladies and I were clearly speaking an entirely different language here (I mean, above and beyond the fact that we were *literally* speaking an entirely different language here). But what was so specifically absurd to them about my questions?

In the weeks to come, as I replayed this conversation over in my mind, I was forced to hatch my own theory about what had made me and my hosts so foreign and incomprehensible to each other on the subject of marriage. And here's my theory: Neither the grandmother nor any other woman in that room was placing her marriage at the center of her emotional biography in any way that was remotely familiar to me. In the modern industrialized Western world, where I come from, the person whom you choose to marry is perhaps the single most vivid representation of your own personality. Your spouse becomes the most gleaming possible mirror through which your emotional individualism is reflected back to the world. There is no choice more intensely personal, after all, than whom you choose to marry; that choice tells us, to a large extent, who you are. So if you ask any typical modern Western woman how she met her husband, when she met her husband, and why she fell in love with her husband, you can be plenty sure that you will be told a complete, complex, and deeply personal narrative which that woman has not only spun carefully around the entire experience, but which she has memorized, internalized, and scrutinized for clues as to her own selfhood. Moreover, she will more than likely share this story with you quite openly — even if you arc a perfect stranger. In fact, I have found over the years that the question "How did you meet your husband?" is one of the best conversational icebreakers ever invented. In my experience, it doesn't even matter whether that woman's marriage has been happy or a disaster: It will still be relayed to you as a vitally important story about her emotional being — perhaps even *the* most vitally important story about her emotional being.

Whoever that modern Western woman is, I can promise you that her story will concern two people — herself and her spouse — who, like characters in a novel or movie, are presumed to have been on some kind of personal life's journeys before meeting each other, and whose journeys then intersected at a fateful moment. (For instance: "I was living in San Francisco that summer, and I had no intention of staying much longer — until I met Jim at that party.") The story will probably have drama and suspense ("He thought I was dating the guy I was there with, but that was just my gay friend Larry!"). The story will have doubts ("He wasn't really my type; I normally go for guys who are more intellectual"). Critically, the story will end either with salvation ("Now I can't imagine my life without him!"), or — if things have turned sour — with recriminating second-guesses ("Why didn't I admit to myself right away that he was an alcoholic and a liar?"). Whatever the details, you can be certain that the modern Western woman's love story will have been examined by her from every possible angle, and that, over the years, her narrative will have been either hammered into a golden epic myth or embalmed into a bitter cautionary tale.

I'm going to go way out on a limb here and state: Hmong women don't seem to do that. Or at least not *these* Hmong women.

Please understand, I am not an anthropologist and I acknowledge that I am operating far above my pay grade when I make any conjectures whatsoever about Hmong culture. My personal experience with these women was limited to a single afternoon's conversation, with a twelve-year-old child acting as a translator, so I think it's safe to assume that I probably missed a smidge of nuance about this ancient and intricate society. I also concede that these women may have found my questions intrusive, if not outright offensive. Why should they have told their most intimate stories to me, a nosy interloper? And even if they were somehow trying to impart information to me about their relationships, it's likely that certain subtle messages fell by the wayside through mistranslation or a simple lack of cross-cultural understanding.

All that said, though, I am somebody who has spent a large chunk of her professional life interviewing people, and I trust my ability to watch and listen closely. Moreover, like all of us, whenever I enter the family homes of strangers, I am quick to notice the ways in which they may look at or do things differently than my family looks at or does things. Let us say, then, that my role that day in that Hmong household was that of a more-than-averagely observant visitor who was paying a more-than-average amount of attention to her more-than-averagely expressive hosts. In that role, and only in that role, I feel fairly confident reporting what I did *not* see happening that day in Mai's grandmother's house. I did *not* see a group of women sitting around weaving overexamined myths and cautionary tales about their marriages. The reason I found this so notable was that I have watched women all over the world weave overexamined myths and cautionary tales about their marriages, in all sorts of mixed company, and at the slightest provocation. But the Hmong ladies did not seem remotely interested in doing that. Nor did I see these Hmong women crafting the character of "the husband" into either the hero or the villain in some vast, complex, and epic Story of the Emotional Self.

I'm not saying that these women don't love their husbands, or that they never had loved them, or that they never *could.* That would be a ridiculous thing to infer, because people everywhere love each other and always have. Romantic love is a universal human experience. Evidence of passion exists in all corners of this world. All human cultures have love songs and love charms and love prayers. People's hearts get broken across every possible social, religious, gender, age, and cultural boundary. (In India, just so you know, May 3 is National Broken Hearts Day. And in Papua New

Guinea, there exists a tribe whose men write mournful love songs called *namai,* which tell the tragic stories of marriages which never came to pass but should have.) My friend Kate once went to a concert of Mongolian throat singers who were traveling through New York City on a rare world tour. Although she couldn't understand the words to their songs, she found the music almost unbearably sad. After the concert, Kate approached the lead Mongolian singer and asked, "What are your songs about?" He replied, "Our songs are about the same things that everyone else's songs are about: lost love, and somebody stole your fastest horse."

So of course the Hmong fall in love. Of course they feel preference for one person over another person, or miss a beloved one who has died, or find that they inexplicably adore somebody's particular smell, or laugh. But perhaps they don't believe that any of that romantic love business has very much to do with the *actual reasons for marriage.* Perhaps they do not assume that those two distinct entities (love and marriage) must necessarily intersect — either at the beginning of the relationship or maybe ever at all. Perhaps they believe that marriage is about something else altogether.

If this sounds like a foreign or crazy notion, remember that it wasn't so long ago that people in Western culture held these same sorts of unromantic views about matrimony. Arranged marriage has never been a prominent feature of American life, of course — much less bridal kidnapping — but certainly *pragmatic* marriages were routine at certain levels of our society until fairly recently. By "pragmatic marriage," I mean any union where the interests of the larger community are considered above the interests of the two individuals involved; such marriages were a feature of American agricultural society, for instance, for many, many generations.

I personally know of one such pragmatic marriage, as it turns out. When I was growing up in my small town in Connecticut, my favorite neighbors were a white-haired husband and wife named Arthur and Lillian Webster. The Websters were local dairy farmers who lived by an inviolable set of classic Yankee values. They were modest, frugal, generous, hardworking, unobtrusively religious, and socially discreet members of the community who raised their three children to be good citizens. They were also enormously kind. Mr. Webster called me "Curly" and let me ride my bike for hours on their nicely paved parking lot. Mrs. Webster — if I was very good — would sometimes let me play with her collection of antique medicine bottles.

Just a few years ago, Mrs. Webster passed away. A few months after her death, I went out to dinner with Mr. Webster, and we got to talking about his wife. I wanted to know how they had met, how they had fallen in love — all the romantic beginnings of their life together. I asked him all the same questions, in other words, that I would eventually ask the Hmong ladies in Vietnam, and I got the same sorts of replies — or lack of replies. I couldn't dredge up a single romantic memory from Mr. Webster about the origins of his marriage. He couldn't even remember the precise moment when he had first met Lillian, he confessed. She had always been around town, as he recalled. It was certainly not love at first sight. There was no moment of electricity, no spark of instant attraction. He had never become infatuated with her in any way.

"So why did you marry her?" I asked.

As Mr. Webster explained in his typically open and matter-of-fact Yankee manner, he had gotten married because his brother had instructed him to get married. Arthur was soon going to be taking over the family farm and therefore he needed a wife. You cannot run a proper farm without a wife, any more than you can run a proper farm without a tractor. It was an unsentimental message, but dairy farming in New England was an unsentimental business, and Arthur knew his brother's edict was on target. So, the diligent and obedient young Mr. Webster went out there into the world and dutifully secured himself a wife. You got the feeling, listening to his narrative, that any number of young ladies might have gotten the job of being "Mrs. Webster," instead of Lillian herself, and it wouldn't have made a huge difference to anyone at the time. Arthur just happened to settle on the blonde one, the one who worked over at the Extension Service in town. She was the right age for it. She was nice. She was healthy. She was good. She would do.

The Websters' marriage, therefore, clearly did not launch from a place of passionate, personal, and fevered love — no more than the Hmong grandmother's marriage had. We might therefore assume, then, that such a union is "a loveless marriage." But we have to be careful about drawing such assumptions. I know better, at least when it comes to the case of the Websters.

In her waning years, Mrs. Webster was

diagnosed with Alzheimer's disease. For almost a decade, this once-powerful woman wasted away in a manner that was agonizing to watch for everyone in the community. Her husband — that pragmatic old Yankee farmer — took care of his wife at home the entire time she was dying. He bathed her, fed her, gave up freedoms in order to keep watch over her, and learned to endure the dreadful consequences of her decay. He tended to this woman long after she knew who he was anymore — even long after she knew who she herself was anymore. Every Sunday, Mr. Webster dressed his wife in nice clothing, put her in a wheelchair, and brought her to services at the same church where they had been married almost sixty years earlier. He did this because Lillian had always loved that church, and he knew she would've appreciated the gesture if only she had been conscious of it. Arthur would sit there in the pew beside his wife, Sunday after Sunday, holding her hand while she slowly ebbed away from him into oblivion.

And if that isn't love, then somebody is going to have to sit me down and explain to me very carefully what love actually is.

That said, we have to be careful, too, not to assume that all arranged marriages across history, or all pragmatic marriages, or all marriages that begin with an act of kidnap-ping, necessarily resulted in years of con-tentment. The Websters were lucky, to an extent. (Though they also put a good deal of work into their marriage, one suspects.) But what Mr. Webster and the Hmong people perhaps have in common is a notion that the emotional place where a marriage begins is not nearly as important as the emotional place where a marriage finds itself toward the end, after many years of partnership. Moreover, they would likely agree that there is not one special person waiting for you somewhere in this world who will make your life magically complete, but that there are any number of people (right in your own community, probably) with whom you could seal a respectful bond. Then you could live and work along-side that person for years, with the hope that tenderness and affection would be the gradual outcome of your union.

At the end of my afternoon's visit at Mai's family's house, I was granted the clearest possible insight into this notion when I asked the tiny old Hmong grandmother one final question, which again, she thought bizarre and foreign.

"Is your man a good husband?" I asked.

The old woman had to ask her granddaughter to repeat the question several times, just to make sure she'd heard it correctly: *Is he a* good *husband?* Then she gave me a bemused look, as though I'd asked, "These stones which compose the mountains in which you live — are they *good* stones?"

The best answer she could come up with was this: Her husband was neither a good husband nor a bad husband. He was just a husband. He was the way that husbands *are.* As she spoke about him, it was as though the word "husband" connoted a job description, or even a species, far more than it represented any particularly cherished or frustrating individual. The role of "husband" was simple enough, involving as it did a set of tasks that her man had obviously fulfilled to a satisfactory degree throughout their life together — as did most other women's husbands, she suggested, unless you were unlucky and got yourself a real dud. The grandmother even went so far as to say that it is not so important, in the end, which man a woman marries. With rare exceptions, one man is pretty much the same as another.

"What do you mean by that?" I asked.

"All men and all women are mostly the same, most of the time," she clarified.

"Everybody knows that this is true."

The other Hmong ladies all nodded in agreement.

May I pause here for a moment to make a blunt and perhaps perfectly obvious point? *It is too late for me to be Hmong.*

For heaven's sake, it's probably even too late for me to be a Webster.

I was born into a late-twentieth-century American middle-class family. Like untold millions of other people in the contemporary world born into similar circumstances, I was raised to believe that I was special. My parents (who were neither hippies nor radicals; who in fact voted for Ronald Reagan twice) simply believed that their children had particular gifts and dreams that set them apart from other people's children. My "me-ness" was always prized, and was moreover recognized as being different from my sister's "her-ness," my friends' "them-ness," and everyone else's "everyone-else-ness." Though I was certainly not spoiled, my parents believed that my personal happiness was of some importance, and that I should learn to shape my life's journey in such a way that would support and reflect my individual search for contentment.

I must add here that all my friends and

relatives were raised with varying degrees of this same belief. With the possible exception of the very most conservative families among us, or the very most recently immigrated families among us, everyone I knew — at some basic level — shared this assumed cultural respect for the individual. Whatever our religion, whatever our economic class, we all at least somewhat embraced the same dogma, which I would describe as being very historically recent and very definitely Western and which can effectively be summed up as: "You matter."

I don't mean to imply that the Hmong don't believe their children matter; on the contrary, they are famous in anthropological circles for building some of the world's most exceptionally loving families. But this was clearly not a society that worshiped at the Altar of Individual Choice. As in most traditional societies, Hmong family dogma might effectively be summed up not as "You matter" but as "Your *role* matters." For, as everyone in this village seemed to know, there are tasks at hand in life — some tasks that men must do and some tasks that women must do — and everyone must contribute to the best of his or her abilities. If you perform your tasks reasonably well, you can go to sleep at night knowing that you are a good man or a good woman, and you need not expect much more out of life or out of relationships than that.

Meeting the Hmong women that day in Vietnam reminded me of an old adage: "Plant an expectation; reap a disappointment." My friend the Hmong grandmother had never been taught to expect that her husband's job was to make her abundantly happy. She had never been taught to expect that her task on earth was to become abundantly happy in the first place. Never having tasted such expectations to begin with, she had reaped no particular disenchantment from her marriage. Her marriage fulfilled its role, performed its necessary social task, became merely what it was, and that was fine.

By contrast, I had always been taught that the pursuit of happiness was my natural (even *national*) birthright. It is the emotional trademark of my culture to seek happiness. Not just any kind of happiness, either, but profound happiness, even soaring happiness. And what could possibly bring a person more soaring happiness than romantic love? I, for one, had always been taught by my culture that marriage ought to be a fertile greenhouse in which romantic love can abundantly flourish. Inside the somewhat rickety greenhouse of my first marriage, then, I had planted row after row of grand expectations. I was a veritable Johnny Appleseed of grand expectations, and all I reaped for my trouble was a harvest of bitter fruit.

One gets the feeling that if I'd tried to explain all that to the Hmong grandmother, she would have had no idea what the hell I was talking about. She probably would have responded exactly the way an old woman I once met in southern Italy responded, when I confessed to her that I'd left my husband because the marriage made me unhappy.

"Who's *happy?*" the Italian widow asked casually, and shrugged away the conversation forever.

Look, I don't want to risk romanticizing the oh-so-simple life of the picturesque rural peasant here. Let me make it clear that I had no desire to trade lives with any of the women that I met in that Hmong village in Vietnam. For the dental implications alone, I do not want their lives. It would be farcical and insulting, besides, for me to try adopting their worldview. In fact, the inexorable march of industrial progress suggests that the Hmong will be more likely to start adopting *my* worldview in the years to come.

As a matter of fact, it's already happening. Now that young girls like my twelve-year-old friend Mai are being exposed to modern Western women like me through crowds of tourists, they're experiencing those first critical moments of cultural hesitation. I call this the "Wait-a-Minute Moment" — that pivotal instant when girls from traditional cultures start pondering what's in it for them, exactly, to be getting married at the age of thirteen and starting to have babies not long after. They start wondering if they might prefer to make different choices for themselves, or *any* choices, for that matter. Once girls from closed societies start thinking such thoughts, all hell breaks loose. Mai — trilingual, bright, and observant — had already glimpsed another set of options for life. It wouldn't be long before she was making demands of her own. In other words: It might be too late for even the Hmong to be Hmong anymore.

So, no, I'm not willing — or probably even able — to relinquish my life of individualistic yearnings, all of which are the birthright of my modernity. Like most human beings, once I've been shown the options, I will always opt for more choices for my life: expressive choices, individualistic choices, inscrutable and indefensible and sometimes risky choices, perhaps . . . but they will all be mine. In fact, the sheer number of choices that I'd already been offered in my life — an almost embarrassing cavalcade of options — would have made the eyes pop out of the head of my friend the Hmong grandmother. As a result of such personal freedoms, my life belongs to me and resembles me to an extent that would be unthinkable in the hills of northern Vietnam, even today. It's almost as if I'm from an entirely new strain of woman (*Homo limitlessness,* you might call us). And while we of this brave new species do have possibilities that are vast and magnificent and almost infinite in scope, it's important to remember that our choice-rich lives have the potential to breed their own brand of trouble. We are susceptible to emotional uncertainties and neuroses that are probably not very common among the Hmong, but that run rampant these days among my contemporaries in, say, Baltimore.

The problem, simply put, is that *we cannot choose everything simultaneously.* So we live in danger of becoming paralyzed by indecision, terrified that every choice might be the wrong choice. (I have a friend who second-guesses herself so compulsively that her husband jokes her autobiography will someday be titled *I Should've Had the Scampi.*) Equally disquieting are the times when we *do* make a choice, only to later feel as though we have murdered some other aspect of our being by settling on one single concrete decision. By choosing Door Number Three, we fear we have killed off a different — but equally critical — piece of our soul that could only have been made manifest by walking through Door Number One or Door Number Two.

The philosopher Odo Marquard has noted a correlation in the German language between the word *zwei,* which means "two," and the word *zweifel,* which means "doubt" — suggesting that two of *anything* brings the automatic possibility of uncertainty to our lives. Now imagine a life in which every day a person is presented with not two or even three but dozens of choices, and you can begin to grasp why the modern world has become, even with all its advantages, a neurosis-generating machine of the highest order. In a world of such abundant possibility, many of us simply go limp from indecision. Or we derail our life's journey again and again, backing up to try the doors we neglected on the first round, desperate to get it right this time. Or we become compulsive comparers — always measuring our lives against some other person's life, secretly wondering if we should have taken her path instead.

Compulsive comparing, of course, only leads to debilitating cases of what Nietzsche called *Lebensneid,* or "life envy": the certainty that somebody else is much luckier than you, and that if only you had *her* body, *her* husband, *her* children, *her* job, everything would be easy and wonderful and happy. (A therapist friend of mine defines this problem simply as "the condition by which all of my single patients secretly long to be married, and all of my married patients secretly long to be single.") With certainty so difficult to achieve, everyone's decisions become an indictment of everyone else's decisions, and because there is no universal model anymore for what makes "a good man" or "a good woman," one must almost earn a personal merit badge in emotional orientation and navigation in order to find one's way through life anymore.

All these choices and all this longing can create a weird kind of haunting in our lives — as though the ghosts of all our other, unchosen, possibilities linger forever in a shadow world around us, continuously asking, "Are you certain this is what you *really* wanted?" And nowhere does that question risk haunting us more than in our marriages, precisely because the emotional stakes of that most intensely personal choice have become so huge.

Believe me, modern Western marriage has much to recommend it over traditional Hmong marriage (starting with its kidnapping-free spirit), and I will say it again: I would not trade lives with those women. They will never know my range of freedom; they will never have my education; they will never have my health and prosperity; they will never be allowed to explore so many aspects of their own natures. But there is one critical gift that a traditional Hmong bride almost always receives on her wedding day which all too often eludes the modern Western bride, and that is the gift of certainty. When you have only one path set before you, you can generally feel confident that it was the correct path to have taken. And a bride whose expectations for happiness are kept necessarily low to begin with is more protected, perhaps, from the risk of devastating disappointments down the road.

To this day, I admit, I'm not entirely sure how to use this information. I cannot quite bring myself to make an official motto out of "Ask for less!" Nor can I imagine advising a young woman on the eve of her marriage to lower her expectations in life in order to be happy. Such thinking runs contrary to every modern teaching I've ever absorbed. Also, I've seen this tactic backfire. I had a friend from college who deliberately narrowed down her life's options, as though to vaccinate herself against overly ambitious expectations. She skipped a career and ignored the lure of travel to instead move back home and marry her high school sweetheart. With unwavering confidence, she announced that she would become "only" a wife and mother. The simplicity of this arrangement felt utterly safe to her — certainly compared to the convulsions of indecision that so many of her more ambitious peers (myself included) were suffering. But when her husband left her twelve years later for a younger woman, my friend's rage and sense of betrayal were as ferocious as anything I've ever seen. She virtually imploded with resentment — not so much against her husband, but against the universe, which she perceived to have broken a sacred contract with her. "I asked for so *little!*" she kept saying, as though her diminished demands alone should have protected her against any disappointments. But I think she was mistaken; she had actually asked for a lot. She had dared to ask for happiness, and she had dared to expect that happiness out of her marriage. You can't possibly ask for more than that.

But maybe it would be useful for me to at least acknowledge to myself now, on the eve of my second marriage, that I, too, ask for an awful lot. Of course I do. It's the emblem of our times. I have been allowed to expect great things in life. I have been permitted to expect far more out of the experience of love and living than most other women in history were ever permitted to ask. When it comes to questions of intimacy, I want many things from my man, and I want them all simultaneously. It reminds me of a story my sister once told me, about an English-woman who visited the United States in the winter of 1919 and who, scandalized, re-ported back home in a letter that there were people in this curious country of America who actually lived with the expectation that every part of their bodies should be warm at the same time! My afternoon spent discussing marriage with the Hmong made me wonder if I, in matters of the heart, had also become such a person — a woman who believed that my lover should magically be able to keep every part of my emotional being warm at the same time.

We Americans often say that marriage is "hard work." I'm not sure the Hmong would understand this notion. Life is hard work, of course, and *work* is very hard work — I'm quite certain they would agree with those statements — but how does marriage become hard work? Here's how: Marriage becomes hard work once you have poured the entirety of your life's expectations for happiness into the hands of one mere person. Keeping that going is hard work. A recent survey of young American women found that what women are seeking these days in a husband — more than anything else — is a man who will "inspire" them, which is, by any measure, a tall order. As a point of comparison, young women of the same age, surveyed back in the 1920s, were more likely to choose a partner based on qualities such as "decency," or "honesty," or his ability to provide for a family. But that's not enough anymore. Now we want to be *inspired* by our spouses! Daily! Step to it, honey!

But this is exactly what I myself have expected in the past from love (inspiration, soaring bliss) and this is what I was now preparing to expect all over again with Felipe — that we should somehow be answerable for every aspect of each other's joy and happiness. That our very job description as spouses was to be each other's everything.

So I had always assumed, anyhow.

And so I might have gone on blithely assuming, except that my encounter with the Hmong had knocked me off course in one critical regard: For the first time in my life, it occurred to me that perhaps I was asking too much of love. Or, at least, perhaps I was asking too much of marriage. Perhaps I was loading a far heavier cargo of expectation onto the creaky old boat of matrimony than that strange vessel had ever been built to accommodate in the first place.

CHAPTER THREE: MARRIAGE AND HISTORY

THE FIRST BOND OF SOCIETY IS MARRIAGE.

— Cicero

What *is* marriage supposed to be, then, if not a delivery device of ultimate bliss?

This question was infinitely difficult for me to answer, because marriage — as a historical entity anyhow — has a tendency to resist our efforts to define it in any simple terms. Marriage, it seems, does not like to sit still long enough for anyone to capture its portrait very clearly. Marriage shifts. It changes over the centuries the way that Irish weather changes: constantly, surprisingly, swiftly. It's not even a safe bet to define marriage in the most reductively simple terms as a sacred union between one man and one woman. First of all, marriage has not always been considered "sacred," not even within the Christian tradition. And for most of human history, to be honest, marriage has usually been seen as a union between one man and *several* women.

Sometimes, though, marriage has been

seen as a union between one woman and several men (as in southern India, where one bride might be shared by several brothers). Marriage has also, at times, been recognized as a union between two men (as in ancient Rome, where marriages between aristocratic males were once recognized by law); or as a union between two siblings (as in medieval Europe, when valuable property was at stake); or as a union between two children (again in Europe, as orchestrated by inheritance-protecting parents or by power-wielding popes); or as a union between the unborn (ditto); or as a union between two people limited to the same social class (once more in Europe, where medieval peasants were often forbidden by law to marry their betters, in order to keep social divisions clean and orderly).

Marriage has also been seen at times as a deliberately temporary union. In modern revolutionary Iran, for instance, young couples can ask a mullah for a special marriage permit called a *sigheh* — a twenty-four-hour pass that permits the couple to be "married," but just for one day. This pass allows a male and female to be safely seen in public together or even, legally, to have sex with each other — essentially creating a Koran-sanctioned, marriage-protected form of provisional romantic expression.

In China, the definition of marriage once included a sacred union between a living woman and a dead man. Such a merger was called a ghost marriage. A young girl of rank would be married off to a dead man from a good family in order to seal the bonds of unity between two clans. Thankfully, no actual skeleton-to-living-flesh contact was involved (it was more of a conceptual wedding, you could say), but the idea still sounds ghoulish to modern ears. That said, some Chinese women came to see this custom as an ideal social arrangement. During the nineteenth century, a surprising number of women in the Shanghai region worked as merchants in the silk trade, and some of them became terrifically successful businesswomen. Trying to gain ever more economic independence, such women would petition for ghost marriages rather than take on living husbands. There was no better path to autonomy for an ambitious young businesswoman than to be married off to a respectable corpse. This brought her all the social status of marriage with none of the constraints or inconveniences of actual wifehood.

Even when marriage has been defined as a union between a man and just one woman, its purposes were not always what we might assume today. In the early years of Western civilization, men and women married each other mostly for the purpose of physical safety. In the time before organized states, in the wild B.C. days of the Fertile Crescent, the fundamental working unit of society was the family. From the family came all your basic social welfare needs — not just companionship and procreation, but also food, housing, education, religious guidance, medical care, and, perhaps most importantly, defense. It was a hazardous world out there in the cradle of civilization. To be alone was to be targeted for death. The more kin you had, the safer you were. People married in order to expand their numbers of relatives. It was not your spouse who was your primary helpmeet, then; it was your entire giant extended family, operating (Hmong-like, you could say) as a single helpmeet entity in the constant combat of survival.

Those extended families grew into tribes, and those tribes became kingdoms, and those kingdoms emerged as dynasties, and those dynasties fought each other in savage wars of conquest and genocide. The early Hebrews emerged from exactly this system, which is why the Old Testament is such a family-centric, stranger-abhorring, genealogical extravaganza — rife with tales of patriarchs, matriarchs, brothers, sisters, heirs, and other miscellaneous kin. Of course, those Old Testament families were not always healthy or functional (we see brothers murdering brothers, siblings selling each other into slavery, daughters seducing their own fathers, spouses sexually betraying each other), but the driving narrative always concerns the progress and tribulations of the bloodline, and marriage was central to the perpetuation of that story.

But the New Testament — which is to say, the arrival of Jesus Christ — invalidated all those old family loyalties to a degree that was truly socially revolutionary. Instead of perpetuating the tribal notion of "the chosen people against the world," Jesus (who was an unmarried man, in marked contrast to the great patriarchal heroes of the Old Testament) taught that we are *all* chosen people, that we are *all* brothers and sisters united within one human family. Now, this was an utterly radical idea that could never possibly fly in a traditional tribal system. You cannot embrace a stranger as your brother, after all, unless you are willing to renounce your real biological brother, thus capsizing an ancient code that binds you in sacred obligation to your blood relatives while setting you in auto-opposition to the unclean outsider. But that sort of fierce clan loyalty was exactly what Christianity sought to overturn. As Jesus taught: "If any man come to me and hate not his father, and mother, and wife, and children, and brethren, and sisters, yea, and his own life also, he cannot be my disciple" (Luke 14:26).

But this created a problem, of course. If you're going to deconstruct the entire social structure of the human family, what do you replace that structure *with?* The early Christian plan was staggeringly idealistic, even downright utopian: Create an exact replica of heaven right here on earth. "Renounce marriage and imitate the angels," instructed John of Damascus around A.D. 730, explaining the new Christian ideal in no uncertain terms. And how do you go about imitating angels? By repressing your human urges, of course. By cutting away all your natural human ties. By holding in check all your desires and loyalties, except the yearning to be one with God. Among the heavenly hosts of angels, after all, there existed no husbands or wives, no mothers or fathers, no ancestor worship, no blood ties, no blood vengeance, no passion, no envy, no bodies — and, most especially, no sex.

104

So that was to be the new human paradigm, as modeled by Christ's own example: celibacy, fellowship, and absolute purity.

This rejection of sexuality and marriage represented a massive departure from any Old Testament way of thinking. Hebrew society, by contrast, had always held marriage to be the most moral and dignified of all social arrangements (in fact, Jewish priests were *required* to be married men), and within that bond of matrimony there had always come a frank assumption of sex. Of course, adultery and random fornication were criminalized activities in ancient Jewish society, but nobody forbade a husband and wife from making love to each other, or from enjoying it. Sex within marriage was not a sin; sex within marriage was . . . marriage. Sex, after all, was how Jewish babies were made — and how can you build up the tribe without making more Jewish babies?

But the early Christian visionaries weren't interested in *making* Christians in the biological sense (as infants who came from the womb); instead, they were interested in *converting* Christians in the intellectual sense (as adults who came to salvation through individual choice). Christianity wasn't something you had to be born into;

Christianity was something that you selected as an adult, through the grace and sacrament of baptism. Since there would always be more potential Christians to convert, there was no need for anybody to sully himself by generating new babies through vile sexual congress. And if there was no need anymore for babies, then it naturally stood to reason that there was no need anymore for marriage.

Remember, too, that Christianity was an apocalyptic religion — even more so at the beginning of its history than now. Early Christians were expecting the End of Days to arrive at any moment, perhaps as early as tomorrow afternoon, so they were not especially interested in launching future dynasties. Effectively, the future did not exist for these people. With Armageddon both inevitable and imminent, the newly baptized Christian convert had only one task in life: to prepare himself for the upcoming apocalypse by making himself as pure as humanly possible.

Marriage = wife = sex = sin = impurity.

Therefore: Don't marry.

When we speak today, then, about "holy wedded matrimony," or the "sanctity of marriage," we would do well to remember that, for approximately ten centuries, Christianity itself did not see marriage as being either holy or sanctified. Marriage was certainly not modeled as the ideal state of moral being. On the contrary, the early Christian fathers regarded the habit of marriage as a somewhat repugnant worldly affair that had everything to do with sex and females and taxes and property, and nothing whatsoever to do with higher concerns of divinity.

So when modern-day religious conservatives wax nostalgic about how marriage is a sacred tradition that reaches back into history for thousands of uninterrupted years, they are absolutely correct, but in only one respect — only if they happen to be talking about Judaism. Christianity simply does not share that deep and consistent historical reverence toward matrimony. Lately it has, yes — but not originally. For the first thousand or so years of Christian history, the church regarded monogamous marriage as marginally less wicked than flat-out whoring — but only very marginally. Saint Jerome even went so far as to rank human holiness on a 1-to-100 scale, with virgins scoring a perfect 100, newly celibate widows and widowers ranking somewhere around 60, and married couples earning the surprisingly unclean score of 30. It was a helpful scale, but even Jerome himself admitted that these sorts of comparisons had their limits. Strictly speaking, he wrote, one should not even rightly compare virginity to marriage — because you cannot "make a comparison between two things if one is good and the other evil."

Whenever I read a line like this (and you can find such pronouncements all over early Christian history), I think of my friends and relatives who identify themselves as Christian, and who — despite having strived with all their might to lead blameless lives — often end up getting divorced anyhow. I have watched over the years as these good and ethical people then proceed to absolutely eviscerate themselves with guilt, certain that they have violated the holiest and most ancient of all Christian precepts by not upholding their wedding vows. I myself fell into this trap when I got divorced, and I wasn't even raised in a fundamentalist household. (My parents were moderate Christians at best, and none of my relatives laid any guilt on me when I was divorcing.) Even so, as my marriage collapsed, I lost more nights of sleep than I care to remember, struggling over the question of whether God would ever forgive me for having left my husband. And for a good long while after my divorce, I remained haunted by the nagging sense that I had not merely failed but had also somehow sinned.

Such currents of shame run deep and cannot be undone overnight, but I submit that it might have been useful for me, during those months of fevered moral torment, to have known a thing or two about the hostility with which Christianity actually regarded marriage for many centuries. "Give over thy stinking family duties!" instructed one English rector, as late as the sixteenth century, in a spittle-flecked denunciation of what we might today call family values. "For under all there lies snapping, snarling, biting, horrid hypocrisy, envy, malice, evil surmising!"

Or consider Saint Paul himself, who wrote in his famous letter to the Corinthians, "It is not good for a man to touch a woman." Never, ever, under any circumstances, Saint Paul believed, was it good for a man to touch a woman — not even his own wife. If Paul had his way, as he himself readily admitted, all Christians would be celibates like him. ("I would that all men were even as I myself.") But he was rational enough to realize that this was a tall order. What he asked for instead, then, was that Christians engage in as little marriage as humanly possible. He instructed those who were unmarried never to marry, and asked those who were widowed or divorced to abstain from settling down in the future with another partner. ("Art thou loosed from a wife? Seek not a wife.") In every possible instance, Paul begged Christians to restrain themselves, to contain their carnal yearnings, to live solitary and sexless lives, on earth as it is in heaven.

"But if they cannot contain," Paul finally conceded, then "let them marry; for it is better to marry than to burn."

Which is perhaps the most begrudging endorsement of matrimony in human history. Although it does remind me of the agreement that Felipe and I had recently reached — namely, that it is better to marry than to be deported.

None of this meant that people stopped getting married, of course. With the exception of the very most devout among them, early Christians rejected the call to celibacy in resounding numbers, continuing to have sex with each other and to get married (often in that order) without any supervision whatsoever from priests. All across the Western world, in the centuries following Christ's death, couples sealed their unions in various improvisational styles (blending together Jewish, Greek, Roman, and Franco-Germanic matrimonial influences) and then registered themselves in village or city documents as being "married." Sometimes these couples failed at their marriages, too, and filed for divorce in the surprisingly permissive early European courts. (Women in Wales in the tenth century, for instance, had more rights to divorce and family assets than women in Puritan America would have seven centuries later.) Often these couples remarried new spouses, and argued later over who had rights to furniture, farmland, or children.

Matrimony became a purely civil convention in early European history because, by this point in the game, marriage had evolved into an entirely new shape. Now that people lived in cities and villages rather than fighting for survival in the open desert, marriage was no longer needed as a fundamental personal safety strategy or as a tool of tribal clan building. Instead, marriage was now regarded as a highly efficient form of wealth management and social order, requiring some sort of organizing structure from the larger community.

At a time when banks and laws and governments were still enormously unstable, marriage became the single most important business arrangement most people would ever make in their lives. (Still is, some might argue. Even today, very few people have the power to influence your financial standing — for better or worse — quite so deeply as your spouse.) But marriage in the Middle Ages was certainly the safest and smoothest means of passing wealth, livestock, heirs, or property from one generation to the next. Great wealthy families stabilized their fortunes through marriages much the same way that great multinational corporations today stabilize their fortunes through careful mergers and acquisitions. (Great wealthy families back then essentially *were* great multinational corporations.) Wealthy European children with titles or inheritance became chattel, to be traded and manipulated like investment stocks. Not just the girls, mind you, but the boys, too. A child of rank could find himself engaged and then unengaged to seven or eight potential wives before he reached the age of puberty and all the families and their lawyers reached a final decision.

Even among the common classes, economic considerations weighed heavily on both sexes. Landing a good spouse back then was sort of like getting into a good college, or earning tenure, or securing a job at the post office; it insured a certain future stability. Of course people did have their personal affections for each other, and of course tender-hearted parents did try to arrange emotionally satisfying unions for their children, but marriages during the Middle Ages were more often than not openly opportunistic. As just one example: A great wave of matrimonial fever swept across medieval Europe right after the Black Death had killed off seventy-five million people. For the survivors, there were suddenly unprecedented avenues for social advancement through marriage. After all, there were thousands of brand-new widows and widowers floating around Europe with a considerable amount of valuable property waiting to be redistributed, and perhaps no more living heirs. What followed, then, was a kind of matrimonial gold rush, a land grab of the highest order. Court records from this era are suspiciously filled with cases of twenty-year-old men marrying elderly women. They weren't idiots, these guys. They saw their window — or widow — of opportunity, and they leapt.

Reflecting this general lack of sentimentality toward matrimony, it's not surprising that European Christians married privately, in their own homes, in their everyday clothing. The big romantic white weddings that we now think of as "traditional" didn't come into being until the nineteenth century — not until a teenaged Queen Victoria walked down the aisle in a fluffy white gown, thereby setting a fashion trend that has never gone out of style since. Before that, though, your average European wedding day wasn't all that much different from any other day of the week. Couples exchanged vows in impromptu ceremonies that generally lasted only a few moments. Witnesses became important on wedding days only so that later there would be no argument in the courts as to whether or not this couple had really consented to marriage — a vital question when money, land, or children were at stake. The reason the courts were involved at all was only in the interest of upholding a certain degree of social order. As the historian Nancy Cott has put it, "marriage prescribed duties and dispensed privileges," distributing clear roles and responsibilities among the citizenry.

For the most part, this is still true in modern Western society. Even today, pretty much the only things the law cares about when it comes to your marriage are your money, your property, and your offspring.

Granted, your priest, your rabbi, your neighbors, or your parents may have other ideas about marriage, but in the eyes of modern secular law, the only reason marriage matters is that two people have come together and produced something in their union (children, assets, businesses, debts), and these things all need to be managed so that civil society can proceed in a methodical fashion and governments will not be stuck with the messy business of raising abandoned babies or supporting bankrupted ex-spouses.

When I began divorce proceedings in 2002, for instance, the judge had no interest whatsoever in myself or my then-husband as emotional or moral beings. She didn't care about our sentimental grievances or our shattered hearts or any holy vows that may or may not have been broken. She certainly didn't care about our mortal souls. What she cared about was the deed to our house and who was going to hold it. She cared about our taxes. She cared about the six months remaining on our car's lease, and who would be obligated to make the monthly payments. She cared about who had the rights to my future book royalties. If we'd had any children together (which we did not have, mercifully), the judge would've cared very much about who was obligated to provide for their schooling and medical care and housing and babysitting. Thus — through the power invested in her by the State of New York — she kept our little corner of civil society tidy and organized. In so doing, that judge in the year 2002 was hearkening back to a medieval understanding of marriage: namely, that this is a civil/secular affair, not a religious/moral one. Her rulings would not have been out of place in a tenth-century European courtroom.

To me, though, the most striking feature of these early European marriages (and divorces, I should add) was their *looseness.* People got married for economic and personal reasons, but they also separated for economic and personal reasons — and fairly easily, compared to what would soon come. Civil society back then seemed to understand that, while human hearts make many promises, human minds can change. And business deals can change, too. In medieval Germany, the courts even went so far as to create two different kinds of legal marriage: *Muntehe,* a heavily binding permanent life contract, and *Friedelehe,* which basically translates as "marriage-lite" — a more casual living arrangement between two consenting adults which took no account

116

whatsoever of dowry requirements or inheritance law, and which could be dissolved by either party at any time.

By the thirteenth century, though, all that looseness was about to change because the church got involved in the business of matrimony again — or rather, for the first time. The utopian dreams of early Christianity were long over. Church fathers were no longer monkish scholars intent on re-creating heaven on earth, but were now mighty political figures very much invested in controlling their growing empire. One of the biggest administrative challenges the church now faced was managing the European royalty, whose marriages and divorces often made and broke political alliances in ways that were not always agreeable to various popes.

In the year 1215, then, the church took control of matrimony forever, laying down rigid new edicts about what would henceforth constitute legitimate marriage. Before 1215, a spoken vow between two consenting adults had always been considered contract enough in the eyes of the law, but the church now insisted that this was unacceptable. The new dogma declared: "We absolutely prohibit clandestine marriages." (Translation: *We absolutely prohibit any mar-*

riage that takes place behind our backs.) Any prince or aristocrat who now dared to marry against the wishes of the church could suddenly find himself excommunicated, and those restrictions trickled down to the common classes as well. Just to further tighten controls, Pope Innocent III now forbade divorce under any circumstances — except in cases of church-sanctioned annulments, which were often used as tools of empire building or empire busting.

Marriage, once a secular institution monitored by families and civil courts, now became a stringently religious affair, monitored by celibate priests. Moreover, the church's strict new prohibitions against divorce turned marriage into a life sentence — something it had never really been before, not even in ancient Hebrew society. And divorce remained illegal in Europe until the sixteenth century, when Henry VIII brought back the custom in grand style. But for about two centuries there — and for much longer in countries that remained Catholic after the Protestant Reformation — unhappy couples no longer had any legal escape from their marriages should things go wrong.

In the end, it must be said that these limitations made life far more difficult for women than for men. At least men were allowed to look for love or sex outside their marriages, but ladies had no such socially condoned outlet. Women of rank were especially locked into their nuptial vows, expected to make do with whatever and whoever had been foisted upon them. (Peasants could both select and abandon their spouses with a little more freedom, but in the upper classes — with so much wealth at stake — there was simply no room for any give.) Girls from important families could find themselves shipped off in mid-adolescence to countries where they might not even speak the language, left there forever to wither in the domain of some random husband. One such English teenager, describing the plans for her upcoming arranged marriage, wrote mournfully about making "daily preparations for my journey to Hell."

To further enforce controls over wealth management and stabilization, courts all across Europe were now seriously upholding the legal notion of *coverture* — that is, the belief that a woman's individual civil existence is erased the moment she marries. Under this system, a wife effectively becomes "covered" by her husband and no longer has any legal rights of her own, nor can she hold any personal property. Coverture was initially a French legal notion, but it spread handily across Europe and soon became entrenched deep in English Common Law. Even as late as the nineteenth century, the British judge Lord William Blackstone was still defending the essence of coverture in his courtroom, insisting that a married woman did not really exist as a legal entity. "The very being of the woman," Blackstone wrote, "is suspended during marriage." For that reason, Blackstone ruled, a husband cannot share assets with his wife even if he wanted to — not even if those assets were once technically the woman's property. A man cannot grant *anything* to his wife, for doing so would presuppose "her separate existence" from him — and such a thing was clearly impossible.

Coverture, then, was not so much a blending of two individuals as a spooky and almost voodoo-like "twicing" of the man, wherein his powers doubled and his wife's evaporated completely. Combined with the strict new antidivorce policies of the church, marriage became, by the thirteenth century, an institution that entombed and then erased its female victims — particularly among the gentry. One can only imagine how lonely the lives of those women must have become once they were so thoroughly eradicated as humans. How on earth did they fill their days? Over the course of their paralyzing marriages, as Balzac wrote of such unfortunate ladies, "Boredom overtakes them, and they give themselves up to religion, or cats, or little dogs, or other manias which are offensive only to God."

If there is one word, by the way, that triggers all the inherent terrors I have ever felt about the institution of marriage, it is *coverture*. This is exactly what the dancer Isadora Duncan was talking about when she wrote that "any intelligent woman who reads the marriage contract and then goes into it deserves all the consequences."

My aversion is not entirely irrational either. The legacy of coverture lingered in Western civilization for many more centuries than it ought to have, clinging to life in the margins of dusty old law books, and always linked to conservative assumptions about the proper role of a wife. It wasn't until the year 1975, for instance, that the married women of Connecticut — including my own mother — were legally allowed to take out loans or open checking accounts without the written permission of their husbands. It wasn't until 1984 that the state of New York overturned an ugly legal notion called "the marital rape exemption," which had previously permitted a man to do anything he liked sexually to his wife, no matter how violent or coercive, since her body belonged to him — since, in effect, she *was* him.

There's one particular example of coverture's legacy which — given my circumstances — touches me most of all. The fact is, I was lucky that the United States government was even considering allowing me to marry Felipe without forcing me to renounce my own nationality in the process. In 1907, a law was passed by the United States Congress stating that any natural-born American woman who married a foreign-born man would have to surrender her American citizenship upon her marriage and automatically become a citizen of her husband's nation — whether she wanted to or not. Though the courts conceded that this was unpleasant, they maintained for many years that it was necessary. As the Supreme Court ruled on the matter, if you were to permit an American woman to keep her own nationality at the moment of marriage to a foreigner, you would essentially be allowing the wife's citizenship to trump the husband's citizenship. In so doing, you would be suggesting that the woman was in possession of something that rendered her superior to her husband — *in even one small regard* — and this was obviously unconscionable, as one American judge explained, since it undermined "the ancient principle" of the marital contract, which existed in order "to merge their identity (man and wife) and give dominance to the husband." (Strictly speaking, of course, that's not a merger; that's a takeover. But you get the point.)

Needless to say, the law did not hold the reverse to be true. If a natural-born American man married a foreign-born woman, the husband was certainly allowed to keep his citizenship, and his bride (covered by him, after all) would certainly be allowed to become an American citizen herself — that is, so long as she met the official naturalization requirements for foreign-born wives (which is to say, so long as she was not a Negro, a mulatto, a member of "the Malay race," or any other kind of creature that the United States of America expressly deemed undesirable).

This brings us to another subject I find disturbing about matrimony's legacy: the racism that one encounters all over marriage law — even in very recent American history. One of the more sinister characters in the American matrimonial saga was a fellow named Paul Popenoe, an avocado farmer from California who opened a eugenics clinic in Los Angeles in the 1930s called "The Human Betterment Foundation." Inspired by his attempts to cultivate better avocados, he devoted his clinic to the work of cultivating better (read: whiter) Americans. Popenoe was concerned that white women — who had lately started attending college and delaying marriage — weren't breeding quickly or copiously enough, while all the wrong-colored people were breeding in dangerous numbers. He also nursed deep concerns about marriage and breeding among the "unfit," and so his clinic's first priority was to sterilize all those whom Popenoe judged unworthy to reproduce. If any of this sounds distressingly familiar, it's only because the Nazis were impressed by Popenoe's work, which they quoted often in their own writings. Indeed, the Nazis really ran with his ideas. While Germany eventually sterilized over 400,000 people, American states — following Popenoe's programs — managed to get only about 60,000 citizens sterilized.

It's also chilling to learn that Popenoe used his clinic as the base from which to launch the very first marriage-counseling center in America. The intention of this counseling center was to encourage marriage and breeding among "fit" couples (white, Protestant couples of northern European descent). More chilling still is the fact that Popenoe, the father of American eugenics, also went on to launch the famous *Ladies' Home Journal* column "Can This Marriage Be Saved?" His intention with the advice column was identical to that of the counseling center: to keep all those white American couples together so they could produce more white American babies.

But racial discrimination has always shaped marriage in America. Slaves in the antebellum South, not surprisingly, were never allowed to marry. The argument against slaves' marrying, simply put, was this: *It's impossible.* Marriage in Western society is supposed to be a contract based on mutual consent, and a slave — by very definition — does not possess his own consent. His every move is controlled by his master and therefore he cannot willfully enter into any contract with another human being. To allow a slave to enter into a consensual marriage, then, would be to assume that a slave can make even one small promise of his own, and this is obviously impossible. Therefore, slaves could not marry. A tidy line of reasoning, this argument (and the brutal policies that enforced it) effectively destroyed the institution of marriage within the African American community for generations to come — a disgraceful legacy that haunts society to this day.

Then there is the question of interracial marriage, which was illegal in the United States until fairly recently. For most of American history, falling in love with a person of the wrong color could land you in jail, or worse. All this changed in 1967, with the case of a rural Virginia couple named — poetically enough — the Lovings. Richard Loving was white; his wife, Mildred — whom he had adored since he was seventeen years old — was black. When they decided to marry in 1958, interracial unions were still illegal in the Commonwealth of Virginia as well as in fifteen other American states. So the young couple sealed their vows in Washington, D.C., instead. But when they returned home after their honeymoon, they were swiftly apprehended by local police, who broke into the Lovings' bedroom in the middle of the night and arrested them. (The police had hoped to find the couple having sex, so they could also charge them with the crime of interracial intercourse, but no luck; the Lovings were only sleeping.) Still, the fact that they had married each other at all rendered the couple guilty enough to haul off to jail. Richard and Mildred petitioned the courts for the right to uphold their District of Columbia marriage, but a Virginia state judge struck down their wedding vows, helpfully explaining in his ruling that "Almighty God created the races white, black, yellow, Malay and red, and He placed them on separate continents. The fact that He separated the races shows that He did not intend for the races to mix."

Good to know.

The Lovings moved to Washington, D.C., with the understanding that if they ever again returned to Virginia, they would face a jail sentence. Their story might have ended there, but for a letter that Mildred wrote to the NAACP in 1963, asking if the organization might help find a way for the couple to return home to Virginia, even if only for a short visit. "We know we can't live there," Mrs. Loving wrote with a devastating humility, "but we would like to go back once and awhile to visit our families & friends."

A pair of civil rights lawyers from the ACLU took on the case, which finally made its way to the U.S. Supreme Court in 1967, where the justices — upon reviewing the story — unanimously begged to differ with the idea that modern civil law should be based on biblical exegesis. (To its everlasting credit, the Roman Catholic Church itself had issued a public statement only a few months earlier, expressing its unqualified support for interracial marriage.) The Supreme Court sealed the legality of Richard and Mildred's union in a 9–0 ruling, and with this ringing statement: "The freedom to marry has long been recognized as one of the vital personal rights essential to the orderly pursuit of happiness by free men."

At the time, I must also mention, a poll showed that 70 percent of Americans vehemently opposed this ruling. Let me repeat that: In recent American history, *seven out of ten* Americans still believed that it should be a criminal offense for people of different races to marry each other. But the courts were morally ahead of the general population on this matter. The last racial barriers were removed from the canon of American matrimonial law, and life went on, and everyone got used to the new reality, and the institution of marriage did not collapse for having had its boundaries adjusted just that tiny bit wider. And although there still may be people out there who believe that the intermingling of races is abhorrent, you would have to be an extreme fringe racist lunatic these days to seriously suggest aloud that consenting adults of different ethnic backgrounds should be excluded from legal matrimony. Moreover, there is not a single politician in this country who could ever win election to high office again by running on such a contemptible platform.

We have moved on, in other words.

You see where I'm heading with this, right?

Or rather, you see where *history* is heading with this?

What I mean to say is: You won't be surprised, will you, if I now take a few moments to discuss the subject of same-sex marriage? Please understand that I realize people have strong feelings on this topic. Then-congressman James M. Talent of Missouri undoubtedly spoke for many when he said in 1996, "It is an act of hubris to believe that marriage can be infinitely malleable, that it can be pushed and pulled around like Silly Putty without destroying its essential stability and what it means to our society."

The problem with that argument, though, is that the only thing marriage has ever done, historically and definitionally speaking, is to change. Marriage in the Western world changes with every century, adjusting itself constantly around new social standards and new notions of fairness. The Silly Putty–like malleability of the institution, in fact, is the only reason we still have the thing at all. Very few people — Mr. Talent included, I'll wager — would accept marriage on its thirteenth-century terms. Marriage survives, in other words, precisely because it evolves. (Though I suppose this would not be a very persuasive argument to those who probably also don't believe in evolution.)

In the spirit of full disclosure, I should make clear here that I'm a supporter of same-sex marriage. Of course I would be; I'm precisely that sort of person. The reason I bring up this topic at all is that it irritates me immensely to know that I have access, through the act of marriage, to certain critical social privileges that a large number of my friends and fellow taxpayers do not have. It irritates me even more to know that if Felipe and I had happened to be a same-sex couple, we would have been in *really* big trouble after that incident at the Dallas/Fort Worth Airport. The Homeland Security Department would have taken one look at our relationship and thrown my partner out of the country forever, with no hope of future parole through marriage. Strictly on account of my heterosexual credentials, then, I am allowed to secure Felipe an American passport. Put in such terms, my upcoming marriage starts to look something like a membership at an exclusive country club — a means of offering me valuable amenities that are denied to my equally worthy neighbors. That sort of discrimination will never sit well with me, only adding to the natural suspicion I already feel toward this institution.

Even so, I'm hesitant to discuss in much detail the specifics of this particular social debate, if only because gay marriage is such a hot issue that it's almost too early to be publishing books about it yet. Two weeks before I sat down to write this paragraph, same-sex marriage was legalized in the state of Connecticut. A week after that, it was declared illegal in the state of California. While I was editing this paragraph a few months later, all hell broke loose in Iowa and Vermont. Not long after that, New Hampshire became the sixth state to make same-sex marriage legal, and I'm beginning to believe that whatever I declare today about the gay marriage debate in America will most likely be obsolete by next Tuesday afternoon.

What I can say about this subject, though, is that legalized same-sex marriage is coming to America. In large part this is because *non*legalized same-sex marriage is already here. Same-sex couples already live together openly these days, whether their relationships have been officially sanctioned by their states or not. Same-sex couples are raising children together, paying taxes together, building homes together, running businesses together, creating wealth together, and even getting divorced from each other. All these already existing relationships and social responsibilities must be managed and organized through rule of law in order to keep civil society running smoothly. (This is why the 2010 U.S. Census will be documenting same-sex couples as "married" for the first time in order to chart clearly the actual demographics of the nation.) The federal courts will eventually get fed up, just as they did with interracial marriage, and decide that it's far easier to let all consenting adults have access to matrimony than it is to sort out the issue state by state, amendment by amendment, sheriff by sheriff, personal prejudice by personal prejudice.

Of course, social conservatives may still believe that homosexual marriage is wrong because the purpose of matrimony is to create children, but infertile and childless and postmenopausal heterosexual couples get married all the time and nobody protests. (The archconservative political commentator Pat Buchanan and his wife are childless, just as one example, and nobody suggests that their marital privileges should be revoked for failure to propagate biological offspring.) And as for the notion that same-sex marriage will somehow corrupt the community at large, nobody has ever been able to prove this in a court of law. On the contrary, hundreds of scientific and social organizations — from the American Academy of Family Physicians, to the American Psychological Association, to the Child Welfare League of America — have publicly endorsed both gay marriage and gay adoption.

But gay marriage is coming to America first and foremost because marriage here is a secular concern, not a religious one. The objection to gay marriage is almost invariably biblical, but nobody's legal vows in this country are defined by interpretation of biblical verse — or at least, not since the Supreme Court stood up for Richard and Mildred Loving. A church wedding ceremony is a nice thing, but it is neither *required* for legal marriage in America nor does it *constitute* legal marriage in America. What constitutes legal marriage in this country is that critical piece of paper that you and your betrothed must sign and then register with the state. The morality of your marriage may indeed rest between you and God, but it's that civic and secular paperwork which makes your vows official here on earth. Ultimately, then, it is the business of America's courts, not America's churches, to decide the rules of matrimonial law, and it is in those courts that the same-sex marriage debate will finally be settled.

Anyhow, to be perfectly honest, I find it a bit crazy that social conservatives are fighting so hard against this at all, considering that it's quite a positive thing for society in general when as many intact families as possible live under the estate of matrimony. And I say this as someone who is — I think we can all agree by now — admittedly suspicious of marriage. Yet it's true. Legal marriage, because it restrains sexual promiscuity and yokes people to their social obligations, is an essential building block of any orderly community. I'm not convinced that marriage is always so terrific for every individual *within* the relationship, but that's another question altogether. There is no doubt — not even within my rebellious mind — that in general, matrimony stabilizes the larger social order and is often exceedingly good for children.*

* Pardon me for a moment. This is such an important and complicated point that it warrants the only footnote of this whole book. When sociologists say that "marriage is extremely good for children," what they really mean is that *stability* is extremely good for children. It has been categorically proven that children thrive in environments where they are not subjected to constant unsettling emotional changes — such as, for instance, an endless rotation of Mom's or Dad's new romantic partners cycling in and out of the home. Marriage *tends* to stabilize families and prevent such upheavals, but not *necessarily.* These days, for instance, a child born to an unmarried couple in Sweden (where legal marriage is increasingly passé, but where family bonds are quite solid) has a greater chance of living forever with the same parents than a child born to a married couple in America (where marriage is still revered but divorce runs rampant). Children need constancy and familiarity. Marriage encourages, but cannot guarantee, familial solidity. Unmarried couples and single parents and even grandparents can create calm and stable environments in which children can thrive, outside the bonds of legal

If I were a social conservative, then — that is to say, if I were somebody who cared deeply about social stability, economic prosperity, and sexual monogamy — I would want as many gay couples as possible to get married. I would want as many of *every* kind of couple as possible to get married. I recognize that conservatives are worried that homosexuals will destroy and corrupt the institution of marriage, but perhaps they should consider the distinct possibility that gay couples are actually poised at this moment in history to *save* marriage. Think of it! Marriage is on the decline everywhere, all across the Western world. People are getting married later in life, if they're getting married at all, or they are producing children willy-nilly out of wedlock, or (like me) they are approaching the whole institution with ambivalence or even hostility. We don't trust marriage anymore, many of us straight folk. We don't get it. We're not at all convinced that we need it. We feel as though we can take it or leave it behind forever. All of which leaves poor old matrimony twisting in the winds of cold modernity.

But just when it seems like maybe all is

---

matrimony. I just wanted to be very clear about that. Sorry for the interruption, and thanks.

lost for marriage, just when matrimony is about to become as evolutionarily expendable as pinkie toes and appendixes, just when it appears that the institution will wither slowly into obscurity due to a general lack of social interest, in come the gay couples, asking to be included! Indeed, pleading to be included! Indeed, fighting with all their might to be included in a custom which may be terrifically beneficial for society as a whole but which many — like me — find only suffocating and old-fashioned and irrelevant.

It might seem ironic that homosexuals — who have, over the centuries, made an art form out of leading bohemian lives on the outer fringes of society — want so desperately now to be part of such a mainstream tradition. Certainly not everyone understands this urge to assimilate, not even within the gay community. The filmmaker John Waters, for one, says that he always thought the only advantages of being gay were that he didn't have to join the military and he didn't have to get married. Still, it is true that many same-sex couples want nothing more than to join society as fully integrated, socially responsible, family-centered, taxpaying, Little League–coaching, nation-serving, respectably married citizens. So why not welcome them in? Why not recruit them by the vanload to sweep in on heroic wings and save the flagging and battered old institution of matrimony from a bunch of apathetic, ne'er-do-well, heterosexual deadbeats like me?

In any case, whatever happens with gay marriage, and whenever it happens, I can also assure you that future generations will someday find it ridiculous to the point of comedy that we ever debated this topic at all, much the same way that it seems absurd today that it was once strictly illegal for an English peasant to marry outside of his class, or for a white American citizen to marry someone of "the Malay race." Which brings us to the final reason that gay marriage is coming: because marriage in the Western world over the last several centuries has been moving — slowly but inexorably — in the direction of ever more personal privacy, ever more fairness, ever more respect for the two individuals involved, and ever more freedom of choice.

You can chart the beginning of the "marital freedom movement," as we might call it, from sometime around the mideighteenth century. The world was changing, liberal democracies were on the rise, and all over western Europe and the Americas came a massive social push for more freedom, more privacy, more opportunities for individuals to pursue their own personal happiness regardless of other people's wishes. Men and women alike began to express ever more vocally their desire for *choice.* They wanted to choose their own leaders, choose their own religions, choose their own destinies, and — yes — even choose their own spouses.

Moreover, with the advancements of the Industrial Revolution and the increase in personal earnings, couples could now afford to purchase their own homes rather than live forever with extended family — and we cannot overestimate how much that social transformation affected marriage. Because along with all those new private homes came . . . well, *privacy.* Private thoughts and private time, which led to private desires and private ideas. Once the doors of your house were closed, your life belonged to you. You could be the master of your own destiny, the captain of your emotional ship. You could seek your own paradise and find your own happiness — not in heaven but right there in downtown Pittsburgh, for instance, with your own lovely wife (whom you had personally selected, by the way, not because it was an economically advantageous choice, or because your family had arranged the match, but because *you liked her laugh*).

One of my personal hero-couples of the marital freedom movement were a pair named Lillian Harman and Edwin Walker, of the great state of Kansas circa 1887. Lillian was a suffragette and the daughter of a noted anarchist; Edwin was a progressive journalist and feminist sympathizer. They were made for each other. When they fell in love and decided to seal their relationship, they visited neither minister nor judge, but entered instead into what they called an "autonomistic marriage." They created their own wedding vows, speaking during the ceremony about the absolute privacy of their union, and swearing that Edwin would not dominate his wife in any way, nor would she take his name. Moreover, Lillian refused to swear eternal loyalty to Edwin, but stated firmly that she would "make no promises that it may become impossible or immoral for me to fulfill, but retain the right to act always as my conscience and best judgment shall dictate."

It goes without saying that Lillian and Edwin were arrested for this flouting of convention — and on their wedding night, no less. (What *is* it about arresting people in their beds that always signals a new era in marriage history?) The pair were charged with failure to respect license and ceremony, with one judge stating that "the union between E.C. Walker and Lillian Harman is no marriage, and they deserve all the punishment which has been inflicted upon them."

But the toothpaste was already out of the tube. Because what Lillian and Edwin wanted was not all that different from what their contemporaries wanted: the freedom to enter into or dissolve their own unions, on their own terms, for private reasons, entirely free from meddling interference by church, law, or family. They wanted parity with each other and fairness within their marriage. But mostly what they wanted was the liberty to define their own relationship based on their own personal interpretation of love.

Of course, there was resistance to these radical notions. Even as early as the mid-1800s, you start to see prim, fussy, social conservatives suggesting that this trend toward expressive individualism in marriage would spell out the very breakdown of society. What these conservatives specifically predicted was that allowing couples to make

141

life matches based purely on love and the whims of personal affection would promptly lead to astronomical divorce rates and a host of bitterly broken homes.

Which all seems ridiculous now, doesn't it?

Except that they were kind of right.

Divorce, which had once been vanishingly rare in Western society, did begin to increase by the midnineteenth century — almost as soon as people began choosing their own partners for reasons of mere love. And divorce rates have only been growing higher since as marriage becomes ever less "institutional" (based on the needs of the larger society) and ever more "expressively individualistic" (based on the needs of . . . *you*).

Which is somewhat hazardous, as it turns out. Because here comes the single most interesting fact I've learned about the entire history of marriage: Everywhere, in every single society, all across the world, all across time, whenever a conservative culture of arranged marriage is replaced by an expressive culture of people choosing their own partners based on love, divorce rates will immediately begin to skyrocket. You can set your clock to it. (It's happening in India right now, for instance, even as we speak.)

About five minutes after people start clamoring for the right to choose their own spouses based on love, they will begin clamoring for the right to divorce those spouses once that love has died. Moreover, the courts will start permitting people to divorce, on the grounds that forcing a couple who once loved each other to stay together now that they detest each other is a form of wanton cruelty. ("Send the husband and wife to penal servitude if you disapprove of their conduct and want to punish them," protested George Bernard Shaw, "but don't send them back to perpetual wedlock.") As love becomes the currency of the institution, judges become more sympathetic to miserable spouses — possibly because they, too, know from personal experience just how painful ruined love can become. In 1849, a Connecticut court ruled that spouses should be allowed to legally leave their marriages not only for reasons of abuse, neglect, or adultery, but also because of simple unhappiness. "Any such conduct as permanently destroys the happiness of the petitioner," the judge declared, "defeats the purpose of the marriage relation."

This was a truly radical statement. To infer that the *purpose* of marriage is to create a state of happiness had never before been an assumption in human history. This notion led, inevitably you could say, to the rise of something the matrimonial researcher Barbara Whitehead has called "expressive divorces" — cases of people leaving their marriages merely because their love has died. In such cases, nothing else is wrong with the relationship. Nobody has beaten or betrayed anyone, but the *feeling* of the love story has changed and divorce becomes the expression of that most intimate disappointment.

I know exactly what Whitehead is talking about when it comes to expressive divorce; my exit from my first marriage was precisely that. Of course, when a situation is making you truly miserable, it's difficult to say that you are "merely" unhappy. There seems to be nothing "mere," for instance, about crying for months on end, or feeling that you are being buried alive within your own home. But yes, in all fairness, I must admit that I left my ex-husband *merely* because my life with him had become miserable, and this gesture marked me as a very expressively modern wife indeed.

So this transformation of marriage from a business deal to a badge of emotional affection has weakened the institution considerably over time — because marriages based on love are, as it turns out, just as fragile as love itself. Just consider my relationship with Felipe and the gossamer thread that holds us together. To put it simply, I do not need this man in almost any of the ways that women have needed men over the centuries. I do not need him to protect me physically, because I live in one of the safest societies on earth. I do not need him to provide for me financially, because I have always been the winner of my own bread. I do not need him to extend my circle of kinship, because I have a rich community of friends and neighbors and family all on my own. I do not need him to give me the critical social status of "married woman," because my culture offers respect to unmarried women. I do not need him to father my children, because I have chosen not to become a mother — and even if I did want children, technology and the permissiveness of a liberal society would permit me to secure babies through other means, and to raise them alone.

So where does that leave us? Why do I need this man at all? I need him only because I happen to adore him, because his company brings me gladness and comfort, and because, as a friend's grandfather once put it, "Sometimes life is too hard to be alone, and sometimes life is too good to be alone." The same goes for Felipe: He needs me only for my companionship as well. Seems like a lot, but it isn't much at all; it is only love. And a love-based marriage does not guarantee the lifelong binding contract of a clan-based marriage or an asset-based marriage; it *cannot.* By unnerving definition, anything that the heart has chosen for its own mysterious reasons it can always unchoose later — again, for its own mysterious reasons. And a shared private heaven can quickly descend into a failed private hell.

Moreover, the emotional havoc that accompanies divorce is often colossal, which makes the psychological risk of marrying for love extreme. The most common survey that doctors are using these days to determine stress levels in their patients is a test put together in the 1970s by a pair of researchers named Thomas Holmes and Richard Rahe. The Holmes-Rahe scale puts "death of a spouse" at the very top of their list, as the single most stressful event most people will ever undergo in their lives. But guess what's second on the list? *Divorce.* According to this survey, "divorce" is even more anxiety-inducing than "death of a close family member" (even the death of one's own child, we must assume, for there is no separate category for that awful event), and it is far more emotionally stressful than "serious illness," or "losing a job," or even "imprisonment." But what I found most amazing about the Holmes-Rahe scale is that "marital reconciliation" also ranks quite high on the list of stress-inducing events. Even *almost* getting a divorce and then saving the marriage at the last moment can be absolutely emotionally devastating.

So when we talk about how love-based marriages can lead to higher divorce rates, this is not something to be taken lightly. The emotional, financial, and even physical costs of failed love can destroy individuals and families. People stalk, injure, and kill their ex-spouses, and even when it doesn't reach the extreme of physical violence, divorce is a psychological and emotional and economic wrecking ball — as anyone who has ever been in, or even near, a failing marriage can attest.

Part of what makes the experience of divorce so dreadful is the emotional ambivalence. It can be difficult, if not impossible, for many divorced people ever to rest in a state of pure grief, pure anger, or pure relief when it comes to feelings about one's ex-spouse. Instead, the emotions often remain mixed up together in an uncomfortably raw stew of contradictions for many years. This is how we end up missing our ex-husband at the same time as resenting him. This is how we end up worrying about our ex-wife even as we feel absolute murderous rage toward her. It's confusing beyond measure. Most of the time, it's hard even to assign clear blame. In almost all the divorces I've ever witnessed, both parties (unless one of them was a clear-cut sociopath) were at least somewhat responsible for the collapse of the relationship. So which character are you, once your marriage has failed? Victim or villain? It's not always easy to tell. These lines mesh and blend, as though there's been an explosion at a factory and fragments of glass and steel (bits of his heart and her heart) have melded together in the searing heat. Trying to pick through all that wreckage can bring a person straight to the brink of madness.

This is not even to mention the special horror of watching as somebody whom you once loved and defended becomes an aggressive antagonist. I once asked my divorce lawyer, when we were really going through the thick of it, how she could bear to do this work — how she could endure watching every day as couples who had once loved each other tore each other apart in the courtroom. She said, "I find this work rewarding for one reason: because I know something that you don't know. I know that this is the worst experience of your life, but I also know that someday you'll move past it and you'll be *fine.* And helping somebody like you through the worst experience of her life is incredibly gratifying."

She was correct in one respect (we will all be *fine* eventually), but she was dead wrong in another respect (we will never entirely move past it, either). In this sense, we divorced folks are something like twentieth-century Japan: We had a culture which was prewar and we have a culture which is postwar, and right between those two histories lies a giant smoking hole.

I will do virtually anything to avoid going through that apocalypse again. But I recognize that there's always the possibility of another divorce, exactly because I love Felipe, and because love-based unions make for strangely fragile tethers. I'm not giving up on love, mind you. I still believe in it. But maybe that's the problem. Maybe divorce is the tax we collectively pay as a culture for daring to believe in love — or at least, for daring to link love to such a vital social contract as matrimony. Maybe it is not love and marriage that go together like a horse and carriage after all. Maybe it is love and divorce that go together . . . like a carriage and a horse.

So perhaps this is the social issue that needs to be addressed here, far more than who is allowed to get married and who isn't allowed to get married. From an anthropological perspective, the real dilemma of modern relationships is this: If you honestly want to have a society in which people choose their own partners on the basis of personal affection, then you must prepare yourself for the inevitable. There will be broken hearts; there will be broken lives. Exactly because the human heart is such a mystery ("such a tissue of paradox," as the Victorian scientist Sir Henry Finck beautifully described it), love renders all our plans and all our intentions a great big gamble. Maybe the only difference between first marriage and second marriage is that the second time at least you know you are gambling.

I remember a conversation I had several years ago with a young woman I met at a publishing party in New York City during a bad moment in my life. The young woman, whom I'd met on one or two previous social occasions, asked me out of politeness where my husband was. I revealed that my husband would not be joining me that evening because we were going through a divorce. My companion uttered a few not-very-heartfelt words of sympathy, and then said, before digging into the cheese plate, "I myself have been happily married for eight years already. And I'll never get divorced."

What do you say to a comment like that? *Congratulations on an accomplishment that you have not yet accomplished?* I can see now that this young woman still had a certain innocence about marriage. Unlike your average sixteenth-century Venetian teenager, she was lucky enough not to have had a husband inflicted upon her. But for that very reason — exactly because she had chosen her spouse out of love — her marriage was more fragile than she realized.

The vows that we make on our wedding day are a noble effort to belie this fragility, to convince ourselves that — truly — what God Almighty has brought together, no man can tear asunder. But unfortunately God Almighty is not the one who swears those wedding vows; man (unmighty) is, and man can always tear a sworn vow asunder. Even if my acquaintance at the publishing party was certain that she herself would never abandon her husband, the question was not entirely up to her. She was not the only person in that bed. All lovers, even the most faithful lovers, are vulnerable to abandonment against their will. I know this simple fact to be true, for I myself have abandoned people who did not want me to go, and I myself have been abandoned by those whom I begged to stay. Knowing all this, I will enter into my second marriage with far more humility than I entered into my first. As will Felipe. Not that humility alone will protect us, but at least this time we'll have some.

It's been famously said that second marriage is the triumph of hope over experience, but I'm not entirely sure that's true. It seems to me that first marriages are the more hope-drenched affairs, awash in vast expectations and easy optimism. Second marriages are cloaked, I think, in something else: a respect for forces that are bigger than us, maybe. A respect that perhaps even approaches awe.

An old Polish adage warns: "Before going to war, say one prayer. Before going to sea, say two prayers. Before getting married, say three."

I myself intend to pray all year.

CHAPTER FOUR:
MARRIAGE
AND INFATUATION

BE OF LOVE (A LITTLE)/MORE
CAREFUL/THAN OF EVERYTHING
— *e.e. cummings*

It was now September 2006.

Felipe and I were still wandering across Southeast Asia. We had nothing but time to kill. Our immigration case had stalled completely. To be fair, it was not only *our* immigration case that had stalled, but the cases of every single couple applying for fiancé visas to America. The whole system was in lockdown, frozen shut. To our collective misfortune, a new immigration law had just been passed by Congress and now everybody was going to be held up — thousands of couples — for at least another four months or so of bureaucratic limbo. The new law stated that any American citizen who wanted to marry a foreigner now had to be investigated by the FBI, who would search the applicant for evidence of past felonies.

That's right: any *American* who now wished to marry a foreigner was subject to

FBI investigation.

Curiously enough, this law had been passed to protect women — poor foreign women from developing nations, to be precise — from being imported into the United States as brides for convicted rapists, murderers, or known spousal abusers. This had become a grisly problem in recent years. American men were essentially buying brides from the former Soviet Union, Asia, and South America, who — once shipped off to the United States — often faced horrible new lives as prostitutes or sex slaves, or even ended up murdered by American husbands who may have already had a police record of rape and homicide. Thus, this new law came into being to pre-screen all prospective American spouses, in order to protect their foreign-born brides from marrying a potential monster.

It was a good law. It was a fair law. It was impossible not to approve of such a law. The only problem for Felipe and me was that it was an awfully inconveniently timed law, given that our case would now take at least four extra months to process, as the FBI back home did their due diligence investigations to confirm that I was neither a convicted rapist nor a serial murderer of unfortunate women, despite the fact that I totally matched the profile.

Every few days I would send another e-mail to our immigration lawyer back in Philadelphia, checking in for progress reports, for timelines, for hope.

"No news," the lawyer would always report. Sometimes he would remind me, just in case I had forgotten: "Make no plans. Nothing is promised."

So while all that played out (or rather, while all that *didn't* play out) Felipe and I entered the country of Laos. We took a flight out of northern Thailand to the ancient city of Luang Prabang, passing over a continuous emerald expanse of mountains that poked out of the verdant jungle, steep and striking, one after another, like choppy frozen green waves. The local airport looked something like a small-town American post office. We hired a bicycle taxi to carry us into Luang Prabang itself, which turned out to be a treasure of a city, situated beautifully on a delta between the Mekong and Nam Khan rivers. Luang Prabang is an exquisite place that has somehow managed over the centuries to wedge forty Buddhist temples onto one small slice of real estate. For this reason, one encounters Buddhist monks everywhere there. The monks range in age from about ten years old (the novices) to about ninety years old (the masters), and literally thousands of them live in Luang Prabang at any given time. The monk-to-normal-mortal ratio, therefore, feels something like five to one.

The novices were some of the most beautiful boys I'd ever seen. They dressed in bright orange robes, and had shaved heads and golden skin. Every morning before dawn, they streamed out of the temples in long lines, alms bowls in hand, collecting their daily food from the townspeople, who would kneel in the streets to offer up rice for the monks to eat. Felipe, already weary of traveling, described this ceremony as "an awful lot of fuss for five o'clock in the morning," but I loved it, and I awoke every day before dawn to sneak onto the veranda of our crumbling hotel and watch.

I was captivated by the monks. They were a fascinating distraction for me. I completely fixated on them. In fact, I was *so* captivated by the monks that, after a few languid days spent doing nothing much in this small Laotian town, I commenced to spying on them.

Okay, spying on monks is probably a very wicked activity (may the Buddha forgive me), but it was difficult to resist. I was dying to know who these boys were, what they felt, what they wanted out of life, but there was a limit to how much information I could find out openly. Notwithstanding the language barrier, women are not even supposed to *look* at the monks, or even stand near them, much less speak to them. Also, it was difficult to collect any personal information about any particular monk when they all looked exactly the same. It's not an insult or a racist dismissal to say that they all looked exactly the same; sameness is the very intention of the shaved heads and the simple, identical orange robes. The reason their Buddhist masters created this uniform look is to deliberately help the boys diminish their sense of themselves as individuals, to blend them into a collective. Even they are not supposed to distinguish themselves one from the other.

But we stayed there in Luang Prabang for several weeks, and after a great deal of back-street surveillance I slowly came to recognize individual monks within the crowds of interchangeable orange robes and shaved heads. There were young monks of all sorts, it gradually became clear. There were the flirtatious and daring monks who stood on each other's shoulders to peek over the temple wall at you and call out "Hello, Mrs.

Lady!" as you walked by. There were novices who snuck cigarettes at night outside the temple walls, the embers of their smokes glowing as orange as their robes. I saw a buff teenage monk doing push-ups, and I spotted another one with an unexpectedly gangsterish tattoo of a knife emblazoned on one golden shoulder. One night I'd eavesdropped while a handful of monks sang Bob Marley songs to each other underneath a tree in a temple garden, long after they should have been asleep. I'd even seen a knot of barely adolescent novices kickboxing each other — a display of good-natured competition that, like boys' games all over the world, carried the threat of turning truly violent at a moment's notice.

But I was most surprised by an incident I witnessed one afternoon in the small, dark Internet café in Luang Prabang, where Felipe and I would spend several hours a day checking e-mails and communicating with our families and our immigration lawyer. I often came to this Internet café alone, too. When Felipe wasn't with me, I would use the computers to scan real estate notices back home, looking at houses around the Philadelphia area. I was feeling — more than I had ever felt in my life, or maybe even for the first time in my life — homesick. As in: sick for a *home.* I longed like mad for a house, an address, a small private location of our own. I yearned to liberate my books from storage and alphabetize them on shelves. I dreamed of adopting a pet, of eating home-cooked food, of visiting my old shoes, of living close to my sister and her family.

I had recently called my niece to wish her a happy eighth birthday, and she had fallen apart on the phone.

"Why aren't you *here?*" Mimi demanded. "Why aren't you coming over to my *birthday party?*"

"I can't come, sweetheart. I'm stuck on the other side of the world."

"Then why don't you come over *tomorrow?*"

I didn't want to burden Felipe with any of this. My homesickness just made him feel helpless and trapped and somehow responsible for having uprooted us to northern Laos. But home was a constant distraction for me. Scrolling through real estate listings behind Felipe's back made me feel guilty, as though I were surfing porn, but I did it anyhow. "Make no plans," our immigration lawyer kept repeating, but still, I could not help myself. I dreamed of plans. Floor plans.

So as I was sitting there alone in the In-

ternet café one hot afternoon in Luang Prabang, staring at my flickering computer
screen, admiring an image of a stone cottage on the Delaware River (with a small
barn that could easily be transformed into a
writing studio!), a thin teenage novice monk
suddenly sat down at the computer next to
me, balancing his skinny bottom lightly on
the edge of a hard wooden chair. I'd been
seeing monks using computers in this Internet café for weeks now, but I had still not
gotten over the cultural disconnect of
watching shaven-headed, serious boys in
saffron robes surfing the Web. Overcome
with curiosity about what exactly they were
doing on those computers, I would sometimes get up from my seat and casually
wander around the room, glancing at everyone's screens as I passed by. Usually the
boys were playing video games, though
sometimes I found them typing laboriously
away at English-language texts, utterly
absorbed in their work.

On this day, though, the young monk sat
down right beside me. He was so close that
I could see the faint hairs on his thin, pale-
brown arms. Our workstations were so near
to each other that I could also see his
computer screen quite clearly. After a spell,
I glanced over to get a sense of what he was

working on, and realized that the boy was reading a love letter. Actually, he was reading a love e-mail, which I quickly gleaned was from somebody named Carla, who was clearly not Laotian and who wrote in comfortable, colloquial English. So Carla was American, then. Or maybe British. Or Australian. One sentence on the boy's computer screen popped out at me: "I still long for you as my lover."

Which snapped me from my reverie. Dear Lord, what was I doing reading somebody's private correspondence? And over his shoulder, no less? I pulled my eyes away, ashamed of myself. This was none of my business. I returned my attention to Delaware Valley real estate listings. Though naturally I found it a tad difficult to focus on my own tasks anymore, because, come on: *Who the hell was Carla?*

How had a young Western woman and a teenage Laotian monk met in the first place? How old was she? And when she wrote, "I still long for you as my lover," had she meant, "I *want* you as my lover?" — or had this relationship been consummated, and she was now cherishing a memory of shared physical passion? If Carla and the monk *had* consummated their love affair — well, how? When? Perhaps Carla had been on vacation

163

in Luang Prabang, and maybe she'd struck up a conversation somehow with this boy, despite the fact that females should not even gaze at the novices? Had he sung out "Hello, Mrs. Lady!" to her, and maybe things had tumbled toward a sexual encounter from there? What would become of them now? Was this boy going to give up his vows and move to Australia now? (Or Britain, or Canada, or Memphis?) Would Carla relocate to Laos? Would they ever see each other again? Would he be defrocked if they were caught? (Do you even call it "defrocked" in Buddhism?) Was this love affair going to ruin his life? Or hers? Or both?

The boy stared at his computer in rapt silence, studying his love letter with such concentration that he had no awareness whatsoever of me sitting right there beside him, worrying silently about his future. And I *was* worried about him — worried that he was in way over his head here, and that this chain of action could only lead to heartache.

Then again, you cannot stop the flood of desire as it moves through the world, inappropriate though it may sometimes be. It is the prerogative of all humans to make ludicrous choices, to fall in love with the most unlikely of partners, and to set themselves up for the most predictable of calamities. So Carla had the hots for a teenage monk — what of it? How could I judge her for this? Over the course of my own life, hadn't I also fallen in love with many inappropriate men? And weren't the beautiful young "spiritual" ones the most alluring of all?

The monk did not type out a response to Carla — or at least not that afternoon. He read the letter a few more times, as carefully as though he were studying a religious text. Then he sat for a long while in silence, hands resting lightly on his lap, eyes closed as though in meditation. Finally the boy took action: He printed out the e-mail. He read Carla's words once more, this time on paper. He folded the note with tenderness, as though he were folding an origami crane, and tucked it away somewhere inside his orange robes. Then this beautiful almost-child of a young man disconnected from the Internet and walked out of the café into the searing heat of the ancient river town.

I stood up after a moment and followed him outside, unnoticed. I watched as he walked up the street, moving slowly in the direction of the central temple on the hill, looking neither to the left nor the right. Soon enough a group of young monks came walking by, gradually overtaking him, and

165

Carla's monk quietly joined their ranks, disappearing into the crowd of slim young novices like an orange fish vanishing into a school of its duplicate brothers. I immediately lost track of him there in this throng of boys who all looked exactly the same. But clearly these boys were not all exactly the same. Only one of those young Laotian monks, for instance, had a love letter from a woman named Carla folded and hidden somewhere within his robes. And as crazy as it seemed, and as dangerous a game as he was playing here, I could not help but feel a little excited for the kid.

Whatever the outcome, something was *happening* to him.

The Buddha taught that all human suffering is rooted in desire. Don't we all know this to be true? Any of us who have ever desired something and then didn't get it (or, worse, got it and subsequently lost it) know full well the suffering of which the Buddha spoke. Desiring another person is perhaps the most risky endeavor of all. As soon as you want somebody — really want him — it is as though you have taken a surgical needle and sutured your happiness to the skin of that person, so that any separation will now cause you a lacerating injury. All you know is that you must obtain the object of your desire by any means necessary, and then never be parted. All you can think about is your beloved. Lost in such primal urgency, you no longer completely own yourself. You have become an indentured servant to your own yearnings.

So you can see why the Buddha, who taught serene detachment as a path to wisdom, might not have approved of this young monk furtively carrying around love letters from somebody named Carla. You can see how Lord Buddha might have regarded this tryst as a bit of distraction. Certainly no relationship rooted in secrecy and lust would have impressed him. But then the Buddha was not a big fan of sexual or romantic intimacy anyhow. Remember, before he became the Perfected One, he had abandoned a wife and child of his own in order to set forth unencumbered on a spiritual journey. Much like the early Christian fathers, the Buddha taught that only the celibate and the solitary can find enlightenment. Therefore, traditional Buddhism has always been somewhat suspicious of marriage. The Buddhist path is a journey of nonattachment, and marriage is an estate that brings an intrinsic sense of attachment to spouse, children, and home. The journey to enlightenment begins by walking away from all that.

There does exist a role for married people in traditional Buddhist culture, but it's more of a supporting role than anything else. The Buddha referred to married people as "householders." He even gave clear instructions as to how one should be a good householder: Be nice to your spouse, be honest, be faithful, give alms to the poor, buy some insurance against fire and flood . . .

I'm dead serious: The Buddha literally advised married couples to buy property insurance.

Not quite as exciting a path as parting the veil of illusion and standing on the shimmering threshold of untarnished perfection, now is it? But as far as the Buddha was concerned, enlightenment was simply not available to householders. In this way, again, he resembled the early Christian fathers, who believed that spousal attachment was nothing but an obstacle to heaven — which does lead one to start pondering exactly what these enlightened beings had against couplehood anyhow. Why all the hostility toward romantic and sexual union, or even toward steadfast marriage? Why all the resistance to love? Or perhaps it wasn't love that was the problem; Jesus and the Buddha were the greatest teachers of love and compassion the world has ever seen. Perhaps it was the attendant danger of desire that caused these masters to worry for people's souls and sanity and equilibrium.

The problem is that we're all full of desire; it is the very hallmark of our emotional existence, and it can lead to our downfall — and to the downfall of others. In the most famous treatise on desire ever written, *The Symposium,* Plato describes a famous dinner party during which the playwright Aristophanes lays out the mythical story of why we humans have such deep longings for union with each other, and why our acts of union can sometimes be so unsatisfying and even destructive.

Once upon a time, Aristophanes relates, there were gods in the heavens and humans down on earth. But we humans did not look the way we look today. Instead, we each had two heads and four legs and four arms — a perfect melding, in other words, of two people joined together, seamlessly united into one being. We came in three different possible gender or sexual variations: male/female meldings, male/male meldings, and female/female meldings, depending on what suited each creature the best. Since we each had the perfect partner sewn into the very fabric of our being, we were all happy. Thus, all of us double-headed, eight-limbed, perfectly contented creatures moved across the earth much the same way that the planets travel through the heavens — dreamily, orderly, smoothly. We lacked for nothing; we had no unmet needs; we wanted nobody. There was no strife and no chaos. We were whole.

But in our wholeness, we became overly proud. In our pride, we neglected to worship the gods. The mighty Zeus punished us for our neglect by cutting all the double-headed, eight-limbed, perfectly contented humans in half, thereby creating a world of cruelly severed one-headed, two-armed, two-legged miserable creatures. In this moment of mass amputation, Zeus inflicted on mankind that most painful of human conditions: the dull and constant sense that we are not quite whole. For the rest of time, humans would be born sensing that there was some missing part — a lost half, which we love almost more than we love ourselves — and that this missing part was out there someplace, spinning through the universe in the form of another person. We would also be born believing that if only we searched relentlessly enough, we might someday find that vanished half, that other soul. Through union with the other, we would recomplete our original form, never to experience loneliness again.

This is the singular fantasy of human intimacy: that one plus one will somehow, someday, equal *one.*

But Aristophanes warned that this dream of completion-through-love is impossible. We are too broken as a species to ever entirely mend through simple union. The original cleaved halves of the severed eight-limbed humans were far too scattered for any of us to ever find our missing halves again. Sexual union can make a person feel completed and sated for a while (Aristophanes surmised that Zeus had given humans the gift of orgasm out of pity, specifically so that we could feel temporarily melded again, and would not die of depression and despair), but eventually, one way or another, we will all be left alone with ourselves in the end. So the loneliness continues, which causes us to mate with the wrong people over and over again, seeking perfected union. We may even believe at times that we have found our other half, but it's more likely that all we've found is somebody else who is searching for his other half — somebody who is equally desperate to believe that he has found that completion in us.

This is how infatuation begins. And infatuation is the most perilous aspect of human desire. Infatuation leads to what psychologists call "intrusive thinking" — that famously distracted state in which you cannot concentrate on anything other than the object of your obsession. Once infatuation strikes, all else — jobs, relationships, responsibilities, food, sleep, work — falls by the wayside as you nurse fantasies about your dearest one that quickly become repetitive, invasive, and all-consuming. Infatuation alters your brain chemistry, as though you were dousing yourself with opiates and stimulants. The brain scans and mood swings of an infatuated lover, scientists have recently discovered, look remarkably similar to the brain scans and mood swings of a cocaine addict — and not surprisingly, as it turns out, because infatuation *is* an addiction, with measurable chemical effects on the brain. As the anthropologist and infatuation expert Dr. Helen Fisher has explained, infatuated lovers, just like any junkie, "will go to unhealthy, humiliating, and even physically dangerous lengths to procure their narcotic."

Nowhere is that drug stronger than at the

very beginning of a passionate relationship. Fisher has noted that an awful lot of babies are conceived during the first six months of a love story, a fact that I find really noteworthy. Hypnotic obsession can lead to a sense of euphoric abandon, and euphoric abandon is the very best way to find yourself accidentally pregnant. Some anthropologists argue, in fact, that the human species needs infatuation as a reproductive tool in order to keep us reckless enough to risk the hazards of pregnancy so that we can constantly replenish our ranks.

Fisher's research has also shown that people are far more susceptible to infatuation when they are going through delicate or vulnerable times in their lives. The more unsettled and unbalanced we feel, the more quickly and recklessly we are likely fall in love. This makes infatuation start to sound like a dormant virus, lying in wait, ever ready to attack our weakened emotional immune systems. College students, for instance — away from home for the first time, uncertain, lacking familiar support networks — are notoriously susceptible to infatuation. And we all know that travelers in foreign lands often fall wildly in love, overnight it seems, with total strangers. In the flux and thrill of travel, our protective mechanisms break down quickly. This is marvelous in one way (for the rest of my life I will always feel a shiver of pleasure whenever I remember kissing that guy outside the bus terminal in Madrid), but it is wise in such circumstances to heed the advice of the venerable North American philosopher Pamela Anderson: "Never get married on vacation."

Anybody going through a difficult time emotionally — due to the death of a family member, perhaps, or the loss of a job — is also susceptible to unstable love. The sick and the wounded and the frightened are famously vulnerable to sudden love, too — which helps explain why so many battle-torn soldiers marry their nurses. Spouses with relationships in crisis are also prime candidates for infatuation with a new lover, as I can personally attest from the mad commotion that surrounded the end of my own first marriage — when I had the good, solid judgment to go out in the world and fall quite insanely in love with another man at the very same moment as I was leaving my husband. My great unhappiness and my shredded sense of self made me ripe for the plucking of infatuation, and boy, did I get plucked. In my situation (and from what I know now, it is a tediously common textbook example), my new love interest seemed to have a giant EXIT sign hanging over his head — and I dived right through that exit, using the love affair as an excuse to escape my collapsing marriage, then claiming with an almost hysterical certainty that *this* person was everything I truly needed in life.

Shocking how that didn't work out.

The problem with infatuation, of course, is that it's a mirage, a trick of the eye — indeed, a trick of the endocrine system. Infatuation is not quite the same thing as love; it's more like love's shady second cousin who's always borrowing money and can't hold down a job. When you become infatuated with somebody, you're not really looking at that person; you're just captivated by your own reflection, intoxicated by a dream of completion that you have projected on a virtual stranger. We tend, in such a state, to decide all sorts of spectacular things about our lovers that may or may not be true. We perceive something almost divine in our beloved, even if our friends and family might not get it. One man's Venus is another man's bimbo, after all, and somebody else might easily consider your personal Adonis to be a flat-out boring little loser.

Of course all lovers do — and should —

see their partners through generous eyes. It's natural, even appropriate, to exaggerate somewhat our partners' virtues. Carl Jung suggested that the first six months of most love stories is a period of pure projection for just about anyone. But infatuation is projection run off the rails. An infatuation-based affair is a sanity-free zone, where misconception has no limits and where perspective finds no foothold. Freud defined infatuation pithily as "the overvaluation of the object," and Goethe put it even better: "When two people are really happy about one another, one can generally assume they are mistaken." (By the way, poor Goethe! Not even he was immune to infatuation, not for all his wisdom or experience. That staunch old German, at the age of seventy-one, fell passionately in love with the utterly inappropriate Ulrike, a nineteen-year-old beauty who turned down his heated marriage proposals, leaving the aging genius so bereft that he wrote a requiem to his own life, concluding with the lines "I have lost the whole world, I have lost myself.")

Any actual relating is impossible during such a state of pitched fever. Real, sane, mature love — the kind that pays the mortgage year after year and picks up the kids after school — is not based on infatuation but on affection and respect. And the word "respect," from the Latin *respicere* ("to gaze at"), suggests that you can actually *see* the person who is standing next to you, something you absolutely cannot do from within the swirling mists of romantic delusion. Reality exits the stage the moment that infatuation enters, and we might soon find ourselves doing all sorts of crazy things that we would never have considered doing in a sane state. For instance, we might find ourselves sitting down one day to write a passionatc c-mail to a sixteen-year-old monk in Laos — or whatever. When the dust has settled years later, we might ask ourselves, "What was I thinking?" and the answer is usually: *You weren't.*

Psychologists call that state of deluded madness "narcissistic love."

I call it "my twenties."

Listen, I want to make it clear here that I am not intrinsically against passion. Mercy, no! The single most exhilarating sensations I have ever experienced in my life happened when I was consumed by romantic obsession. That kind of love makes you feel superheroic, mythical, beyond human, immortal. You radiate life; you need no sleep; your beloved fills your lungs like oxygen. As painfully as those experiences may have turned out in the end (and they always did end in pain for me), I would hate to see someone go through an entire lifetime never knowing what it feels like to morph euphorically into another person's being. So when I say that I'm sort of excited for the monk and Carla, that's what I'm talking about. I'm glad they have the opportunity to taste that narcotic bliss. But I'm also really, really glad that it's not me this time.

Because here is something I know for certain about myself, as I near the age of forty. I can no longer *do* infatuation. It kills me. In the end, it always puts me through the wood chipper. While I know there must be some couples out there whose love stories began with a bonfire of obsession and then mellowed safely over the years into the embers of a long, healthy relationship, I myself never learned that trick. For me, infatuation has only ever done one thing: It destroys, and generally pretty fast.

But I loved the high of infatuation in my youth, and so I made a habit of it. By "habit," I mean exactly the same thing that any heroin addict means when he speaks of his habit: a mild word for an unmanageable compulsion. I sought passion everywhere. I freebased it. I became the kind of girl about whom Grace Paley was surely thinking when she described a character who always needed a man in her life, even when it might have appeared that she already had one. Falling in love at first sight became a particular specialty of mine in my late teens and early twenties; I could do it upwards of four times a year. There were occasions when I made myself so sick over romance that I lost whole chunks of my life to it. I would vanish into abandon at the beginning of the encounter but soon enough find myself sobbing and barfing at the end of it. Along the way I would lose so much sleep and so much sanity that parts of the whole process start to look, in retrospect, like an alcoholic blackout. Except without the alcohol.

Should such a young lady have gotten married at the age of twenty-five? Wisdom and Prudence might have suggested not. But I did not invite Wisdom or Prudence to my wedding. (In my defense, nor were they guests of the groom.) I was a careless girl back then, in every possible way. I once read a newspaper article about a man who caused thousands of acres of forest to burn down because he drove all day through a national park with his muffler dragging, causing explosive sparks to leap into the dry underbrush and set a new small fire every few hundred feet. Other motorists along the way kept honking and waving and trying to alert the driver's attention to the damage he was causing, but the guy was happily listening to his radio and didn't notice the catastrophe he had set in motion behind him.

That was me in my youth.

Only when I reached my early thirties, only once my ex-husband and I had wrecked our marriage for good, only once my life had been utterly disrupted (as well as the lives of a few very nice men, a few not-so-nice men, and a handful of innocent bystanders) did I finally stop the car. I got out and looked around at the charred landscape, blinked a bit, and asked, "You don't mean to suggest that all this mess might have something to do with *me?*"

Then came the depression.

The Quaker teacher Parker Palmer once said of his own life that depression was a friend sent to save him from the exaggerated elevations of false euphoria that he'd been manufacturing forever. Depression pushed him back down to earth, Palmer said, back down to a level where it might finally be safe for him to walk and stand in reality. I, too, needed to be hauled down to the real after years spent artificially hoisting myself aloft with one thoughtless passion after another. I've come to see my season of depression, too, as having been essential — if also grim and sorrowful.

I used that time alone to study myself, to truthfully answer painful questions, and — with the help of a patient therapist — to work out the origins of my most destructive behaviors. I traveled (and veered away from handsome Spanish men in bus terminals). I diligently pursued healthier forms of joy. I spent a lot of time alone. I'd never been alone before, but I mapped my way through it. I learned how to pray, atoning as best I could for the burned wasteland behind me. Most of all, though, I practiced the novel art of self-comfort, resisting all fleeting romantic and sexual temptations with this newly adult question: "Will this choice be beneficial to *anybody* in the long term?" In short: I grew up.

Immanuel Kant believed that we humans, because we are so emotionally complex, go through two puberties in life. The first puberty is when our bodies become mature enough for sex; the second puberty is when our *minds* become mature enough for sex. The two events can be separated by many, many years, though I do wonder if perhaps our emotional maturity comes to us only through the experiences and lessons of our youthful romantic failures. To ask a twenty-year-old girl to somehow automatically know things about life that most forty-year-old women needed decades to understand is expecting an awful lot of wisdom from a very young person. Maybe we must all go through the anguish and errors of a first puberty, in other words, before any of us can ascend into the second one?

Anyhow, long into my experiment with solitude and self-accountability, I met Felipe. He was kind and loyal and attentive, and we took it slow. This was not teen love. Nor was it puppy love or last-day-of-summer-camp love. On the surface, I will admit, our love story did seem awfully romantic as it was unfolding. For pity's sake, we met on the tropical island of Bali, under the swaying palm trees, etc., etc. One could hardly summon a more idyllic setting than this. At the time, I remember describing this whole dreamy scene in an e-mail that I sent to my older sister back in the suburbs of Philadelphia. In retrospect, this was probably unfair of me. Catherine — at home with two little kids and facing down a massive house renovation — replied only, "Yeah, I was planning to go to a tropical island this weekend with my Brazilian lover, too . . . but then there was all that traffic."

So, yes, my love affair with Felipe had a wonderful element of romance to it, which I will always cherish. But it was not an infatuation, and here's how I can tell: because I did not demand that he become my Great Emancipator or my Source of All Life, nor did I immediately vanish into that man's chest cavity like a twisted, unrecognizable, parasitical homunculus. During our long period of courtship, I remained intact within my own personality, and I allowed myself to meet Felipe for who he was. In each other's eyes, we may very well have seemed beautiful and perfect and heroic beyond measure, but I never lost sight of our actual realities: I was a loving but haggard divorced lady who needed to carefully manage her tendency toward melodramatic romance and unreasonable expectation; Felipe was an affectionate and balding divorced guy who needed to carefully manage his drinking and his deep-seated fear of betrayal. We were two nice enough people, bearing the wounds of some very average massive personal disappointments, and we were looking for something that might simply be possible in each other — a certain kindness, a certain attentiveness, a certain shared yearning to trust and be trusted.

To this day, I refuse to burden Felipe with

the tremendous responsibility of somehow completing me. By this point in my life I have figured out that he cannot complete me, even if he wanted to. I've faced enough of my own incompletions to recognize that they belong solely to me. Having learned this essential truth, I can actually tell now where I end and where somebody else begins. That may sound like an embarrassingly simple trick, but I do need to make clear that it took me over three and a half decades to get to this point — to learn the limitations of sane human intimacy, as nicely defined by C. S. Lewis, when he wrote of his wife, "We both knew this: I had my miseries, not hers; she had hers, not mine."

One plus one, in other words, is sometimes supposed to equal two.

But how do I know for certain that I will never again become infatuated with anybody else? How trustworthy is my heart? How solid is Felipe's loyalty to me? How do I know without doubt that outside desires won't tempt us apart?

These were the questions that I started asking myself as soon as I realized that Felipe and I were — as my sister calls us — "lifers." To be honest, I was less worried about his loyalties than I was about my own. Felipe has a far simpler history in love than I do. He is a hopeless monogamist who chooses somebody and then relaxes easily into fidelity, and that's pretty much it. He's faithful in every regard. Once he has a favorite restaurant, he's happy to eat there every night, never craving variety. If he enjoys a movie, he'll contentedly watch it hundreds of times. If he likes an item of clothing, you will see him wearing it for years. The first time I ever bought him a pair of shoes, he said quite sweetly, "Oh, that's lovely of you, darling — but I already have a pair of shoes."

Felipe's first marriage didn't end with infidelity (he already had a pair of shoes, if you catch my point). Instead, the relationship was buried under an avalanche of circumstantial misfortunes that put too much pressure on the family and finally snapped the bonds. This was a pity, because Felipe, I honestly believe, is meant to mate for life. He's loyal on a cellular level. I mean that, perhaps, quite literally. There's a theory within evolutionary scholarship these days suggesting that there are two sorts of men in this world: those who are meant to father children, and those who are meant to raise children. The former are promiscuous;

the latter are constant.

This is the famous "Dads or Cads" theory. In evolutionary circles this is not considered a moral judgment call, but rather something that can actually be broken down to the level of DNA. Apparently, there is this critical little chemical variation in the male of the species called the "vasopressin receptor gene." Men who have the vasopressin receptor gene tend to be trustworthy and reliable sexual partners, sticking with one spouse for decades, raising children and running stable households. (Let's call such guys "Harry Trumans.") Men who lack the vasopressin receptor gene, on the other hand, are prone to dalliance and disloyalty, always needing to seek sexual variety elsewhere. (Let's call such men "John F. Kennedys.")

The joke among female evolutionary biologists is that there's only one part of a man's anatomy that any potential mate should worry about measuring, and that is the length of his vasopressin receptor gene. The scantily-vasopression-receptor-gened John F. Kennedys of this world wander far and wide, spreading their seed across the earth, keeping the human DNA code mixed up and jumbled — which is good for the species, if not necessarily good for the women who are loved and then often abandoned. The long-gened Harry Trumans, in the end, often find themselves raising the kids of the John F. Kennedys.

Felipe is a Harry Truman, and by the time I met him, I was so finished with JFKs, so exhausted by their charms and heart-splintering whims, that all I wanted was this reassuring bundle of steadfastness. But I don't take Felipe's decency for granted either, nor do I blithely relax with regard to my own fidelity. History teaches us that just about anybody is capable of just about anything when it comes to the realm of love and desire. Circumstances arise in all of our lives that challenge even our most stubborn loyalties. Maybe this is what we fear most when we enter into marriage — that "circumstances," in the form of some uncontrollable outside passion, will someday break the bond.

How do you guard against such things?

The only comfort I've ever found on this subject came to me through reading the work of Shirley P. Glass, a psychologist who spent much of her career studying marital infidelity. Her question was always, "How did it happen?" How did it happen that good people, decent people, even Harry Truman–like people, find themselves suddenly swept away by currents of desire, destroying lives and families without ever really intending to? We're not talking about serial cheaters here but trustworthy people who — against their better judgment or their own moral code — stray. How many times have we heard someone say, "I wasn't looking for love outside my marriage, but *it just happened*"? Put in such terms, adultery starts to sound like a car accident, like a patch of black ice hidden on a treacherous curve, waiting for an unsuspecting motorist.

But Glass, in her research, discovered that if you dig a little deeper into people's infidelities, you can almost always see how the affair started long before the first stolen kiss. Most affairs begin, Glass wrote, when a husband or wife makes a new friend, and an apparently harmless intimacy is born. You don't sense the danger as it's happening, because what's wrong with friendship? Why can't we have friends of the opposite sex — or of the same sex, for that matter — even if we are married?

The answer, as Dr. Glass explained, is that *nothing* is wrong with a married person launching a friendship outside of matrimony — so long as the "walls and windows" of the relationship remain in the correct places. It was Glass's theory that every healthy marriage is composed of walls and windows. The windows are the aspects of your relationship that are open to the world — that is, the necessary gaps through which you interact with family and friends; the walls are the barriers of trust behind which you guard the most intimate secrets of your marriage.

What often happens, though, during so-called harmless friendships, is that you begin sharing intimacies with your new friend that belong hidden within your marriage. You reveal secrets about yourself — your deepest yearnings and frustrations — and it feels good to be so exposed. You throw open a window where there really ought to be a solid, weight-bearing wall, and soon you find yourself spilling your secret heart with this new person. Not wanting your spouse to feel jealous, you keep the details of your new friendship hidden. In so doing, you have now created a problem: You have just built a wall between you and your spouse where there really ought to be free circulation of air and light. The entire architecture of your matrimonial intimacy has therefore been rearranged. Every old wall is now a giant picture window; every old window is now boarded up like a crack house. You have just established the perfect

blueprint for infidelity without even noticing.

So by the time your new friend comes into
your office one day in tears over some piece
of bad news, and you wrap your arms
around each other (only meaning to be
comforting!), and then your lips brush and
you realize in a dizzying rush that you *love*
this person — that you have *always* loved
this person! — it's too late. Because now
the fuse has been lit. And now you really do
run the risk of someday (probably very
soon) standing amid the wreckage of your
life, facing a betrayed and shattered spouse
(whom you still care about immensely, by
the way), trying to explain through your
ragged sobs how you never meant to hurt
anybody, and how you *never saw it coming.*

And it's true. You didn't see it coming.
But you did build it, and you could have
stopped it if you'd acted faster. The moment you found yourself sharing secrets
with a new friend that really ought to have
belonged to your spouse, there was, according to Dr. Glass, a much smarter and more
honest path to be taken. Her suggestion
would be that you come home and tell your
husband or wife about it. The script goes
along these lines: "I have something worrying to share with you. I went out to lunch

twice this week with Mark, and I was struck by the fact that our conversation quickly became intimate. I found myself sharing things with him that I used to share only with you. This is the way you and I used to talk at the beginning of our relationship — and I loved that so much — but I fear we've lost that. I miss that level of intimacy with you. Do you think there's anything you and I might do to rekindle our connection?"

The answer, truthfully, might be: "No."

There might be nothing you can do to rekindle that connection. I have a friend who brought her husband pretty much this exact conversation, to which he replied, "I don't really give a shit who you spend your time with." And there's a marriage that, not surprisingly, ended soon after. (And needed to, I would argue.) But if your spouse is at all responsive, he or she might hear the longing behind your admission, and will hopefully react to it, maybe even countering with an expression of his or her own longing.

It's always possible that the two of you will be unable to figure things out, but at least you'll know later on that you made a heartfelt effort to keep the walls and the windows of your marriage secured, and that knowledge can be comforting. Also, you may avoid cheating on your spouse, even if you may not ultimately avoid divorcing your spouse — and that alone can be a good thing, for many reasons. As an old lawyer friend of mine once observed, "No divorce in human history has ever been rendered more simple, more compassionate, more quick or less expensive by somebody's episode of adultery."

In any case, reading Dr. Glass's research on infidelity filled me with a sense of hope that felt almost euphoric. Her ideas about marital fidelity are not especially complex, but it's just that *I'd never learned this stuff before.* I'm not sure I ever understood the almost embarrassingly remedial notion that you are somewhat in control of what happens within and around your relationships. I shame myself by admitting this, but it's true. I once believed that desire was as unmanageable as a tornado; all you could do was hope it didn't suck up your house and explode the thing in midair. As for those couples whose relationships lasted decades? They must have been very lucky, I figured, that the tornado never hit them. (It never occurred to me that they might have actually constructed storm cellars together underneath their homes, where they could retreat whenever the winds picked up.)

Though the human heart may indeed be shot through with bottomless desire, and while the world may well be full of alluring creatures and other delicious options, it seems one truly can make clear-eyed choices that limit and manage the risk of infatuation. And if you're worried about future "trouble" in your marriage, it's good to understand that trouble is not necessarily something that always "just happens"; trouble is often cultured unthinkingly in careless little petri dishes we have left scattered all over town.

Does all this sound excruciatingly obvious to everybody else? Because it was not excruciatingly obvious to me. This is information I really could've used over a decade ago when I was getting married for the first time. I didn't know any of this stuff. And I am appalled sometimes to realize that I stepped into matrimony without this piece of useful data, or without very many pieces of useful data at all. Looking back on my first wedding now, I'm reminded of what so many of my friends say about the day they brought their first babies home from the hospital. There is this moment, my friends report, when the nurse hands over the infant, and the new mother realizes with horror, "Oh my God — they're going to send this thing home with me? I have no idea what I'm doing!" But of course hospitals give mothers their babies and send them on home, because there is an assumption that motherhood is somehow *instinctive,* that you will naturally know how to care for your own child — that love will teach you how — even if you have zero experience or training for this towering undertaking.

I've come to believe that we all too often make the same assumption about marriage. We believe that if two people really love each other, then intimacy will somehow be intuitive to them, and their marriage will run forever on the mere power of affection. Because all you need is love! Or so I believed in my youth. You certainly don't need strategies or assistance or tools or perspective. And so it came to pass that my first husband and I just went ahead and got married from a place of great ignorance and great immaturity and great unpreparedness simply because we felt like getting married. We sealed our vows without a single clue whatsoever about how to keep our union alive and safe.

Is it any wonder that we went straight home and dropped that baby on its fuzzy little head?

■ ■ ■ ■

So now, a dozen years later, preparing to enter marriage again, it seemed like some more mindful preparations might be in order. The silver lining to the unforeseen long engagement period offered to us by the Department of Homeland Security was that Felipe and I had a luxurious amount of time (every waking hour of the day, actually, for many months on end) to discuss our questions and issues about marriage. And so we did discuss them. All of them. Isolated from our families, alone together in remote places, stuck on one ten-hour-long bus ride after another — all we had was time. So Felipe and I talked and talked and talked, clarifying daily what the shape of our marriage contract would be.

Fidelity, of course, was of primary importance. This was the one nonnegotiable condition of our marriage. We both recognized that once trust has been shattered, piecing it back together again is arduous and agonizing, if not impossible. (As my father once said about water pollution, from his standpoint as an environmental engineer, "It's so much easier and cheaper to keep the river uncontaminated in the first place than it is to clean it up again once it's been polluted.")

The potentially radioactive topics of housework and domestic chores were also fairly simple to address; we'd lived together already and had discovered that we shared these tasks easily and fairly. Similarly, Felipe and I shared a united position on the subject of ever having children (to wit: thanks, but no thanks), and our concordance on this massive subject seemed to erase a textbook-sized volume of potential future marital conflict. Happily, we were also compatible in bed, so we didn't foresee future problems in the human sexuality department, and I didn't think it was smart to start digging for trouble where none existed.

That left just one major issue that can really undo a marriage: money. And as it turned out, there was much to discuss here. Because while Felipe and I easily agree on what is important in life (good food) and what is *not* important in life (expensive china on which to serve that good food), we hold seriously different values and beliefs about money. I've always been conservative with my earnings, careful, a compulsive saver, fundamentally incapable of debt. I chalk this up to the lessons taught to me by my frugal parents, who treated every single day as though it were October 30, 1929, and who opened up my first savings account for me when I was in the second grade.

Felipe, on the other hand, was raised by a father who once traded a pretty nice car for a fishing pole.

Whereas thrift is my family's state-sponsored religion, Felipe has no such reverence for frugality. If anything, he is imbued with a natural-born entrepreneur's willingness to take risks, and is far more willing than I am to lose everything and start all over again. (Let me rephrase that: I am utterly unwilling to lose everything and start over again.) Moreover, Felipe doesn't have any of the innate trust in financial institutions that I have. He blames this, not unreasonably, on having grown up in a country with a wildly fluctuating currency; as a child, he had learned to count by watching his mother readjust her reserves of Brazilian cruzeiros every single day for inflation. Cash, therefore, means very little to him. Savings accounts mean even less. Bank statements are nothing but "zeroes on a page" that can disappear overnight, for reasons completely out of one's control. Therefore, Felipe explained, he would prefer to keep his wealth in gemstones, for instance, or in real estate, rather than in banks. He made it clear that he was never going to change his mind about this.

Okay, fair enough. It is what it is. That being the case, though, I did ask Felipe if he would be willing to let me handle our living expenses and manage our household accounts. I was pretty certain that the electric company would not accept monthly payment in amethysts, so we would have to work out a joint bank account, if only to handle the bills. He agreed to this idea, which was comforting.

What was even more comforting, though, was that Felipe was willing to use our months of travel together to very carefully and very respectfully — over the course of those many long bus rides — work with me on setting the terms of a prenuptial agreement. In fact, he insisted on it, just as much as I did. While this might be difficult for some readers to understand or embrace, I must ask you to please consider our situations. As a self-made and self-employed woman in a creative field, who has always earned my own living, and who has a history of financially supporting the men in my life (and who still, painfully, writes checks to my ex), this subject mattered dearly to my heart. As for Felipe, a man whose divorce had left him not only broken-hearted but also quite literally *broke* . . . well, it mattered to him, too.

I recognize that whenever prenuptial agreements are discussed in the media, it is generally because a rich older man is about to marry yet another beautiful younger woman. The topic always seems sordid, a distrustful sex-for-cash scheme. But Felipe and I were neither tycoons nor opportunists; we were just experienced enough to recognize that relationships do sometimes end, and it seemed willfully childish to pretend that such a thing could never happen to us. Anyhow, questions of money are always different when you're getting married in middle age rather than youth. We would each be bringing to this marriage our existing individual worlds — worlds that contained careers, businesses, assets, his children, my royalties, the gemstones he had been carefully collecting for years, the retirement accounts that I had been building ever since I was a twenty-year-old diner waitress . . . and all these things of value needed to be considered, weighed, discussed.

While drafting a prenup might not sound like a particularly romantic way to spend the months leading up to one's marriage, I must ask you to believe me when I say that we shared some truly tender moments during these conversations — especially those moments when we would find ourselves arguing on behalf of the other person's best interests. That said, there were also times when this process turned uncomfortable and tense. There was a real limit to how long we could discuss the subject at all, before we would need to take a break from it, change the subject, or even spend a few hours apart. Interestingly, a couple of years later, as Felipe and I were drafting our wills together, we encountered this exact same problem — an exhaustion of the heart that kept driving us away from the table. It's dreary work, planning for the worst. And in both cases, with both the wills and the prenup, I lost track of how many times we each uttered the phrase "God forbid."

We stayed with the task, though, and got our prenuptial agreement written under terms that made each of us happy. Or maybe "happy" isn't exactly the right word to use when you're conceptualizing an emergency exit strategy for a love story that is still only at its beginning. Imagining the failure of love is a grim job, but we did it anyhow. We did it because marriage is not just a private love story but also a social and economic contract of the strictest order; if it weren't, there wouldn't be thousands of municipal, state, and federal laws pertaining to our matrimonial union. We did it because we knew that it's better to set your own terms than to risk the possibility that someday down the road unsentimental strangers in a harsh courtroom might set the terms for you. Mostly, though, we pushed through the unpleasantness of these very awkward financial conversations because Felipe and I have both, over time, learned this hard fact to be incontrovertibly true: *If you think it's difficult to talk about money when you're blissfully in love, try talking about it later, when you are disconsolate and angry and your love has died.*

God forbid.

But was I delusional to hope that our love would not die?

Could I dare to even dream of that? I spent an almost embarrassing amount of time during our travels ticking off lists of everything that Felipe and I had going in our favor, collecting our merits like lucky pebbles, piling them up in my pockets, running my fingers over them nervously in a constant search for assurance. Didn't my family and friends already love Felipe? Wasn't that a meaningful endorsement, or even a lucky charm? Hadn't my most wise and prescient old friend — the one woman who had warned me years earlier against marrying my first husband — completely embraced Felipe as a good match for me? Hadn't my hammer-blunt ninety-one-year-old grandfather even liked him? (Grandpa Stanley had watched Felipe carefully all weekend the first time they met, and then finally cast his verdict: "I like you, Felipe," he pronounced. "You seem to be a survivor. And you'd better be one, too — because this girl has burned through quite a few of 'em already.")

I clung to those endorsements not because I was trying to collect reassurances about Felipe, but because I was trying to collect reassurances about *myself*. For exactly the reason so frankly stated by Grandpa Stanley, I was the one whose romantic discrimination was not entirely trustworthy. I had a long and colorful history of making some extremely bad decisions on the subject of men. So I leaned on the opinions of others in order to prop up my own confidence about the decision I was making now.

I leaned on some other encouraging evidence, too. I knew from our two years already spent together that Felipe and I were, as a couple, what psychologists call "conflict averse." This is shorthand for "Nobody Is Ever Going to Throw Dishes at Anyone from Across the Kitchen Table." In fact, Felipe and I argue so infrequently that it used to worry me. Conventional wisdom has always taught that couples *must* argue in order to air out their grievances. But we scarcely ever argued. Did this mean we were repressing our true anger and resentment, and that one day it would all explode in our faces in a hot wave of fury and violence? It didn't feel that way. (But of course it *wouldn't;* that's the insidious trick of repression, isn't it?)

When I researched the topic more, though, I relaxed a bit. New research shows that some couples manage to dodge serious conflict for decades without any serious blowback. Such couples make an art form out of something called "mutually accommodating behavior" — delicately and studiously folding themselves inside out and backwards in order to avoid discord. This system, by the way, works only when *both* people have accommodating personalities. Needless to say, it is not a healthy marriage when one spouse is meekly compliant and the other is a domineering monster or an unrepentant harridan. But mutual meekness can make for a successful partnering strategy, if it's what both people want. Conflict-averse couples prefer to let their grievances dissolve rather than fight over every point. From a spiritual standpoint, this idea appeals to me immensely. The Buddha taught that most problems — if only you give them enough time and space — will eventually wear themselves out. Then again, I'd been in relationships in the past where our troubles were never going to wear themselves out, not in five consecutive lifetimes, so what did I know about it? All I do know is that Felipe and I seem to get along really nicely. What I can't tell you is *why.*

But human compatibility is such a mysterious piece of business anyhow. And not just *human* compatibility! The naturalist William Jordan wrote a small, lovely book called *Divorce Among the Gulls,* in which he explained that even among seagulls — a species of bird that allegedly mates for life — there exists a 25 percent "divorce rate." Which is to say that one-quarter of all seagull couples fail in their first relationships — failing to the point that they must separate due to irreconcilable differences. Nobody can figure out why those particular birds don't get along with each other, but clearly: *They just don't get along.* They bicker and compete for food. They argue over who will build the nest. They argue over who will guard the eggs. They probably argue over navigation, too. Ultimately they fail to produce healthy chicks. (Why such contentious birds were ever attracted to each other in the first place, or why they didn't listen to their friends' warnings, is a mystery — but I suppose I'm hardly one to judge.) Anyhow, after a season or two of strife, those miserable seagull couples give up and go find themselves other spouses. And here's the kicker: often their "second marriage" is perfectly happy, and then many of them do mate for life.

Imagine that, I beg you! Even among birds with brains the size of camera batteries, there does exist such a thing as fundamental compatibility and incompatibility, which seems to be based — as Jordan explains — on "a bedrock of basic psycho-biological differences" which no scientist has yet been able to define. The birds are either capable of tolerating each other for many years, or they aren't. It's that simple, and it's that complex.

The situation is the same for humans. Some of us drive each other nuts; some of us do not. Maybe there's a limit to what can be done about this. Emerson wrote that "we are not very much to blame for our bad marriages," so maybe it stands to reason that we should also not be overly credited for our good ones. After all, doesn't every romance begin in the same place — at that same intersection of affection and desire, where two strangers always meet to fall in love? So how can anyone at the beginning of a love story ever possibly anticipate what the years might bring? Some of it really has to be chalked up to chance. Yes, there is a certain amount of work involved in keeping any relationship together, but I know some very nice couples who put heaps of serious labor into saving their marriages only to end up divorced anyhow, while other couples — no intrinsically nicer or better than their neighbors — seem to hum along happily and trouble-free together for years, like self-cleaning ovens.

I once read an interview with a New York City divorce court judge, who said that in the sorrowful days after September 11, a surprisingly large number of divorcing couples withdrew their cases from her purview. All these couples claimed to have been so moved by the scope of the tragedy that they decided to revive their marriages. Which makes sense. Calamity on that scale *would* put your petty arguments about emptying the dishwasher into perspective, filling you with a natural and compassionate longing to bury old grievances and perhaps even generate new life. It was a noble urge, truly. But as the divorce judge noted, six months later, every single one of those couples was back in court, filing for divorce all over again. Noble urges notwithstanding, if you really cannot tolerate living with somebody, not even a terrorist attack can save your marriage.

On the subject of compatibility, I often wonder sometimes, too, if maybe those seventeen years that separate me from Felipe work to our advantage. He always insists that he's a far better partner to me now than he ever could have been to anybody twenty years ago, and I certainly appreciate (and need) his maturity. Or maybe we're just extra careful with each other because the age difference stands as a reminder of our relationship's innate mortality. Felipe is already in his midfifties; I'm not going to have him forever, and I don't want to waste the years that I do have him locked in strife.

I remember watching my grandfather bury my grandmother's ashes on our family's farm twenty-five years ago. It was November, upstate New York, a cold winter's evening. We, his children and grandchildren, all walked behind my grandfather through the purple evening shadows across the familiar meadows, out to the sandy point by the river's bend where he had decided to bury his wife's remains. He carried a lantern in one hand and a shovel over his shoulder. The ground was covered with snow and the digging was hard work — even for such a small container as this urn, even for such a robust man as Grandpa Stanley. But he hung the lantern on a naked tree limb and steadily dug that hole — and then it was over. And that's how it goes. You have somebody for a little while, and then that person is gone.

So it will come to pass for all of us — for all couples who stay with each other in love — that someday (if we are lucky enough to have earned a lifetime together) one of us will carry the shovel and the lantern on behalf of the other. We all share our houses with Time, who ticks alongside us as we work at our daily lives, reminding us of our ultimate destination. It's just that for some of us Time ticks particularly insistently . . .

Why am I talking about all this right now?

Because I love him. Have I actually gotten this far in my book without having yet said that clearly? I love this man. I love him for countless ridiculous reasons. I love his square, sturdy, Hobbit-like feet. I love the way he always sings "La Vie en Rose" when he's cooking dinner. (Needless to say, I love that he cooks dinner.) I love how he speaks *almost* perfect English but still, even after all these years with the language, sometimes manages to invent marvelous words. ("Smoothfully" is a personal favorite of mine, though I'm also fond of "lulu-bell," which is Felipe's own lovely translation for the word "lullaby.") I love that he has never quite mastered the exact wording or pacing of certain English-language idioms either. ("Don't count your eggs while they're still up inside the chicken's ass," is a terrific example, though I'm also a big fan of "Nobody sings till the fat lady sings.") I love that Felipe can never — not for the life of him — keep straight the names of American celebrities. ("George Cruise" and "Tom Pitt" are two prime examples.)

I love him and therefore I want to protect him — even from me, if that makes sense. I didn't want to skip any steps of preparation for marriage, or leave anything unresolved that might reemerge later to harm us — to harm *him*. Worried that, even with all this talking and researching and legal wrangling, I might be missing some important relevant matrimonial issue, I somehow got my hands on a recent Rutgers University report called "Alone Together: How Marriage Is Changing in America," and went a little crazy with it. This massive tome carefully sorts through the results of a twenty-year survey on matrimony in America — the most extensive such study ever produced — and I pored over the thing like it was the veritable I Ching. I sought solace in its statistics, fretting over charts about "marital resilience," searching for the faces of Felipe and me hidden within columns of comparable variance scales.

From what I could understand of the Rutgers report (and I'm sure I didn't understand everything), it seemed that the researchers had discovered trends in "divorce proneness," based on a certain number of hard demographic factors. Some couples are simply more likely to fail than others, to a degree that can be somewhat predicted. Some of these factors sounded familiar to me. We all know that people whose parents were divorced are more likely to someday divorce themselves — as though divorce breeds divorce — and examples of this are spread across generations.

But other ideas were less familiar, and even reassuring. I'd always heard, for instance, that people who had divorced once were statistically more likely to also fail in their second marriage, but no — not necessarily. Encouragingly, the Rutgers survey demonstrates that many second marriages do last a lifetime. (As with seagull love affairs, some people make bad choices the first time, but do far better with a subsequent partner.) The problem comes when people carry unresolved destructive behaviors with them from one marriage to the next — such as alcoholism, compulsive gambling, mental illness, violence, or philandering. With baggage like that, it really doesn't matter whom you marry, because you're going to wreck that relationship eventually and inevitably, based on your own pathologies.

Then there is the business of that infamous 50 percent divorce rate in America. We all know that classic statistic, don't we? It gets tossed around constantly, and man, does it ever sound grim. As the anthropologist Lionel Tiger wrote trenchantly on this topic: "It is astonishing that, under the circumstances, marriage is still legally allowed. If nearly half of anything else ended so disastrously, the government would surely ban it immediately. If half the tacos served in restaurants caused dysentery, if half the people learning karate broke their palms, if only 6 percent of people who went on roller coaster rides damaged their middle ears, the public would be clamoring for action. Yet the most intimate of disasters . . . happens over and over again."

But that 50 percent figure is far more complicated than it looks, once you break it down across certain demographics. The age of the couple at the time of their marriage seems to be the most significant consideration. The younger you are when you get married, the more likely you are to divorce later. In fact, you are *astonishingly* more likely to get divorced if you marry young. You are, for example, two to three times more likely to get divorced if you marry in your teens or early twenties than if you wait until your thirties or forties.

The reasons for this are so glaringly obvious that I hesitate to enumerate them for fear of insulting my reader, but here goes: When we are very young, we tend to be more irresponsible, less self-aware, more careless, and less economically stable than when we are older. Therefore, we should not get married when we are very young. This is why eighteen-year-old newlyweds do not have a 50 percent divorce rate; they have something closer to a 75 percent divorce rate, which totally blows the curve for everyone else. Age twenty-five seems to be the magic cutoff point. Couples who marry before that age are exceptionally more divorce-prone than couples who wait until they are twenty-six or older. And the statistics get only more reassuring as the couple in question ages. Hold off on getting married until you're in your fifties, and the odds of your ever ending up in a divorce court become statistically almost invisible. I found this incredibly heartening, given that — if you add together Felipe's age and my age, and then divide that number by two — we average out around forty-six years old. When it comes to the statistical predictor of age, we absolutely rock.

But age, of course, isn't the only consideration. According to the Rutgers study, other factors of marital resilience include:

1. **Education.** The better-educated you are, statistically speaking, the better off your marriage will be. The better-educated a *woman* is, in particular, the happier her marriage will be. Women with college educations and careers who marry relatively late in life are the most likely female candidates to stay married.

213

This reads like good news, definitely tipping a few points in favor of Felipe and me.

2. **Children.** The statistics show that couples with young children at home report "more disenchantment" within their marriage than couples with grown children, or couples who have no children at all. The demands that newborns in particular put on a relationship are considerable, for reasons I am certain I do not have to explain to anyone who has recently had a baby. I don't know what this means for the future of the world at large, but for Felipe and me it was more good news. Older, educated, and babyless, Felipe and I are running some pretty good odds here as a couple — or at least according to the bookies at Rutgers.

3. **Cohabitation.** Ah, but here is where the tide begins to turn against us. It appears that people who live together before marriage have a slightly higher divorce rate than those who wait until marriage to cohabit. The sociologists can't quite figure this one out, except to

wager a guess that perhaps premarital cohabitation indicates a more casual view in general toward sincere commitment. Whatever the reason: Strike One against Felipe and Liz.

4. **Heterogamy.** This factor depresses me, but here goes: The less similar you and your partner are in terms of race, age, religion, ethnicity, cultural background, and career, the more likely you are to someday divorce. Opposites do attract, but they don't always endure. Sociologists suspect that this trend will diminish as society's prejudices break down over time, but for now? Strike Two against Liz and her much older, Catholic-born, South American businessman sweetheart.

5. **Social Integration.** The more tightly woven a couple is within a community of friends and family, the stronger their marriage will be. The fact that Americans today are less likely to know their neighbors, belong to social clubs, or live near kin has had a seriously destabilizing effect on marriage, across the board. Strike Three against Felipe and Liz,

who were — at the time of Liz's reading this report — living all alone in a shabby hotel room in the north of Laos.

6. **Religiousness.** The more religious a couple is, the more likely they are to stay married, though faith offers only a slight edge. Born-again Christians in America have a divorce rate that is only 2 percent lower than their more godless neighbors — perhaps because Bible Belt couples are getting married too young? Anyhow, I'm not sure where this question of religion leaves me and my intended. If you blend together Felipe's and my personal views on divinity, they comprise a philosophy that one might call "vaguely spiritual." (As Felipe explains: "One of us is spiritual; the other is merely vague.") The Rutgers report offered no particular data about marital-resilience statistics within the ranks of the vaguely spiritual. We'll have to call this one a wash.

7. **Gender Fairness.** Here's a juicy one. Marriages based on a traditional, restrictive sense about a

woman's place in the home tend to be less strong and less happy than marriages where the man and the woman regard each other as equals, and where the husband participates in more traditionally female and thankless household chores. All I can say on this matter is that I once overheard Felipe telling a house-guest that he has always believed a woman's place is in the kitchen . . . sitting in a comfortable chair, with her feet up, drinking a glass of wine and watching her husband cook dinner. Can I get a few bonus points on this one?

I could go on, but I did start — after a while — to get a little cross-eyed and crazy with all these bits of data. My cousin Mary, who is a statistician at Stanford University, warns me against putting too much weight on these sorts of studies anyhow. They are not meant to be read like tea leaves, apparently. Mary especially cautions me to look carefully at any matrimonial research that measures such concepts as "happiness," since happiness is not exactly scientifically quantifiable. Moreover, just because a statistical study shows a link between two ideas (higher education and marital resilience, for instance) doesn't mean that one *necessarily* follows from the other. As cousin Mary is quick to remind me, statistical studies have also proven beyond the shadow of a doubt that drowning rates in America are highest in geographical areas with strong ice cream sales. This does not mean, obviously, that buying ice cream causes people to drown. It more likely means that ice cream sales tend to be strong at the beach, and people tend to drown at beaches, because that's where water tends to be found. Linking the two utterly unrelated notions of ice cream and drowning is a perfect example of a logical fallacy, and statistical studies are often rife with such red herrings. Which is probably why, when I sat down one night in Laos with the Rutgers report and tried to concoct a template for the least possible divorce-prone couple in America, I came up with quite a Frankensteinian duo.

First, you must find yourself two people of the same race, age, religion, cultural background, and intellectual level whose parents had never divorced. Make these two people wait until they are about forty-five years old before you allow them to marry — without letting them live together first, of course. Ensure that they both fervently believe in God and that they utterly embrace family values, but forbid them to have any children of their own. (Also, the husband must warmly embrace the precepts of feminism.) Make them live in the same town as their families, and see to it that they spend many happy hours bowling and playing cards with their neighbors — that is, while they're not out there in the world succeeding at the wonderful careers that they each launched on account of their fabulous higher educations.

Who *are* these people?

And what was I doing, anyhow, steaming away in a hot Laotian hotel room, poring over statistical studies and trying to concoct a perfect American marriage? My obsession was beginning to remind me of a scene I witnessed one fine summer day on Cape Cod when I was out for a walk with my friend Becky. We watched as a young mother took her son out on a bicycle ride. The poor kid was decked out in protective gear from head to toe — helmet, kneepads, wrist braces, training wheels, orange warning flags, and a reflective vest. Moreover, the mother literally had the child's bicycle on a tether as she ran frantically after him, making sure he would never be out of her reach, not even for a moment.

My friend Becky took in this scene and sighed. "I've got news for that lady," she said. "Someday that child's gonna get bit by a tick."

The emergency that always gets you in the end is the one you didn't prepare for.

Nobody sings, in other words, until the fat lady sings.

But still, can't we at least try to *minimize* our dangers? Is there a way to do this sanely, without becoming neurotic about it? Unsure how to walk that line, I just kept stumbling through my premarital preparations, trying to cover every base, trying to foresee every imaginable possibility. And the last and most important thing that I wanted to do, out of a fierce impulse toward honesty, was to make sure that Felipe knew what he was getting — and getting into — with me. I desperately did not want to sell this man a bill of goods, or offer up some idealized seductive performance of myself. Seduction works full-time as Desire's handmaiden: All she does is *delude* — that is her very job description — and I did not want her stage-dressing this relationship during the out-of-town tryouts. In fact, I was so adamant about this that I sat Felipe down one day in Laos, right there on the banks of the Mekong River, and presented to him a list of my very worst character flaws, just so I would be certain he had been fairly warned. (Call it a prenuptial informed consent release.) And here is what I came up with as my most deplorable faults — or at least once I had painstakingly narrowed them down to the top five:

1. I think very highly of my own opinion. I generally believe that I know best how everyone in the world should be living their lives — and you, most of all, will be the victim of this.
2. I require an amount of devotional attention that would have made Marie Antoinette blush.
3. I have far more enthusiasm in life than I have actual energy. In my excitement, I routinely take on more than I can physically or emotionally handle, which causes me to break down in quite predictable displays of dramatic exhaustion. You will be the one burdened with the job of mopping me up every time I've overextended myself and then fallen apart. This will be unbelievably tedious. I apologize in advance.
4. I am openly prideful, secretly judg-

mental, and cowardly in conflict. All these things collude at times and turn me into a big fat liar.

5. And my most dishonorable fault of all: Though it takes me a long while to get to this point, the moment I have decided that somebody is unforgivable, that person will very likely remain unforgiven for life — all too often cut off forever, without fair warning, explanation, or another chance.

It was not an attractive list. It stung me to read it, and I'd certainly never codified my failings for anyone so honestly before. But when I presented Felipe with this inventory of lamentable character defects, he took in the news without apparent disquiet. In fact, he just smiled and said, "Is there anything you would now like to tell me about yourself that I didn't already know?"

"Do you still love me?" I asked.

"Still," he confirmed.

"How?"

Because this is the essential question, isn't it? I mean, once the initial madness of desire has passed and we are faced with each other as dimwitted mortal fools, how is it that any of us find the ability to love and forgive each other at all, much less enduringly?

Felipe didn't answer for a long time. Then he said, "When I used to go down to Brazil to buy gemstones, I would often buy something they call 'a parcel.' A parcel is this random collection of gems that the miner or the wholesaler or whoever is bullshitting you puts together. A typical parcel would contain, I don't know, maybe twenty or thirty aquamarines at once. Supposedly, you get a better deal that way — buying them all in a bunch — but you have to be careful, because of course the guy is trying to rip you off. He's trying to unload his bad gemstones on you by packaging them together with a few really good ones.

"So when I first started in the jewelry business," Felipe went on, "I used to get in trouble because I'd get too excited about the one or two perfect aquamarines in the parcel, and I wouldn't pay as much attention to the junk they threw in there. After I got burned enough times, I finally got wise and learned this: You have to ignore the perfect gemstones. Don't even look at them twice because they're blinding. Just put them away and have a careful look at the really bad stones. Look at them for a long time, and then ask yourself honestly, 'Can I work with these? Can I make something out of this?' Otherwise, you've just spent a whole lot of money on one or two gorgeous aquamarines buried inside a big heap of worthless crap.

"It's the same with relationships, I think. People always fall in love with the most perfect aspects of each other's personalities. Who wouldn't? Anybody can love the most wonderful parts of another person. But that's not the clever trick. The really clever trick is this: Can you accept the flaws? Can you look at your partner's faults honestly and say, 'I can work around that. I can make something out of that.'? Because the good stuff is always going to be there, and it's always going to be pretty and sparkly, but the crap underneath can ruin you."

"Are you saying you're clever enough to work around my worthless, junky, crappy bits?" I asked.

"What I'm trying to say, darling, is that I've been watching you carefully for a long time already, and I believe I can accept the whole parcel."

"Thank you," I said, and I meant it. I meant it with every flaw in my being.

"Would you like to know *my* worst faults now?" Felipe asked.

I must admit that I thought to myself, *I already know your worst faults, mister.* But before I could speak, he relayed the facts quickly and bluntly, as only a man who is all too familiar with himself can do.

"I've always been good at making money," he said, "but I never learned how to save the shit. I drink too much wine. I was overprotective of my children and I'll probably always be overprotective of you. I'm paranoid — my natural Brazilianness makes me that way — so whenever I misunderstand what's going on around me, I always assume the worst. I've lost friends because of this, and I always regret it, but that's just the way I am. I can be antisocial and temperamental and defensive. I am a man of routine, which means I'm boring. I have very little patience with idiots." He smiled and tried to leaven up the moment. "Also, I can't look at you without wanting to have sex with you."

"I can work with that," I said.

There is a hardly a more gracious gift that we can offer somebody than to accept them fully, to love them almost despite themselves. I say this because listing our flaws so openly to each other was not some cutesy gimmick, but a real effort to reveal the points of darkness contained in our characters. They are no laughing matter, these faults. They can harm. They can undo. My narcissistic neediness, left unchecked, has every bit as much potential to sabotage a relationship as Felipe's financial daredevilry, or his hastiness to assume the worst in moments of uncertainty. If we are at all self-aware, we work hard to keep these more dicey aspects of our natures under control, *but they don't go away.* Also good to note: If Felipe has character flaws that he cannot change in himself, it would be unwise of me to believe that I could change them on his behalf. Likewise in reverse, of course. And some of the things that we cannot change about ourselves are mirthless to behold. To be fully seen by somebody, then, and to be loved anyhow — this is a human offering that can border on the miraculous.

With all respect to the Buddha and to the early Christian celibates, I sometimes wonder if all this teaching about nonattachment and the spiritual importance of monastic solitude might be denying us something quite vital. Maybe all that renunciation of intimacy denies us the opportunity to ever experience that very earthbound, domesticated, dirt-under-the-fingernails gift of difficult, long-term, daily forgiveness. "All human beings have failings," Eleanor Roosevelt wrote. (And she — one-half of a very complex, sometimes unhappy, but ultimately epic marriage — knew what she was talking about.) "All human beings have needs and temptations and stresses. Men and women who have lived together over long years get to know one another's failings; but they also come to know what is worthy of respect and admiration in those they live with and in themselves."

Maybe creating a big enough space within your consciousness to hold and accept someone's contradictions — someone's idiocies, even — is a kind of divine act. Perhaps transcendence can be found not only on solitary mountaintops or in monastic settings, but also at your own kitchen table, in the daily acceptance of your partner's most tiresome, irritating faults.

I'm not suggesting that anyone should learn to "tolerate" abuse, neglect, disrespect, alcoholism, philandering, or contempt, and I certainly don't think that couples whose marriages have become fetid tombs of sorrow should simply buck up and deal with it. "I just didn't know how many more coats of paint I could put on my heart," a friend of mine said in tears after she had left her husband — and who, with any sort of conscience, would reproach her for ditching that misery? There are marriages that simply rot over time, and some of them must end.

Leaving a blighted marriage is not necessarily a moral failure, then, but can sometimes represent the opposite of quitting: the beginning of hope.

So, no, when I mention "tolerance," I'm not talking about learning how to stomach pure awfulness. What I am talking about is learning how to accommodate your life as generously as possible around a basically decent human being who can sometimes be an unmitigated pain in the ass. In this regard, the marital kitchen can become something like a small linoleum temple where we are called up daily to practice forgiveness, as we ourselves would like to be forgiven. Mundane this may be, yes. Devoid of any rock-star moments of divine ecstasy, certainly. But maybe such tiny acts of household tolerance are a miracle in some other way — in some quietly measureless way — all the same?

And even beyond the flaws, there are just some simple differences between Felipe and me that we will both have to accept. He will never — I promise you — attend a yoga class with me, no matter how many times I may try to convince him that he would absolutely love it. (He would absolutely not love it.) We will never meditate together on a weekend spiritual retreat. I will never get him to cut back on all the red meat, or to do some sort of faddish fasting cleanse with me, just for the fun of it. I will never get him to smooth out his temperament, which burns at sometimes exhausting extremes. He will never take up *hobbies* with me, I am certain of this. We will not stroll through the farmer's market hand in hand, or go on a hike together specifically to identify wildflowers. And although he is happy to sit and listen to me talk all day long about why I love Henry James, he will never read the collected works of Henry James by my side — so this most exquisite pleasure of mine must remain a private one.

Similarly, there are pleasures in his life that I will never share. We grew up in different decades in different hemispheres; I sometimes miss his cultural references and jokes by a mile. (Or, I should say, by a kilometer.) We never raised children together, so Felipe can't reminisce to his partner for hours on end about what Zo and Erica were like when they were little kids — as he might have done had he stayed married to their mother for thirty years. Felipe relishes fine wines almost to the point of holy rapture, but any good wine is wasted on me. He loves to speak French; I don't understand French. He would prefer to linger lazily in bed with me all morning, but if I'm not awake and doing something productive by dawn, I begin to twitch with a kind of ferocious Yankee mania. Moreover, Felipe will never have as quiet a life with me as he might want. He's solitary; I am not. Like a dog, I have pack needs; like a cat, he prefers a quieter house. As long as he is married to me, his house will never be quiet.

And may I add: This is only a partial list.

Some of these differences are significant, others not so much, but all of them are inalterable. In the end, it seems to me that forgiveness may be the only realistic antidote we are offered in love, to combat the inescapable disappointments of intimacy. We humans come into this world — as Aristophanes so beautifully explained — feeling as though we have been sawed in half, desperate to find somebody who will recognize us and repair us. (Or repair us.) Desire is the severed umbilicus that is always with us, always bleeding and wanting and longing for flawless union. Forgiveness is the nurse who knows that such immaculate mergers are impossible, but that maybe we can live on together anyhow if we are polite and kind and careful not to spill too much blood.

There are moments when I can almost *see* the space that separates Felipe from me — and that always will separate us — despite my lifelong yearning to be rendered whole by somebody else's love, despite all my efforts over the years to find someone who would be perfect for me and who, in turn, would allow me to become some sort of perfected being. Instead, our dissimilarities and our faults hover between us always, like a shadowy wave. But sometimes, out of the corner of my eye, I catch a glimpse of Intimacy herself, balancing right there on that very wave of difference — actually standing there right between us — actually (heaven help us) standing a chance.

CHAPTER FIVE:
MARRIAGE
AND WOMEN

TODAY THE PROBLEM THAT HAS NO NAME
IS HOW TO JUGGLE WORK, LOVE, HOME
AND CHILDREN.
— *Betty Friedan,* The Second Stage

During our last week in Luang Prabang, we met a young man named Keo.

Keo was a friend of Khamsy, who ran the tiny hotel on the Mekong River where Felipe and I had been staying for some time already. Once I'd fully explored Luang Prabang both on foot and bicycle, once I'd exhausted myself spying on the monks, once I knew every street and every temple of this small city, I finally asked Khamsy if he might have an English-speaking friend with a car, who could perhaps take us around the mountains outside the city.

Khamsy, thereafter, had generously produced Keo, who had in turn generously produced his uncle's automobile — and away we went.

Keo was a young man of twenty-one years who had many interests in life. I know this to be a fact, for it was among the first things that he told me: "I am a young man of twenty-one years who has many interests in life." Keo also explained to me that he had been born very poor — the youngest of seven children in a poor family in the poorest country in Southeast Asia — but that he had always been foremost in school on account of his tremendous mental diligence. Only one student a year is named "Best Student in English" and this Best Student in English was always Keo, which was why all the teachers enjoyed calling on Keo in class because Keo always knew the correct answers. Keo also assured me that he knew everything about food. Not only Laotian food, but also French food, because he was once a waiter in a French restaurant, and therefore he would happily share his knowledge with me on these subjects. Also, Keo had worked for a while with the elephants at an elephant camp for tourists, so there was a great deal that he knew about elephants.

To demonstrate how much he knew about elephants, Keo asked me, immediately on meeting me, "Can you guess how many toenails an elephant has on its front feet?"

At random, I guessed three.

"You are false," said Keo. "I will permit you to guess again."

I guessed five.

"Unfortunately you are still false," Keo said. "So I will tell you the answer. There are four toenails on an elephant's front feet. Now, how about the back feet?"

I guessed four.

"Unfortunately you are false. I will allow you to guess again."

I guessed three.

"You are still false. There are five toenails on an elephant's back feet. Now, can you guess how many liters of water an elephant's trunk can hold?"

I could not. I could not even imagine how many liters of water an elephant's trunk could hold. But Keo knew: eight liters! As he also knew, I'm afraid, hundreds of other facts about elephants. Therefore, spending a whole day driving through the Laotian mountains with Keo was certainly an education in pachyderm biology! But Keo knew about other subjects, too. As he explained carefully, "It is not only facts and explanations about elephants about which I shall inform you. I also know a great deal about fighting fish."

For that is *exactly* the sort of young man of twenty-one years that Keo was. And that is the reason Felipe elected not to join me on my day trips outside of Luang Prabang — because one of Felipe's other flaws (although he did not mention it on his list) is that he has a very low level of tolerance for being quizzed relentlessly about elephant toenails by serious young men of twenty-one years.

I liked Keo, though. I have an inherent affection for the Keos of the world. Keo was naturally curious and enthusiastic, and he was patient with my curiosity and my enthusiasms. Whatever questions I asked him, no matter how arbitrary, he was always willing to attempt an answer. Sometimes his answers were informed by his rich sense of Laotian history; at other times his replies were more reductive. One afternoon, for instance, we were driving through an immensely poor mountain village, where the people's houses had dirt floors, no doors, and windows cut roughly out of corrugated steel. And yet, as with so many of the places I'd seen in rural Laos, many of these huts had expensive television satellite dishes tacked onto their roofs. I pondered in silence the question of why somebody would choose to invest in a satellite dish before investing in, say, a door. Finally I asked Keo, "Why is it so important to these people that they have satellite dishes?" He just shrugged and said, "Because TV reception is really bad out here."

But most of my questions to Keo were about marriage, of course, that being the theme of my year. Keo was more than happy to explain to me how marriage was done in Laos. Keo said that a wedding is the most important event in a Laotian person's life. Only birth and death come close for momentousness, and sometimes it's hard to plan parties around them. Therefore a wedding is always a huge occasion. Keo himself, he informed me, had invited seven hundred people to his own wedding, just last year. This is standard, he said. Like most Laotians, Keo has, as he admitted, "too many cousins, too many friends. And we must invite them all."

"Did all seven hundred guests come to your wedding?" I asked.

"Oh, no," he assured me. "Over one thousand people came!"

Because what happens at a typical Laotian wedding is that every cousin and every friend invites all their cousins and all their friends (and guests of guests sometimes bring guests), and since the host must never turn anybody away, things can get out of hand quite quickly.

"Would you like me to instruct you now with facts and information about the traditional wedding gift of a traditional Laotian marriage?" Keo asked.

I would like that very much, I said, and so Keo explained. When a Laotian couple is about to get married, they send invitation cards to each guest. The guests take these original invitation cards (with their names and addresses on them), fold the cards into the shape of a small envelope, and stick some money inside. On the wedding day, all these envelopes go into a giant wooden box. This immense donation is the money with which the couple will begin their new life together. This is why Keo and his bride invited so many guests to the wedding: to guarantee the highest possible cash infusion.

Later, when the wedding party is over, the bride and groom sit up all night and count the money. While the groom counts, the bride sits with a notebook, writing down exactly how much money was given by each guest. This is not so that detailed thank-you notes can be written later (as my WASP-y mind immediately assumed), but so that a careful accounting can be kept forever. That notebook — which is really a banking ledger — will be stored in a safe place, to be consulted many times over the coming years. Such that, five years later, when your cousin down in Vientiane gets married, you will go check that old notebook and confirm how much money he gave to you on your wedding day, and then you will give him back the exact same amount of money on the occasion of his marriage. In fact, you will give him back a tiny bit more money than he gave you, as interest.

"Adjusted for inflation!" as Keo explained proudly.

The wedding money, then, is not really a gift: It's an exhaustively catalogued and ever-shifting loan, circulating from one family to the next as each new couple starts a life together. You use your wedding money to get yourself going in the world, to buy a piece of property or start a small business, and then, as you settle into prosperity, you pay that money back slowly over the years, one wedding at a time.

This system makes brilliant sense in a country of such extreme poverty and economic chaos. Laos suffered for decades behind the most restrictive communistic "Bamboo Curtain" in all of Asia, where one incompetent government after another presided over a financial scorched earth policy, and where national banks withered and died in corrupt and incompetent hands. In response, the people gathered together their pennies and turned their wedding ceremonies into a banking system that really worked: the nation's only truly trustworthy National Trust. This entire social contract was built on the collective understanding that, as a young bride and groom, your wedding money doesn't belong to you; it belongs to the community, and the community must be paid back. With interest. To a certain extent, this means that your marriage doesn't entirely belong to you, either; it also belongs to the community, which will be expecting a dividend out of your union. Your marriage, in effect, becomes a business in which everyone around you owns a literal share.

The stakes of that share became clearer to me one afternoon when Keo drove me far out of the mountains of Luang Prabang to a tiny village called Ban Phanom — a distant lowland community populated by an ethnic minority called the Leu, a people who had fled to Laos from China a few centuries earlier, seeking relief from prejudice and persecution, bringing with them only their silkworms and their agricultural skills. Keo had a friend from university who lived in the village and was now working as a weaver, just like every other Leu woman around. This girl and her mother had agreed to meet with me and talk to me about marriage, and Keo had agreed to translate.

The family lived in a clean square bamboo house with a concrete floor. There were no windows, in order to keep out the ferocious sun. The effect, once you were inside the house, was something like sitting in a giant wicker sewing basket — which was fitting in this culture of gifted weavers. The women brought me a tiny stool to sit on and a glass of water. The house was almost empty of furniture, but in the living room were displayed the family's most valuable objects, lined up in a row in order of importance: a brand-new loom, a brand-new motorcycle, and a brand-new television.

Keo's friend was named Joy, and her mother was Ting — an attractive, roundish woman in her forties. While the daughter sat in silence, hemming a silk textile, her mother bubbled over with enthusiasm, so I directed all my questions at Mom. I asked Ting about the traditions of marriage in her particular village and she said that it was all fairly simple. If a boy likes a girl, and the girl likes the boy in return, then the parents will meet and talk over a plan. If all goes well, both families will soon find themselves visiting a special monk, who will consult the Buddhist calendar to find an auspicious date for the couple to marry. Then the young people will marry, with everyone in the community lending money. And those marriages last forever, Ting was eager to explain, because there is no such thing as divorce in the village of Ban Phanom.

Now I had heard remarks like this before in my travels. And I always take it with a grain of salt, because nowhere in the world is there "no such thing as divorce." If you dig a bit, you will always find a story buried somewhere about a marriage that failed. Everywhere. Trust me. It all reminds me of that moment in Edith Wharton's *The House of Mirth* when a gossipy old society lady observes: "There is a divorce and a case of appendicitis in every family one knows." (And the "case of appendicitis," by the way, was polite old Edwardian code for "abortion" — and *that* happens everywhere, too, and sometimes in the most surprising circles.)

But yes, there are societies where divorce is extremely rare.

And so it was in Ting's clan. When pressed, she owned up that one of her childhood friends did have to move to the capital because her husband had abandoned her, but that was the only divorce she could think of in the last five years. Anyway, she said, there are systems in place to help keep families bonded together. As you can imagine, in a tiny impoverished village like this, where lives are so critically (and financially) interdependent, urgent steps must be taken to keep families whole. When problems arise in a marriage, as Ting explained, the community has a four-tiered approach to finding solutions. First of all, the wife in the troubled marriage is encouraged to keep peace by bending to her husband's will as much as possible. "A marriage is best when there is only one captain," she said. "It is easiest if the husband is the captain."

I nodded politely at this, deciding it was better to just let the conversation slide as quickly as possible on to Stage Number Two.

But sometimes, Ting explained, not even absolute submission can solve all domestic conflicts, and then you must outsource the problem. The second level of intervention, then, is to bring in the parents of both the husband and the wife to see if they can fix the domestic problems. The parents will have a conference with the couple, and with each other, and everyone will try as a family to work things out.

If parental supervision is unsuccessful, the couple moves on to the third stage of intervention. Now they must go before the village organization of elders — the same people who married them in the first place. The elders will take up the problem in a public council meeting. Domestic failures, then, become civic agenda items, like dealing with graffiti or school taxes, and everyone must pull together to solve the issue. Neighbors will toss out ideas and solutions, or even offer relief — such as taking in young children for a week or two while the couple works out their troubles without distractions.

Only at Stage Four — if all else fails — is there an admission of hopelessness. If the family can't fix the dispute and if the community can't fix the dispute (which is rare), then and only then will the couple go off to the big city, outside the realm of the village, to secure a legal divorce.

Listening to Ting explain all this, I found myself thinking all over again about my own failed first marriage. I wondered whether my ex-husband and I might have saved our relationship if only we'd interrupted our free fall sooner, before things turned so completely toxic. What if we had called in an emergency council of friends, families, and neighbors to give us a hand? Maybe a timely intervention could have righted us, dusted us off, and guided us back together. We did attend six months of counseling together at the very end of our marriage, but — as I've heard so many therapists lament about their patients — we sought outside help too late, and put in too little effort. Visiting someone's office for one hour a week was not enough of a fix for the massive impasse we had already reached in our nuptial journey. By the time we took our ailing marriage to the good doctor, she could do little beyond offering up a postmortem pathology report. But maybe if we'd acted sooner, or with more trust . . . ? Or maybe if we'd sought help from our family and community . . . ?

On the other hand, maybe not.

There was a lot wrong with that marriage. I'm not sure we could have endured together even if we'd had the entire village of Manhattan working on our collective behalf. Besides, we had no cultural template for anything like family or community intervention. We were modern, independent Americans who lived hundreds of miles away from our families. It would have been the most foreign and artificial idea in the world for us to have summoned our relatives and neighbors together for a tribal council meeting on matters that we had deliberately kept private for years. We might as well have sacrificed a chicken in the name of matrimonial harmony and hoped that that would fix things.

Anyhow, there's a limit to how far you can go with such musings. We must not allow ourselves to get trapped in eternal games of second-guessing and regret about our failed marriages, although such anguished mental contortions are admittedly difficult to control. For this reason, I'm convinced that the supreme patron of all divorced people must be the ancient Greek Titan Epimetheus, who was blessed — or, rather, cursed — with the gift of perfect hindsight. He was a nice enough fellow, that Epimetheus, but he could see things clearly only in reverse, which isn't a very useful real-world skill. (Interestingly, by the way, Epimetheus was a married man himself, although with his perfect hindsight he probably wished he'd chosen another girl: His wife was a little spitfire named Pandora. Fun couple.) In any case, at some point in our lives we must stop beating ourselves up over bygone blunders — even blunders that seem so painfully obvious to us in retrospect — and we must move on with our lives. Or as Felipe once said, in his inimitable manner, "Let us not dwell on the mistakes of the past, darling. Let us concentrate instead on the mistakes of the future."

In that vein, it did cross my mind that day in Laos that maybe Ting and her community were on to something here about marriage. Not the business about the husband being the captain, of course, but the thought that perhaps there are times when a community, in order to maintain its cohesion, must share not only money and not only resources, but also a sense of collective accountability. Maybe all our marriages must be linked to each other somehow, woven on a larger social loom, in order to endure. Which is why I made a little note to myself that day in Laos: *Don't privatize your marriage to Felipe so much that it becomes deoxygenated, isolated, solitary, vulnerable . . .*

I was tempted to ask my new friend Ting if she had ever intervened in a neighbor's marriage, as a sort of village elder. But before I could get to my next question, she interrupted me to ask whether perhaps I could find a good husband in America for her daughter, Joy? The one with the university education? Then Ting showed off one of her daughter's beautiful silk weavings — a tapestry of golden elephants dancing across a wash of crimson. Maybe some man in America would like to marry a girl who could make something like this with her own two hands, she wondered?

The whole time Ting and I were talking, by the way, Joy was sitting there sewing in silence, wearing jeans and a T-shirt, her hair clipped in a loose ponytail. Joy alternated between politely listening to her mom and at other times — in classic daughterly manner — rolling her eyes in embarrassment at her mother's statements.

"Aren't there any educated American men who might want to marry a nice Leu girl like my daughter?" Ting asked again.

Ting wasn't kidding, and the tension in her voice signaled a crisis. I asked Keo if he could gently probe at the problem, and Ting quickly opened up. There had been some big trouble in the village lately, she said. The trouble was that the young women had recently started making more money than the young men, and had also started getting themselves educated. The women of this ethnic minority are exceptionally gifted weavers, and now that Western tourists are coming to Laos, outsiders are interested in buying their textiles. So the local girls can make a fair bit of cash, and they often save that money from a young age. Some of them — like Ting's daughter, Joy — use their money to pay for college, in addition to buying goods for their families, like motorcycles, TVs, and new looms, whereas the local boys are all still farmers who hardly make any money at all.

This hadn't been a social problem when *nobody* made money, but to have one gender — the young women — now thriving, everything was getting thrown out of balance. Ting said that the young women in her village were growing accustomed to the idea of being able to support themselves, and some of them were delaying marriage. But that wasn't even the biggest problem! The biggest problem was that when young people did get married these days, the men quickly got used to spending their wives' money, which meant that they didn't work as hard anymore. The young men, developing no sense of their own worth, drifted away into lives of drinking and gambling. The young women, observing this situation unfold, didn't like it one bit. Therefore, many girls had decided lately that they didn't want to get married at all, and this was upending the whole social system of the tiny village, creating all kinds of tensions and complications. This was why Ting was afraid that her daughter might never marry (unless perhaps I could arrange a match with an equally well-educated American?), and then what would happen to the family line? And what would become of the boys in the village, whose girls had outgrown them? What would become of the village's entire intricate social network?

Ting told me that she referred to this situation as a "Western-style problem," which meant she'd been reading the newspapers, because this is *entirely* a Western-style problem — one that we've been watching play out in the Western world for several generations now, ever since avenues to wealth became more available to women. One of the first things that changes in any society when women start to earn their own income is the nature of marriage. You see this trend across all nations and all people. The more financially autonomous a woman becomes, the later in life she will get married, if ever.

Some people decry this as the Breakdown of Society, and suggest that female economic independence is destroying happy marriages. But traditionalists who look back nostalgically on the halcyon days when women stayed at home and tended to their families, and when divorce rates were much lower than they are today, should keep in mind that many women over the centuries remained in wretched marriages because they could not afford to leave. Even today, the income of your average divorced American woman still drops 30 percent after her marriage has ended — and it was much worse in the past. An old adage used to warn, accurately enough: "Every woman is one divorce away from bankruptcy." Where would a woman leave *to,* exactly, if she had small children and no education and no way to support herself? We tend to idealize cultures in which people stay married forever, but we must not automatically assume that matrimonial endurance is always a sign of matrimonial contentment.

During the Great Depression, for instance, American divorce rates plummeted. Social commentators of the day liked to attribute this decline to the romantic notion that hard times bring married couples closer together. They painted a cheerful picture of resolute families hunkering down to eat their sparse meals together out of one dusty bowl. These same commentators used to say that many a family had lost its car only to find its soul. In reality, though, as any marriage counselor could tell you, deep financial trouble puts monstrous strains on marriages. Short of infidelity and flat-out abuse, nothing corrodes a relationship faster than poverty, bankruptcy, and debt. And when modern historians looked closer at the lowered divorce rates of the Great Depression, they discovered that many American couples had stayed together because they could not afford to separate. It was hard enough to support one household, much less two. Many families elected to ride their way through the Great Depression with a sheet hung in the middle of their living rooms, dividing husband from wife — which is a greatly depressing image, indeed. Other couples did separate but never had the money to file for legal divorce through the courts. Abandonment was epidemic during the 1930s. Legions of bankrupted American men just got up and walked away from their wives and kids, never to be seen again (where do you think all those hobos came from?), and very few women made the effort to officially report their missing husbands with the census takers. They had bigger things to worry about, like finding food.

Extreme poverty breeds extreme tension; this should surprise nobody. Divorce rates all over America are highest among uneducated and financially insecure adults. Money brings its own problems, of course — but money also brings options. Money can buy child care, a separate bathroom, a vacation, the freedom from arguments over bills — all sorts of things that help stabilize a marriage. And when women get their hands on their own money, and when you remove economic survival as a motivation for marriage in the first place, everything changes. By the year 2004, unmarried women were the fastest growing demographic in the United States. A thirty-year-old American woman was three times more likely to be single in 2004 than her counterpart in the 1970s. She was far less likely to become a mother, too — either early, or at all. The number of households in America without children reached an all-time high in 2008.

This change isn't always welcomed by society at large, of course. In Japan these days, where we find the highest-paid women in the industrial world (as well as, not coincidentally, the lowest birth rates on earth), conservative social critics call young females who refuse to get married and have children "parasite singles" — implying that an unmarried, childless woman helps herself to all the benefits of citizenship (e.g., prosperity) without offering up anything (e.g., babies) in return. Even in societies as repressive as contemporary Iran, young women are choosing to delay marriage and child rearing in increasing numbers in order to concentrate instead on furthering their education and careers. Just as day follows night, the conservative commentators are denouncing the trend already, with one Iranian government official describing such willfully unmarried women as "more dangerous than the enemy's bombs and missiles."

As a mother, then, in rural developing Laos, my new friend Ting carried a complicated set of feelings about her daughter. On one hand, she was proud of Joy's education and weaving skills, which had paid for the brand-new loom, the brand-new television, and the brand-new motorcycle. On the other hand, there was little that Ting could comprehend about her daughter's brave new world of learning and money and independence. And when she looked into Joy's future she saw only a puzzling mess of new questions. Such an educated, literate, financially independent, and frighteningly contemporary young woman had no precedent in traditional Leu society. What do you *do* with her? How will she ever find parity with her uneducated farmer-boy neighbors? Sure, you can park a motorcycle in your living room, and you can stick a satellite dish on the roof of your hut, but where on earth do you park such a girl as this?

Let me tell you how much interest Joy herself had in this debate: She got up and walked out of the house in the middle of my conversation with her mother and I never saw her again. I didn't manage to get a single word out of the girl herself on the subject of marriage. While I'm sure she had strong feelings on the topic, she certainly didn't feel like chatting about it with me and her mom. Instead, Joy wandered off to do something else with her time. You kind of got the feeling she was going around the corner to the deli, to pick up some cigarettes and then maybe go see a movie with some friends. Except that this village had no deli, no cigarettes, no movies — only chickens clucking along a dusty road.

So where was that girl going?

Ah, but therein lies the whole question, doesn't it?

By the way, have I mentioned the fact that Keo's wife was pregnant? In fact, the baby was due the very week that I met Keo and hired him to be my translator and guide. I found out about his wife's pregnancy when Keo mentioned that he had been especially happy for the extra income, on account of the baby's imminent arrival. Keo was enormously proud to be having a child, and on our last night in Luang Prabang, he invited Felipe and me to his house for dinner — to show us his life and to introduce us to pregnant young Noi.

"We met at school," Keo had said of his wife. "I always liked her. She is somewhat younger than me — only nineteen years old now. She is very pretty. Although it's odd for me now that she is having the baby. She used to be so tiny that she barely weighed any kilos at all! Now it appears that she weighs all the kilos at once!"

So we went to Keo's house — driven there by his friend Khamsy the innkeeper — and we went bearing gifts. Felipe brought several bottles of Beerlao, the local ale, and I brought some cute gender-neutral baby clothes that I'd found in the market and now wanted to present to Keo's wife.

Keo's house stood at the end of a rutted dirt road just outside Luang Prabang. It was the last house on a road of similar houses, before the jungle took over, and it occupied a twenty-by-thirty-foot rectangle of land. Half of this property was covered by concrete tanks, which Keo had filled with the frogs and fighting fish he raises to supplement his income as an elementary school teacher and occasional tour guide. He sells the frogs for food. As he proudly explained, they go for about 25,000 kip — $2.50 — a kilo, and on average there are three to four frogs in a kilo because these frogs are quite hefty. So it's a good little side living. In the meantime, he also has the fighting fish, which sell for 5,000 kip each — fifty cents — and which are breeding happily. He sells the fighting fish to local men who bet on the aquatic battles. Keo explained that he had begun raising fighting fish as a young boy, already looking for a way to make some extra money so he would not be a burden to his parents. Though Keo does not like to boast, he could not help but reveal that he was perhaps the best breeder of fighting fish in all of Luang Prabang.

Keo's house took up the rest of his property — that which was not overrun by tanks of frogs and fish — which meant the house proper was about fifteen feet square. The structure was made of bamboo and plywood, with a corrugated metal roof. The one original room of the house had recently been divided into two rooms, to make a living area and a sleeping area. The dividing wall was just a plywood separation that Keo had wallpapered neatly with pages from English-language newspapers such as the *Bangkok Post* and the *Herald Tribune.* (Felipe told me later that he suspects Keo lies there at night, reading every word of his wallpaper, always working to better his English.)

There was only one lightbulb, which hung over the living room. There was also a tiny concrete bathroom with a squat toilet and a basin for bathing. On the night of our visit, however, the basin was filled with frogs, because the frog tanks out front were at capacity. (Here is a side benefit of raising hundreds of frogs, as Keo explained: "Among all our neighbors, we alone do not have a problem with the mosquitoes.") The kitchen was outside the house, beneath a small overhang, with a dirt floor, tidily swept.

"Someday we will invest in a real kitchen floor," Keo said with the ease of a suburban man predicting that he will someday build a winterized deck off the family room. "But I will need to make some more money first."

There was no table anywhere in this house, nor chairs. There was a small bench outside in the kitchen, and underneath that bench was the family's tiny pet dog, who'd just had puppies a few days earlier. Those puppies were about the size of gerbils. The only embarrassment Keo ever expressed to me about his modest lifestyle was that his dog was so very small. He seemed to feel that there was something almost ungenerous about introducing his honored guests to such an undersized dog — as though the petite stature of his dog did not match Keo's station in life, or at the very least did not match Keo's aspirations.

"We are always laughing at her because she is so small. I'm sorry she is not bigger," he apologized. "But she really is a nice dog."

There was also a chicken. The chicken lived in the kitchen/porch area, with a bit of twine tying her to the wall so that she could wander but not escape. She had a small cardboard box and in this box she laid her one egg a day. When Keo presented us with his hen and her cardboard box, he did so in the manner of a gentleman farmer, with a proudly outstretched arm: "And this is our chicken!"

At that moment, I caught a glimpse of Felipe out of the corner of my eye, and watched as a series of emotions rippled across his face: tenderness, pity, nostalgia, admiration, and a little dose of sadness. Felipe grew up poor in southern Brazil, and — like Keo — he'd always been a proud soul. In fact, Felipe is still a proud soul, to the point that he likes to tell people he was born "broke," not "poor" — thereby conveying the message that he'd always regarded his poverty as a temporary condition (as though somehow, as a helpless babe in arms, he had been caught just a little short on cash). And, as did Keo, Felipe leaned toward a scrappy entrepreneurship that had expressed itself at an early age. Felipe's first big business idea came to him at the age of nine when he noticed that cars were always stalling out in a deep puddle at the bottom of a hill in his town of Porto Alegre. He enlisted a friend to help him, and the two of them would wait at the bottom of that hill all day long to push stalled cars out of the puddle. The drivers would give the boys spare change for their efforts, and with this spare change many American comic books were purchased. By the age of ten, Felipe had entered the junk metal business, scouring his town for scraps of iron, brass, and copper to sell for cash. By thirteen, he was selling animal bones (scavenged outside the local butcher shops and slaughterhouses) to a glue manufacturer, and it was partly with this money that he bought his first boat ticket out of Brazil. If he had known about frog meat and fighting fish, trust me: He would have done that, too.

Until this evening, Felipe had had no time for Keo. My guide's officious nature, in fact, bugged him immensely. But something shifted in Felipe as soon as he took in Keo's house, and the newspaper wallpaper, and the swept dirt floor, and the frogs in the bathroom, and the chicken in the box, and the humble little dog. And when Felipe met Noi, Keo's wife, who was tiny even in her advanced all-the-kilos-at-once pregnancy, and who was working so hard to cook our dinner over a single gas flame, I saw his eyes moisten with emotion, though he was too polite to express anything toward Noi but friendly interest in her cooking. She shyly accepted Felipe's praise. ("She speaks English," Keo said. "But she is too timid about practicing.")

When Felipe met Noi's mother — a minuscule yet somehow queenly lady in a worn blue sarong, introduced only as "Grandmother" — my husband-to-be followed some deep personal instinct and bowed from the waist to this diminutive woman. At this grand gesture, Grandmother smiled just the slightest bit (just around the corners of her eyes) and responded with an almost imperceptible nod, telegraphing subtly: "Your bow has pleased me, sir."

I loved Felipe so much at that moment, perhaps the most that I have ever loved him anywhere or at any time.

I must clarify here that even though Keo and Noi had no furniture, they did have three luxuries in their home. There was a television with a built-in stereo and DVD player, there was a tiny refrigerator, and there was an electric fan. When we entered the house, Keo had all three of these appliances working full tilt, to welcome us. The fan was blowing; the refrigerator buzzed as it made ice for our beer; the television blasted cartoons.

Keo asked, "Would you prefer to listen to music or to watch television cartoons during dinner?"

I told him that we would prefer to listen to music, thank you.

"Would you prefer to listen to hard-rock Western music?" he asked, "or soft Laotian music?"

I thanked him for his consideration, and answered that soft Laotian music would be fine.

Keo said, "That is no trouble for me. I have some perfect soft Laotian music that you will enjoy." He put on some Laotian love songs, but he played them at an extremely loud volume — the better to demonstrate the quality of his stereo system. This was the same reason Keo directed the electric fan right into our faces. He had these lavish comforts, and he wanted us to benefit from their greatest possible application.

So it was a pretty loud evening, but this

was not the worst thing in the world, for the loudness signaled a festive air, and we duly followed that signal. Soon we were all drinking Beerlao and telling stories and laughing. Or at least Felipe, Keo, Khamsy, and I were all drinking and laughing; Noi, in her extreme pregnancy, seemed to be suffering from the heat and did not drink the beer but just sat quietly on the hard dirt floor, shifting every once in a while in search of comfort.

As for Grandmother, she did drink beer, but she did not laugh so much with us. She only regarded us all with a pleased and quiet air. Grandmother was a rice farmer, we learned, who came from up north, up near the Chinese border. She came from a long line of rice farmers, and she herself had borne ten children (Noi the youngest), each one delivered in her own home. She told us all this only because I asked her directly the story of her life. Through Keo's translation, she told us that her marriage — at the age of sixteen — was somewhat "accidental." She married a man who was just passing through the village. He had stayed at her family's house for the evening and fallen in love with her. A few days after the stranger's arrival, they were married. I tried to ask Grandmother some follow-up questions about her thoughts on her marriage, but she revealed nothing more than these facts: rice farmer, accidental marriage, ten children. I was dying to know what "accidental" marriage might be code for (many women in my family, too, had to get married because of "accidents"), but no more information was forthcoming.

"She is not accustomed to people finding interest in her life," Keo explained, and so I let the subject drop.

All night long, though, I kept stealing glances at Grandmother, and all night long it appeared to me that she was watching us from a great distance. She exuded a shimmering otherworldliness, marked by a demeanor so silent and reserved that she really at times did almost disappear. Even though she was sitting right across the floor from me, even though I could've touched her easily at any moment with an outstretched hand, it felt as though she was residing somewhere else, viewing us all from a benevolent throne set someplace high up on the moon.

Keo's house — though tiny — was so clean that you could eat off the floor, and that is precisely what we did. We all sat down on a bamboo mat and shared the meal, rolling balls of rice in our hands. In keeping with Laotian custom, we all drank from the same glass, passing it around the room from the oldest person to the youngest. And here is what we ate: wonderfully spicy catfish soup, green papaya salad in a smoky fish sauce, sticky rice, and — of course — frogs. The frogs were the proudly offered main course, since these were Keo's own homegrown livestock, so we had to eat quite a few of them. I had eaten frogs in the past (well, frogs' *legs*) but this was different. These were giant frogs — huge, hefty, meaty bullfrogs — chopped into big parts like a stew chicken and then boiled, skin and bones and all. The skin was the hardest bit of the meal to deal with, since it remained, even after cooking, so obviously a frog's skin: spotted, rubbery, amphibian.

Noi watched us carefully. She said little during the meal except at one point to remind us, "Don't just eat the rice — also eat the meat," because meat is precious and we were valued visitors. So we ate all those slabs of rubbery frog flesh, along with the skin and the occasional bit of bone, chewing through it all without complaint. Felipe asked not once but twice if he could have another serving, which made Noi blush and smile at her pregnant belly in uncontainable pleasure. Though I personally knew that Felipe would rather eat his own sautéed shoe than swallow another hunk of boiled bullfrog, I loved him overwhelmingly again at that moment for his great goodness.

You can take this man anywhere, I thought with pride, *and he will always know how to comport himself.*

After dinner, Keo put on some videos of traditional Laotian wedding dancing, to entertain and educate us. The videos showed a group of stiff, formal Laotian women dancing on a disco stage, wearing fancy makeup and glittering sarongs. Their dance involved pretty much standing still and twirling their hands, smiles cemented on their faces. We all watched this for half an hour in attentive silence.

"These are all excellent, professional dancers," Keo finally informed us, breaking the strange reverie. "The singer whose voice you can hear in the background music is very famous in Laos — exactly like your Michael Jackson in America. And I myself have met him."

There was an innocence to Keo which was almost heartbreaking to behold. In fact, his entire family seemed pure beyond anything I'd ever encountered. Television, fridge, and electric fan notwithstanding, they remained untouched by modernity, or at least untouched by modernity's cool slickness. Here were just some of the elements missing in conversation with Keo and his family: irony, cynicism, sarcasm, and presumptuousness. I know five-year-olds in America who are cannier than this family. In fact, *all* the five-year-olds I know in America are cannier than this family. I wanted to wrap their entire house in a sort of protective gauze to defend them from the world — an endeavor that, given the size of their house, would not have required very much gauze at all.

After the dancing exhibition finished, Keo turned off the television and guided our conversation once more to the dreams and plans that he and Noi shared for their life together. After the baby was born, they would clearly need more money, which is why Keo had a plan to increase his frog-meat business. He explained that he would like to someday invent a frog-breeding house with a controlled environment that would mimic the ideal frog-breeding conditions of summertime, but year-round. This contraption, which I gathered would be some kind of greenhouse, would include such technologies as "bogus rain and bogus sun." The bogus weather conditions would trick the frogs into not noticing that winter had arrived. This would be beneficial, as winter is a difficult time of year for frog breeders. Every winter Keo's frogs fall into hibernation (or, as he called it, "meditation"), during which time they do not eat, thereby losing much weight and rendering the frog-meat-by-the-kilo business a not very good business at all. But if Keo were to be able to raise frogs year-round, and if he were the only person in Luang Prabang who could do so, his would become a booming business and the whole family would prosper.

"It sounds like a brilliant idea, Keo," Felipe said.

"It was Noi's idea," Keo said, and we all turned our attention again to Keo's wife, to pretty Noi, only nineteen years old and so damp-faced from the heat, kneeling awkwardly on the dirt floor, her belly all full of baby.

"You're a genius, Noi!" exclaimed Felipe.

"She *is* a genius!" Keo agreed.

Noi blushed so deeply at this praise that she almost seemed to swoon. She was unable to meet our eyes, but you could tell that she felt the honor even if she could not face it. You could tell that she fully felt how well-regarded she was by her husband. Handsome, young, inventive Keo thought so highly of his wife that he could not help himself from boasting about her to his honored dinner guests! At such a public declaration of her own importance, shy Noi seemed to swell to twice her natural size (and she already *was* twice her natural size, what with that baby due any moment). Honestly, for one sublime instant, the young mother-to-be seemed so elated, so inflated, that I feared she might float away and join her mother up there on the face of the moon.

All of this, as we drove back to our hotel that night, got me thinking about my grandmother and her marriage.

My Grandma Maude — who recently turned ninety-six years old — comes from a long line of people whose comfort levels in life far more closely resembled Keo and Noi's than my own. Grandma Maude's family were immigrants from the north of England who found their way to central Minnesota in covered wagons, and who lived through those first unthinkable winters in rough sod houses. Merely by working themselves almost to death, they acquired land, built small wooden houses, then bigger houses, and gradually increased their livestock and prospered.

My grandmother was born in January

1913, in the middle of a cold prairie winter, at home. She arrived in this world with a potentially life-threatening impairment — a serious cleft-palate deformity that left her with a hole in the roof of her mouth and an uncompleted upper lip. It would be almost April before the railroad tracks thawed enough to allow Maude's father to take the baby to Rochester for her first rudimentary surgery. Until that time, my grandmother's mother and father somehow kept this infant alive despite the fact that she could not nurse. To this day, my grandmother still doesn't know how her parents fed her, but she thinks it may have had something to do with a length of rubber tubing that her father borrowed from the milking barn. My grandmother wishes now, she told me recently, that she had asked her mother for more information about those first few difficult months of her own life, but this was not a family where people either dwelled on sad memories or encouraged painful conversations, and so the subject was never raised.

Though my grandmother is not one to complain, her life was a challenging one by any measure. Of course, the lives of everyone around her were challenging, too, but Maude carried the extra burden of her medical condition, which had left her with lingering speech problems and a visible scar in the middle of her face. Not surprisingly, she was terribly shy. For all these reasons, it was widely assumed that my grandmother would never marry. This assumption never had to be spoken aloud; everyone just knew it.

But even the most unfortunate destinies can sometimes bring peculiar benefits. In my grandmother's case, the benefit was this: She was the only member of her family who received a really decent education. Maude was allowed to dedicate herself to her studies because she really *needed* to be educated, to provide for herself someday as an unmarried woman. So while the boys were all pulled out of school around eighth grade to work in the fields, and while even the girls rarely finished high school (they were often married with a baby before their schooling was completed), Maude was sent to town to board with a local family and to become a diligent student. She excelled in school. She had a special fondness for history and English and hoped to someday become a teacher; she worked cleaning houses to save money for teachers' college. Then the Great Depression hit, and the expense of college grew far out of reach. But Maude kept working, and her earnings transformed her into one of the rarest imaginable creatures of that era in central Minnesota: an autonomous young woman who lived by her own means.

Those years of my grandmother's life, just out of high school, have always fascinated me because her path was so different from everyone else's around her. She had *experiences* out there in the real world rather than settling right into the business of raising a family. Maude's own mother rarely left the family farm except to go into town once a month (and never in the winter) to stock up on staples like flour and sugar and gingham. But after graduating from high school, Maude went to Montana all by herself and worked in a restaurant, serving pie and coffee to cowboys. This was in 1931. She did exotic and unusual things that no woman in her family could even imagine doing. She got herself a haircut and a fancy permanent wave (for two entire dollars) from an actual hairdresser, at an actual train station. She bought herself a flirty, kicky, slim yellow dress from an actual store. She went to movies. She read books. She caught a ride back from Montana to Minnesota on the back of a truck driven by some Russian immigrants with a handsome son about her age.

Once home from her Montana adventure, she got a job working as a housekeeper and secretary to a wealthy older woman named Mrs. Parker, who drank and smoked and laughed and enjoyed life immensely. Mrs. Parker, my grandmother informs me, "was not even afraid to curse," and she threw parties in her home that were so extravagant (the best steaks, the best butter, and plenty of booze and cigarettes) that you might never have known a Depression was raging out there in the world. Moreover, Mrs. Parker was generous and liberal, and she often passed her fine clothes along to my grandmother, who was half the older woman's size, so unfortunately she couldn't always take advantage of this literal *largesse*.

My grandmother worked hard and saved her money. I need to emphasize this here: *She had her own savings.* I believe you could comb through several centuries of Maude's ancestors without ever finding a woman who had managed to save money on her own. She was even squirreling away some extra money to pay for an operation that would have rendered her cleft palate scar less noticeable. But to my mind, her youthful independence is best epitomized by one symbol: a gorgeous wine-colored coat with a real fur collar that she bought for herself for twenty dollars in the early 1930s. This was an unprecedented extravagance for a woman from that family. My grandmother's mother was rendered speechless by the notion of squandering such an astronomical amount of money on . . . a coat. Again, I believe you could pick your way through my family's genealogy with tweezers and never find a woman before Maude who'd ever bought something so fine and expensive for herself.

If you ask my grandmother today about that purchase, her eyes will still flutter in absolute pleasure. That wine-colored coat with the real fur collar was the most beautiful thing Maude had ever owned in her life — indeed, it was the most beautiful thing she would ever own in her life — and she can still remember the sensuous feeling of the fur brushing against her neck and chin.

Later that year, probably while wearing that same fetching coat, Maude met a young farmer named Carl Olson, whose brother was courting her sister, and Carl — my grandfather — fell in love with her. Carl was not a romantic man, not a poetic man, and certainly not a rich man. (Her small savings account dwarfed his assets.) But he was a staggeringly handsome man and a hard worker. All the Olson brothers were known to be handsome and hardworking. My grandmother fell for him. Soon enough, much to everyone's surprise, Maude Edna Morcomb was *married.*

Now, the conclusion I always drew from this story whenever I contemplated it in the past was that her marriage marked the end of any autonomy for Maude Edna Morcomb. Her life after that was pretty much unremitting hardship and hard work until maybe 1975. Not that she was any stranger to work, but things got very tough very fast. She moved out of Mrs. Parker's fine home (no more steaks, no more parties, no more *plumbing)* and onto my grandfather's family's farm. Carl's people were severe Swedish immigrants, and the young couple had to live in a small farmhouse with my grandfather's younger brother and their father. Maude was the only woman on the farm, so she cooked and cleaned for all three men — and often fed the farmhands as well. When electricity finally came to town through Roosevelt's Rural Electrification Administration program, her father-in-law would spring for only the lowest wattage lightbulbs, and these were seldom turned on.

Maude raised her first five — of seven — babies in that house. My mother was born in that house. The first three of those babies were raised in one single room, under one single lightbulb, just as Keo and Noi's children will be raised. (Her father-in-law and brother-in-law each got a room to himself.) When Maude and Carl's oldest son Lee was born, they paid the doctor with a veal calf. There was no money. There was never money. Maude's savings — the money she'd been collecting for her reconstructive surgery — had long since been absorbed into the farm. When her oldest daughter, my Aunt Marie, was born, my grandmother cut up her cherished wine-colored coat with the real fur collar and used that material to sew a Christmas outfit for the new baby girl.

And that has always been, in my mind, the operative metaphor for what marriage does to my people. By "my people" I mean the women in my family, specifically the women on my mother's side — my heritage and my inheritance. Because what my grandmother did with her fine coat (the loveliest thing she would ever own) is what all the women of that generation (and before) did for their families and their husbands and their children. They cut up the finest and proudest parts of themselves and gave it all away. They repatterned what was theirs and shaped it for others. They went without. They were the last ones to eat at supper, and they were the first ones to get up every morning, warming the cold kitchen for another day spent caring for everyone else. This was the only thing they knew how to do. This was their guiding verb and their defining principle in life: *They gave.*

The story of the wine-colored coat with the real fur collar has always made me cry. And if I were to tell you that this story has not shaped forever my feelings about marriage, or that it has not forged within me a small, quiet sorrow about what the matrimonial institution can take away from good women, I would be lying to you.

But I would also be lying to you — or at least withholding critical information — if I did not reveal this unexpected coda to the story: A few months before Felipe and I were sentenced to marry by the Homeland Security Department, I went out to Minnesota to visit my grandmother. I sat down with her while she worked on a quilting square, and she told me stories. Then I asked her a question I'd never asked before: "What was the happiest time of your life?"

In my heart, I believed I already knew the answer. It was back in the early 1930s, when she was living with Mrs. Parker, walking around in a slim yellow dress and a barbershop hairdo and a tailor-fitted wine-colored coat. That had to be the answer, right? But here's the trouble with grandmothers. With all that they give away to others, they still insist on maintaining their own opinions about their own lives. Because what Grandma Maude actually said was "The happiest time in my life were those first few years of marriage to your grandfather, when we were living together on the Olson family farm."

Let me remind you: They had *nothing.* Maude was a virtual house slave to three grown men (gruff Swedish farmers, no less, who were usually irritated with each other) and she was forced to cram her babies and their sodden cloth diapers into one cold and badly lit room. She became progressively sicker and weaker with each pregnancy. The Depression raged outside their door. Her father-in-law refused to run plumbing into the house. And so on, and so on . . .

"Grandma," I said, taking her arthritic hands in mine, "how *could* that have been the happiest time of your life?"

"It was," she said. "I was happy because I had a family of my own. I had a husband. I had children. I had never dared to dream that I would be allowed to have any of those things in my life."

As much as her words surprised me, I believed her. But just because I believed her did not mean that I understood her. I did not, in fact, begin to understand my grandmother's reply about her life's greatest happiness until the night, months later, that I ate dinner in Laos with Keo and Noi. Sitting there on the dirt floor, watching Noi shift uncomfortably around her pregnant belly, I had naturally begun to formulate all sorts of assumptions about her life as well. I pitied Noi for the difficulties she faced by marrying so young, and I worried about how she would raise her baby in a home already overtaken by a herd of bullfrogs. But when Keo boasted to us about how clever his young wife was (what with all those big ideas about greenhouses!) and when I saw the joy pass over the face of this young woman (a woman so shy that she had barely met our eyes the entire night), I suddenly encountered my grandmother. I suddenly *knew* my grandmother, as reflected in Noi, in a way I had never known her before. I knew how my grandmother must have looked as a young wife and mother: proud, vital, appreciated. Why was Maude so happy in 1936? She was happy for the same reason that Noi was happy in 2006 — because she knew that she was indispensable to somebody else's life. She was happy because she had a partner, and because they were building something together, and because she believed deeply in what they were building, and because it amazed her to be included in such an undertaking.

I shall not insult either my grandmother or Noi by insinuating that they really ought to have aimed for something higher in their lives (something more closely approximating, perhaps, my aspirations and my ideals). I also refuse to say that a desire to be at the center of their husbands' lives reflected or reflects pathology in these women. I will grant that both Noi and my grandmother know their own happiness, and I bow respectfully before their experiences. What they got, it seems, is precisely what they had always wanted.

So that's settled.

Or is it?

Because — just to confuse the issue even more — I must relay what my grandmother said to me at the end of our conversation that day back in Minnesota. She knew that I had recently fallen in love with this man named Felipe, and she'd heard that things were getting serious between us. Maude is not an intrusive woman (unlike her granddaughter), but we had been speaking intimately, so perhaps that's why she felt free to ask me directly, "What are your plans with this man?"

I told her that I wasn't sure, other than that I wanted to stay with him because he was kind and supportive and loving and because he made me happy.

"But will you . . . ?" She trailed off.

I didn't finish the sentence for her. I knew what she was digging for, but at that point in my life I still had no intention of ever getting married again, so I said nothing, hoping the moment would pass.

After a bit of silence, she tried again. "Are the two of you planning to have . . . ?"

Again, I didn't supply the answer. I wasn't trying to be rude or coy. It's just that I knew I was not going to be having any babies, and I really didn't want to disappoint her.

But then this nearly century-old woman shocked me. My grandmother threw up her hands and said, "Oh, I might as well ask you outright! Now that you've met this nice man, you aren't going to get married and have children and stop writing books, are you?"

So how do I square this?

What am I to conclude when my grandmother says that the happiest decision of her life was giving up everything for her husband and children but then says — in the very next breath — that she doesn't want me making the same choice? I'm not really sure how to reconcile this, except to believe that somehow both these statements are true and authentic, even as they seem to utterly contradict one another. I believe that a woman who has lived as long as my grandmother should be allowed some contradictions and mysteries. Like most of us, this woman contains multitudes. Besides, when it comes to the subject of women and marriage, easy conclusions are difficult to come by, and enigmas litter the road in every direction.

To get anywhere close to unraveling this subject — women and marriage — we have to start with the cold, ugly fact that marriage does not benefit women as much as it benefits men. I did not invent this fact, and I don't like saying it, but it's a sad truth, backed up by study after study. By contrast, marriage as an institution has always been terrifically beneficial for men. If you are a man, say the actuarial charts, the smartest decision you can possibly make for yourself — assuming that you would like to lead a long, happy, healthy, prosperous existence — is to get married. Married men perform dazzlingly better in life than single men. Married men live longer than single men; married men accumulate more wealth than single men; married men excel at their careers above single men; married men are far less likely to die a violent death than single men; married men report themselves to be much happier than single men; and married men suffer less from alcoholism, drug addiction, and depression than do single men.

"A system could not well have been devised more studiously hostile to human happiness than marriage," wrote Percy Bysshe Shelley in 1813, but he was dead wrong, or at least with regard to *male* human happiness. There doesn't seem to be anything, statistically speaking, that a man does not gain by getting married.

Dishearteningly, the reverse is not true. Modern married women do not fare better in life than their single counterparts. Married women in America do not live longer than single women; married women do not accumulate as much wealth as single women (you take a 7 percent pay cut, on average, just for getting hitched); married women do not thrive in their careers to the extent single women do; married women are significantly less healthy than single women;

married women are more likely to suffer from depression than single women; and married women are more likely to die a violent death than single women — usually at the hands of a husband, which raises the grim reality that, statistically speaking, the most dangerous person in the average woman's life is her own man.

All this adds up to what puzzled sociologists call the "Marriage Benefit Imbalance" — a tidy name for an almost freakishly doleful conclusion: that women generally lose in the exchange of marriage vows, while men win big.

Now before we all lie down under our desks and weep — which is what this conclusion makes me want to do — I must assure everyone that the situation is getting better. As the years go by and more women become autonomous, the Marriage Benefit Imbalance diminishes, and there are some factors that can narrow this inequity considerably. The more education a married woman has, the more money she earns, the later in life she marries, the fewer children she bears, and the more help her husband offers with household chores, the better her quality of life in marriage will be. If there was ever a good moment in Western history, then, for a woman to become a wife, this would probably be it. If you are advising your daughter on her future, and you want her to be a happy adult someday, then you might want to encourage her to finish her schooling, delay marriage for as long as possible, earn her own living, limit the number of children she has, and find a man who doesn't mind cleaning the bathtub. Then your daughter may have a chance at leading a life that is nearly as healthy and wealthy and happy as her future husband's life will be.

Nearly.

Because even though the gap has narrowed, the Marriage Benefit Imbalance persists. Given that this is the case, we must pause here for a moment to consider the mystifying question of why — when marriage has been shown again and again to be disproportionately disadvantageous to them — so many women still long for it so deeply. You could argue that maybe women just haven't read the statistics, but I don't think the question is that simple. There's something else going on here about women and marriage — something deeper, something more emotional, something that a mere public service campaign (DO NOT GET MARRIED UNTIL YOU ARE AT LEAST THIRTY YEARS OLD AND ECONOMICALLY

SOLVENT!!!) is unlikely to change or to shape.

Puzzled by this paradox, I brought up the question by e-mail with some friends of mine back in the States — female friends whom I knew were longing to find husbands. Their deep craving for matrimony was something I had never personally experienced and therefore could never really understand, but now I wanted to see it through their eyes.

"What's this all about?" I asked.

I got some thoughtful answers, and some funny answers. One woman composed a long meditation on her desire to find a man who might become, as she elegantly put it, "the co-witness I have always longed for in life." Another friend said that she wanted to raise a family with somebody "if only to have babies. I want to finally use these giant breasts of mine for their intended purpose." But women can build partnerships and have babies these days outside of matrimony, so why the specific yearning for legal marriage?

When I posed the question again, another single friend replied, "Wanting to get married, for me, is all about a desire to feel *chosen*." She went on to write that while the concept of building a life together with another adult was appealing, what really pulled at her heart was the desire for a wedding, a public event "that will unequivocally prove to everyone, especially to myself, that I am precious enough to have been selected by somebody forever."

Now, you could say that my friend had been brainwashed by the American mass media, which has been relentlessly selling her this fantasy of womanly perfection forever (the beautiful bride in the white gown, wearing a halo of flowers and lace, surrounded by solicitous ladies-in-waiting), but I don't entirely buy that explanation. My friend is an intelligent, well-read, thoughtful, and sane adult; I do not happen to believe that animated Disney features or afternoon soap operas have taught her to desire what she desires. I believe she arrived at these desires entirely on her own.

I also believe that this woman should not be condemned or judged for wanting what she wants. My friend is a person of great heart. Her enormous capacity for love has all too often been left unmatched and unreturned by the world. As such, she struggles with some very serious unfulfilled emotional yearnings and questions about her own value. That being the case, what better confirmation of her preciousness could she summon than a ceremony in a beautiful church, where she could be regarded by all in attendance as a princess, a virgin, an angel, a treasure beyond rubies? Who could fault her for wanting to know — *just once* — what that feels like?

I hope she gets to experience that — with the right person, of course. Thankfully, my friend is mentally stable enough that she has not run out and hastily married some deeply inappropriate man in order to bring to life her wedding fantasies. But surely there are other women out there who have made that exchange — trading in their future well-being (and 7 percent of their incomes, and, let us not forget, a few years off their life expectancy) for one afternoon's irrefutably public proof of worth. And I must say it again: I will not ridicule such an urge. As someone who has herself always longed to be regarded as precious, and who has often done foolish things in order to test that regard, *I get it.* But I also get that we women in particular must work very hard to keep our fantasies as clearly and cleanly delineated from our realities as possible, and that sometimes it can take years of effort to reach such a point of sober discernment.

I think of my friend Christine, who realized — on the eve of her fortieth birthday

— that she had been postponing her real life forever, waiting for the validation of a wedding day before she could regard herself as an adult. Never having walked down an aisle in a white dress and a veil, she, too, had never felt *chosen.* For a couple of decades, then, she had just been going through the motions — working, exercising, eating, sleeping — but all the while secretly waiting. But as her fortieth birthday approached, and no man stepped forward to crown her as his princess, she came to realize that all this waiting was ridiculous. No, it was beyond ridiculous: It was an imprisonment. She was being held hostage by an idea she came to call the "Tyranny of the Bride," and she decided that she had to break that enchantment.

So this is what she did: On the morning of her fortieth birthday, my friend Christine went down to the northern Pacific Ocean at dawn. It was a cold and overcast day. Nothing romantic about it. She brought with her a small wooden boat that she had built with her own hands. She filled the little boat with rose petals and rice — artifacts of a symbolic wedding. She walked out into the cold water, right up to her chest, and set that boat on fire. Then she let it go — releasing along with it her most tenacious fantasies of

291

marriage as an act of personal salvation. Christine told me later that, as the sea took away the Tyranny of the Bride forever (still burning), she felt transcendent and mighty, as though she were physically carrying herself across some critical threshold. She had finally married her own life, and not a moment too soon.

So that's one way to do it.

To be perfectly honest, though, this kind of brave and willful act of self-selection was never modeled for me within my own family's history. I never saw anything like Christine's boat as I was growing up. I never saw any woman actively marrying her own life. The women who have been most influential to me (mother, grandmothers, aunties) have all been married women in the most traditional sense, and all of them, I would have to submit, gave up a good deal of themselves in that exchange. I don't need to be told by any sociologist about something called the Marriage Benefit Imbalance; I have witnessed it firsthand since childhood.

Moreover, I don't have to look very far to explain why that imbalance exists. In my family, at least, the great lack of parity between husbands and wives has always been spawned by the disproportionate degree of self-sacrifice that women are willing to make on behalf of those they love. As the psychologist Carol Gilligan has written, "Women's sense of integrity seems to be entwined with an ethic of care, so that to see themselves as women is to see themselves in a relationship of connection." This fierce instinct for entwinement has often caused the women in my family to make choices that are bad for them — to repeatedly give up their own health or their own time or their own best interests on behalf of what they perceive as the greater good — perhaps in order to consistently reinforce an imperative sense of specialness, of chosenness, of connection.

I suspect this may be the case in many other families, too. Please be assured that I know there are exceptions and anomalies. I myself have personally witnessed households where the husbands give up more than the wives, or do more child rearing and housekeeping than the wives, or take over more of the traditional feminine nurturing roles than the wives — but I can count those households on exactly one hand. (A hand that I now raise, by the way, to salute those men with enormous admiration and respect.) But the statistics of the last United States Census tell the real story: In 2000, there were about 5.3 million stay-at-home mothers in America, and only about 140,000 stay-at-home dads. That translates into a stay-at-home-dad rate of only about 2.6 percent of all stay-at-home parents. As of this writing, that survey is already a decade old, so let's hope the ratio is changing. But it can't change fast enough for my tastes. And such a rare creature — the father who mothers — has never been a character anywhere in the history of my family.

I do not entirely understand why the women to whom I am related give over so much of themselves to the care of others, or why I've inherited such a big dose of that impulse myself — the impulse to always mend and tend, to weave elaborate nets of care for others, even sometimes to my own detriment. Is such behavior learned? Inherited? Expected? Biologically predetermined? Conventional wisdom gives us only two explanations for this female tendency toward self-sacrifice, and neither satisfies me. We are either told that women are genetically hardwired to be caretakers, or we are told that women have been duped by an unjustly patriarchal world into *believing* that they're genetically hardwired to be caretakers. These two opposing views mean that we are always either glorifying or pathologizing women's selflessness. Women who give up everything for others are seen as either paragons or suckers, saints or fools. I'm not crazy about either explanation, because I don't see the faces of my female relatives in any of those descriptions. I refuse to accept that the story of women isn't more nuanced than that.

Consider, for instance, my mother. And believe me — I *have* been considering my mother, every single day since I found out I would be marrying again, since I do believe that one should at least try to understand one's mother's marriage before embarking on a marriage of one's own. Psychologists suggest that we must reach back at least three generations to look for clues whenever we begin untangling the emotional legacy of any one family's history. It's almost as though we have to look at the story in 3-D, with each dimension representing one unfolding generation.

While my grandmother had been a typical Depression-era farmwife, my mother belonged to that generation of women I call "feminist cuspers." Mom was just a tiny bit too old to have been part of the women's liberation movement of the 1970s. She had been raised to believe that a lady should be married and have children for exactly the same reason that a lady's handbag and shoes should always match: because this was what was done. Mom came of age in the 1950s, after all, during an era when a popular family advice doctor named Paul Landes preached that every single adult in America should be married, "except for the sick, the badly crippled, the deformed, the emotionally warped and the mentally defective."

Trying to put myself back into that time, trying to understand more clearly the expectations of marriage that my mother had been raised with, I ordered online an old matrimonial propaganda film from the year 1950 called *Marriage for Moderns*. The film was produced by McGraw-Hill, and it was based on the scholarship and research of one Professor Henry A. Bowman, Ph.D., chairman of the Division of Home and Family, Department of Marriage Education, Stephens College, Missouri. When I stumbled on this old relic, I thought, "Lordy, here we go," and I set myself up to be fully entertained by a bunch of tacky, campy, postwar drivel about the sanctity of the home and hearth — starring coiffed actors in pearls and neckties, basking in the glow of their perfect, model children.

But the movie surprised me. The story begins with an ordinary-looking young couple, modestly dressed, sitting on a city park bench, talking to each other in quiet seriousness. Over the image, an authoritative male narrator speaks about how difficult and terrifying it can be "in the America of today" for a young couple even to consider marriage, given how rough life has become. Our cities are haunted by "a social blight called slums," the narrator explains, and we all live in "an age of impermanence, an age of unrest and confusion, under the constant threat of war." The economy is troubled, and "rising living costs vie against flagging earning power." (Here, we see a young man walking dejectedly past a sign on an office building reading NO JOBS AVAILABLE, DO NOT APPLY.) Meanwhile, "for every four marriages, one ends in divorce." It's no wonder, then, that it's so difficult for couples to commit to matrimony. "It is not cowardice that gives people pause," the narrator explains, "but stark reality."

I could not quite believe what I was hearing. "Stark reality" was not what I had expected to find here. Hadn't that decade been our Golden Age — our sweet national matrimonial Eden, back when family, work, and marriage were all sanctified, straightforward ideals? But as this film suggested, for some couples, at least, questions about marriage were no simpler in 1950 than they have ever been.

The film specifically highlights the story of Phyllis and Chad, a recently married young couple trying to make ends meet. When we first meet Phyllis, she's standing in her kitchen, washing dishes. But the voice-over tells us that only a few years earlier, this same young woman "was staining slides in the pathology lab at the university, making her own living, living her own life." Phyllis had been a career girl, we are told, with an advanced degree, and she had loved her work. ("Being a bachelor girl wasn't the social disgrace it was when our parents called them spinsters.") As the camera catches Phyllis shopping for groceries, the narrator explains, "Phyllis didn't marry because she *had* to. She could take it or leave it. Moderns like Phyllis think of marriage as a voluntary state. Freedom of choice — it's a modern privilege and a modern responsibility." Phyllis, we are told, volunteered for marriage only because she decided that she wanted a family and children more than she wanted a career. That was her decision to make, and she stands by it even though her sacrifice has been a significant one.

Soon enough, though, we see signs of strain.

Phyllis and Chad had apparently met in math class at the university, where "she had gotten better grades. But now *he's* an engineer and *she's* a housewife." Phyllis is shown dutifully ironing her husband's shirts at home one afternoon. But then our heroine finds herself distracted when she stumbles on the plans her husband has been drawing up for a big building competition. She takes out her slide rule and starts checking up on his figures, just as she knows he would want her to. ("They both know she's better at math than he is.") She loses track of time, becoming so engaged in her calculations that she leaves the ironing unfinished; then she suddenly remembers that she's late for her appointment at the health clinic, where she's going to discuss her (first) pregnancy. She had entirely forgotten about the baby inside her because she was so captivated by her mathematical calculations.

Sweet heavens, I thought, *what kind of 1950s housewife is this?*

"A typical one," the narrator tells me, as though he had heard my question. "A modern one."

Our story continues. Later that night,

pregnant Phyllis the math wiz and her cute husband Chad sit in their tiny apartment, smoking cigarettes together. (Ah, the fresh nicotine taste of 1950s pregnancies!) Together, they are working on Chad's engineering plans for the new building. The phone rings. It's a friend of Chad's; he wants to go to the movies. Chad looks to Phyllis for approval. But Phyllis argues against it. The competition deadline is coming up next week and the plans need to be completed. The two have been working so hard on this! But Chad *really* wants to see the movie. Phyllis holds her ground; their whole future rests on this work! Chad looks disappointed, almost childishly so. But he relents in the end, sulking a bit, and allows Phyllis to literally push him back to the drawing table.

Our omniscient narrator, analyzing this scene, approves. Phyllis is not a nag, he explains. She has every right to demand that Chad stay home and complete a business project that could advance them both mightily in the world.

"She gave up her career for him," says our sonorous male narrator, "and she wants to see something come of it."

I felt a strange combination of embarrassment and emotion as I watched this film. I was embarrassed that I'd never before imagined American couples of the 1950s having conversations like this. Why had I unquestioningly swallowed the conventional cultural nostalgia, that this era had somehow been a "simpler time"? What time has ever been a simple time for those who are living it? Also, I was touched that the filmmakers were defending Phyllis in their own small way, trying to get across this vital message to the young grooms of America: "Your beautiful, intelligent bride just gave up everything for you, buster — so you'd damn well better honor her sacrifice by working hard and giving her a life of prosperity and security."

Moreover, I found myself moved that this unexpectedly sympathetic response to a woman's sacrifice had come from somebody as clearly male and authoritative as Dr. Henry A. Bowman, Ph.D., Chairman of the Division of Home and Family, Department of Marriage Education, Stephens College, Missouri.

That said, I couldn't help wondering what would happen to Phyllis and Chad about twenty years down the road — when the children were older and the prosperity had been achieved, and Phyllis had no life whatsoever outside of the home, and Chad was starting to wonder why he'd given up so much personal pleasure over the years to be a good and faithful provider, only to be rewarded now with a frustrated wife, rebellious teenage children, a sagging body, and a tedious career. For wouldn't those be the very questions that would explode across American families in the late 1970s, running so many marriages off the rails? Could Dr. Bowman — or anybody else back in 1950, for that matter — ever have anticipated the cultural storm that was coming?

Oh, good luck, Chad and Phyllis!

Good luck, everyone!

Good luck, my mother and father!

Because, while my mom may have defined herself as a 1950s bride (despite having married in 1966, her assumptions about marriage hearkened back to Mamie Eisenhower), history dictated that she grow into a 1970s wife. She had been married only five years, and her daughters were barely out of diapers, when the big wave of feminist turbulence really hit America and shook every assumption about marriage and sacrifice she'd ever been taught.

Mind you, feminism did not arrive overnight, as it sometimes seems. It's not as though women across the Western world just woke up one morning during the Nixon administration, decided they'd had enough, and took to the streets. Feminist ideas had been circulating through Europe and North America for decades before my mother was even born, but it took — ironically — the unprecedented economic prosperity of the 1950s to unleash the upheaval that defined the 1970s. Once their families' basic survival needs had been met on such a wide scale, women could finally turn their attention to such finer-point topics as social injustice and even their own emotional desires. What's more, suddenly there existed in America a massive middle class (my mother was one of its newest members, having been raised poor but trained as a nurse and married to a chemical engineer); within that middle class, labor-saving innovations such as washing machines, refrigerators, processed food, mass-manufactured clothing, and hot running water (comforts that my Grandma Maude could have only dreamed about back in the 1930s) freed up women's time for the first moment in history — or at least freed up women's time *somewhat.*

Moreover, because of mass media, a woman didn't have to live in a big city anymore to hear revolutionary new notions; newspapers, television, and radio could bring newfangled social concepts right into your Iowa kitchen. So a vast population of ordinary women had the time now (as well as the health, the interconnectedness, and the literacy) to start asking questions like "Wait a minute — what do I really want out of my life? What do I want for my daughters? Why am I still putting a meal in front of this man every night? What if I want to work outside the home, too? Is it permissible for me to get myself an education, even if my husband is uneducated? Why can't I open up my own checking account, by the way? And is it really necessary for me to keep having all these babies?"

That last question was the most important and transformative of all. While limited forms of birth control had been available in America since the 1920s (to non-Catholic married women with money, anyhow), it wasn't until the second half of the twentieth century — and the invention and wide availability of the Pill, that the entire social conversation about child rearing and marriage could finally change. As the historian Stephanie Coontz has written, "Until women had access to safe and effective contraception that let them control when to bear children and how many to have, there was only so far they could go in reorganizing their lives and their marriages."

Whereas my grandmother had borne seven children, my mother bore only two. That's a massive difference within just one generation. Mom also had a vacuum cleaner and indoor plumbing, so things were a little easier for her all around. This left a sliver of time in my mother's life to start thinking about other things, and by the 1970s, there were a lot of other things to think about. My mother never identified herself as a feminist — I do want to make that clear. Still, she was not deaf to the voices of this new feminist revolution. As an observant middle child from a large family, my mother had always been a keen listener — and believe me, she listened very carefully to everything that was being said about women's rights, and a good deal of it made sense to her. For the first time, ideas were being openly discussed that she had been silently pondering for a good long while.

Foremost among these were issues relating to women's bodies and women's sexual health, and the hypocrisies intertwined therein. Back in her small Minnesota farming community, my mother had grown up witnessing a particularly unpleasant drama unfold year after year, in household after household, when inevitably a young girl would find herself pregnant and would "have to get married." In fact, this was how most marriages came to pass. But every time it happened — *every single time* — it would be treated as a full-on scandal for the girl's family and a crisis of public humiliation for the girl herself. Every single time, the community behaved as though such a shocking event had never before occurred, much less five times a year, in families from every possible background.

Yet somehow the young man in question — the impregnator — was spared disgrace. He was generally allowed to be seen as an innocent, or sometimes even as the victim of seduction or entrapment. If he married the girl, she was deemed lucky. It was an act of charity, almost. If he didn't marry her, the girl would be sent away for the duration of the pregnancy, while the boy remained in school, or on the farm, carrying on as if nothing had happened. It was as though, in the community's mind, the boy had not even been present in the room when the original sexual act had occurred. His role in the conception was strangely, almost biblically, immaculate.

My mother had observed this drama throughout her formative years and at a young age arrived at a rather sophisticated conclusion: If you have a society in which female sexual morality means *everything,* and male sexual morality means *nothing,* then you have a very warped and unethical society. She'd never attached such specific words to these feelings before, but when women began to speak up in the early 1970s, she heard these ideas vocalized at last. Amid all the other issues on the feminist agenda — equal employment opportunity, equal access to education, equal rights under the law, more parity between husbands and wives — what really spoke to my mother's heart was this one question of societal sexual fairness.

Empowered by her convictions, she got a job working at Planned Parenthood in Torrington, Connecticut. She took this job back when my sister and I were still quite young. Her nursing skills got her the job, but it was her innate managerial ability that made her such a vital part of the team. Soon my mother was coordinating the whole Planned Parenthood office, which had started out in a residential living room but quickly grew into a proper health clinic. Those were heady days. This was back when it was still considered renegade to openly discuss contraception or — heaven forbid — abortion. Condoms were still illegal in Connecticut back when I'd been conceived, and a local bishop had recently testified before the state legislature that if restrictions on contraceptives were removed, the state would "be a mass of smoldering ruin" within twenty-five years.

My mother loved her job. She was on the front lines of an actual health-care revolution, breaking all the rules by talking openly about human sexuality, trying to get a Planned Parenthood clinic launched in every county across the state, empowering young women to make their own choices about their bodies, debunking myths and rumors about pregnancy and venereal disease, fighting prudish laws, and — most of all — offering options to tired mothers (and to tired fathers, for that matter) that had never before been available. It was as though through her work she found a way to pay back all those cousins and aunts and female friends and neighbors who had suffered in the past for their absence of choices. My mom had been a hard worker her whole life, but this job — this *career* — became an expression of her very being, and she loved every minute of it.

But then, in 1976, she quit.

Her decision was sealed the week that she had an important conference to attend in Hartford, and my sister and I both fell sick with the chicken pox. We were ten and seven years old at the time, and of course we had to stay home from school. My mom asked my father if he would take off two days from work to stay home with us so she could attend the conference. He wouldn't do it.

Listen, I don't want to chastise my father here. I love that man with all my heart, and I must say in his defense: *Regrets have since been expressed.* But just as my mother had been a 1950s bride, my father was a 1950s groom. He had never asked for, nor had he ever expected, a wife who would work outside the home. He didn't ask for the feminist movement to arrive on his watch, and he wasn't particularly passionate about women's sexual health issues. He wasn't all that excited about my mother's job, when it all came down to it. What she saw as a career, he saw as a hobby. He didn't object to her having this hobby — just as long as it didn't interfere with his life in any measure. She could have her job, then, as long as she still took care of everything else at home. And there was a lot to be taken care of at our home, too, because my parents were not just raising a family but also running a small farm. Somehow though, until the chicken pox incident, my mother had managed to do everything. She had been working full-time, keeping the garden going, tending to the housework, making the meals, raising the children, milking the goats, and still being fully available to my father when he got home every night at five-thirty. But when the chicken pox hit and my dad would not give up two days of his life to help out with his kids, suddenly it was too much.

My mother made her choice that week. She quit her job and decided to stay home with my sister and me. It wasn't like she would never work outside the home again (she would always have some part-time job or another while we were growing up), but as for her *career?* That was finished. As she explained to me later, she came to feel she had a choice: She could either have a family or she could have a calling, but she couldn't figure how to do both without support and encouragement from her husband. So she quit.

Needless to say, it was a low point in her marriage. In the hands of a different woman, this incident could have spelled out the end of the marriage altogether. Certainly a lot of other women in my mother's circle seemed to be getting divorced around 1976, and for similar sorts of reasons. But my mother is not one for rash decisions. She carefully and quietly studied the working mothers who were getting divorces, and tried to gauge whether their lives were any better off. She didn't always see tremendous improvement, to be honest. These women had been tired and conflicted when they were married, and now, divorced, they still seemed tired and conflicted. It appeared to my mother that they had maybe only replaced their old troubles with a whole new set of troubles — including new boyfriends and new husbands who perhaps weren't such a big trade-up anyhow. Beyond all this, though, my mother was (and is) at her core a conservative person. She believed in the sanctity of marriage. What's more, she still happened to love my dad, even though she was angry at him and even though he had disappointed her deeply.

So she made her decision, stuck with her vows, and this is how she framed it: "I chose my family."

Am I making far too obvious a point here if I say that many, many women have also faced this kind of choice? For some reason, Johnny Cash's wife comes to mind: "I could've made more records," June said, later in her life, "but I wanted to have a marriage." There are endless stories like this. I call it the "New England Cemetery Syndrome." Visit any New England graveyard filled with two or three centuries of history and you will find clusters of family gravestones — often lined up in a neat row — of one infant after another, one winter after another, sometimes for years on end. Babies died. They died in droves. And the mothers did what they had to do: They buried what they had lost, grieved, and somehow moved on to survive another winter.

Modern women, of course, don't have to deal with such bitter losses — at least not routinely, at least not literally, or at least not *yearly,* as so many of our ancestors had to. This is a blessing. But don't necessarily be fooled into thinking that modern life is therefore easy, or that modern life carries no grieving and loss for women anymore. I believe that many modern women, my mother included, carry within them a whole secret New England cemetery, wherein they have quietly buried — in neat little rows — the personal dreams they have given up for their families. June Carter Cash's neverrecorded songs rest in that silent graveyard, for instance, alongside my mother's modest but eminently worthy career.

And so these women adapt to their new reality. They grieve in their own ways — often invisibly — and move on. The women in my family, anyhow, are very good at swallowing disappointment and moving on. They have, it has always seemed to me, a sort of talent for changing form, enabling them to dissolve and then flow around the needs of their partners, or the needs of their children, or the needs of mere quotidian reality. They adjust, adapt, glide, accept. They are mighty in their malleability, almost to the point of a superhuman power. I grew up watching a mother who became with every new day whatever that day required of her. She produced gills when she needed gills, grew wings when the gills became obsolete, manifested ferocious speed when speed was required, and demonstrated epic patience in other more subtle circumstances.

My father had none of that elasticity. He was a man, an engineer, fixed and steady. He was always the same. He was *Dad.* He was the rock in the stream. We all moved around him, but my mother most of all. She was mercury, the tide. Due to this supreme adaptability, she created the best possible world for us within her home. She made the decision to quit her job and stay home because she believed this choice would most benefit her family, and, I must say, it did benefit us. When Mom quit her job, all of our lives (except hers, I mean) became much nicer. My dad had a full-time wife again, and Catherine and I had a full-time mom. My sister and I, to be honest, hadn't loved the days when Mom worked at Planned Parenthood. There were no quality daycare options in our hometown back then, so we'd often find ourselves having to go to the houses of various neighbors after school. Aside from happy access to our neighborhood televisions (we didn't have the stupendous luxury of TV in our own house), Catherine and I always hated these patched-together babysitting arrangements. Frankly, we were delighted when our mother gave up her dreams and came home to take care of us.

Most of all, though, I believe that my sister and I benefited incalculably from Mom's decision to stay married to our father. Divorce sucks for kids, and it can leave lingering psychological scars. We were spared all that. We had an attentive mom at home who met us at the door every day after school, who supervised our daily lives, and who had dinner on the table when our dad got home from work. Unlike so many of my friends from broken homes, I never had to meet my father's icky new girlfriend; Christmases were always in the same place; a sense of constancy in the household allowed me to focus on my homework rather than on my family's heartache . . . and therefore I prospered.

But I just want to say here — to lock it forever in print, if only to honor my mother — that an awful lot of my advantages as a child were built on the ashes of her personal sacrifice. The fact remains that while our family as a whole profited immensely from my mother's quitting her career, her life as an individual did not necessarily benefit so immensely. In the end, she did just what her female predecessors had always done: She sewed winter coats for her children from the leftover material of her heart's more quiet desires.

And this is my beef, by the way, with social conservatives who are always harping about how the most nourishing home for a child is a two-parent household with a mother in the kitchen. If I — as a beneficiary of that exact formula — will concede that my own life was indeed enriched by that precise familial structure, will the social conservatives please (for once!) concede that this arrangement has always put a disproportionately cumbersome burden on women? Such a system demands that mothers become selfless to the point of near invisibility in order to construct these exemplary environments for their families. And might those same social conservatives — instead of just praising mothers as "sacred" and "noble" — be willing to someday join a larger conversation about how we might work together as a society to construct a world where healthy children can be raised and healthy families can prosper without women having to scrape bare the walls of their own souls to do it?

Excuse me for the rant.

This is just a really, really big issue of mine.

Maybe it is precisely because I have seen the cost of motherhood in the lives of women I love and admire that I stand here, nearly forty years old, feeling no desire whatsoever for a baby of my own.

Of course this is a rather important question to discuss on the brink of marriage, and so I must address it here — if only because child rearing and marriage are so inherently linked in our culture and in our minds. We all know the refrain, right? First comes love, then comes marriage, then comes baby in the baby carriage? Even the very word "matrimony" comes to us from the Latin word for mother. We don't call marriage "patrimony." Matrimony carries an intrinsic assumption of motherhood, as though it is the babies themselves who make the marriage. Actually, often it *is* the babies themselves who make the marriage: Not only have many couples throughout history been forced into marriage thanks to an unplanned pregnancy, but sometimes couples waited until a successful pregnancy occurred before sealing the deal with matrimony in order to ensure that fertility would not later be a problem. How else could you find out whether your prospective bride or groom was a productive breeder except by giving the engine a test run? This was often the case in early American colonial society, in which — as the historian Nancy Cott has discovered — many small communities considered pregnancy to be a stigma-free, socially accepted signal that it was now time for a young couple to tie the knot.

But with modernity and the easy availability of birth control, the whole issue of procreation has become more nuanced and tricky. Now the equation is no longer "babies beget matrimony," or even necessarily "matrimony begets babies"; instead, these days it all comes down to three critical questions: when, how, and whether. Should you and your spouse happen to disagree on any of these questions, married life can become extremely complicated, because often our feelings about these three questions can be nonnegotiable.

I know this from painful personal experience because my first marriage fell apart — to a large extent — over the question of children. My then-husband had always assumed that we would have babies together one day. He had every right to make that assumption, since I had always assumed it myself, though I wasn't entirely sure *when* I would want babies. The prospect of eventual pregnancy and parenthood had seemed comfortably distant on my wedding day; it was an event that would happen sometime "in the future," "at the right moment," and "when we were both ready." But the future sometimes approaches us more quickly than we expect, and the right moment doesn't always announce itself with clarity. The problems that existed within my marriage soon made me doubt whether this man and I would ever be ready, truly, to endure such a challenge as raising children.

Moreover, while the vague idea of motherhood had always seemed natural to me, the reality — as it approached — only filled me with dread and sorrow. As I got older, I discovered that nothing within me cried out for a baby. My womb did not seem to have come equipped with that famously ticking clock. Unlike so many of my friends, I did not ache with longing whenever I saw an infant. (Though I did ache with longing, it is true, whenever I saw a good used-book shop.) Every morning, I would perform something like a CAT scan on myself, searching for a desire to be pregnant, but I never found it. There was no imperative there, and I believe that child rearing must come with an imperative, must be driven by a sense of longing and even destiny, because it is such a massively important undertaking. I've witnessed this longing in other people; I know what it looks like. But I never felt it in myself.

Moreover, as I aged, I discovered that I loved my work as a writer more and more, and I didn't want to give up even an hour of that communion. Like Jinny in Virginia Woolf's *The Waves,* I felt at times "a thousand capacities" spring up in me, and I wanted to chase them all down and make every last one of them manifest. Decades ago, the novelist Katherine Mansfield wrote in one of her youthful diaries, "I want to work!" — and her emphasis, the hard-underlined passion of that yearning, still reaches across the decades and puts a crease in my heart.

I, too, wanted to <u>work</u>. Uninterruptedly. Joyfully.

How would I manage that, though, with a baby? Increasingly panicked by this question, and well aware of my then-husband's growing impatience, I spent two frantic years interviewing every woman I could — married, single, childless, artistic, archetypally maternal — and I asked them about their choices, and the consequences of their choices. I was hoping their answers might resolve all my questions, but their answers covered such a wide range of experience that I found myself only more confused in the end.

For instance, I met one woman (an artist who worked at home) who said, "I had my doubts, too, but the minute my baby was born, everything else in my life fell away. Nothing is more important to me now than my son."

But another woman (whom I would define as one of the best mothers I've ever met, and whose grown kids are wonderful and successful) admitted to me privately and even shockingly, "Looking back on it all now, I'm not at all convinced that my life was really bettered in any way by the choice to have children. I gave up altogether too much, and I regret it. It's not that I don't adore my kids, but honestly, I sometimes wish I could have all those lost years back."

A fashionable, charismatic West Coast businesswoman, on the other hand, said to me, "The one thing nobody ever warned me about when I started having babies was this: Brace yourself for the happiest years of your life. I never saw that coming. The joy of it has been like an avalanche."

But I also talked to an exhausted single mom (a gifted novelist) who said, "Raising a child is the very definition of ambivalence. I am overwhelmed at times by how something can simultaneously be so awful and so rewarding."

Another creative friend of mine said, "Yes, you lose a lot of your freedoms. But as a mother, you gain a new kind of freedom as well — the freedom to love another human being unconditionally, with all your heart. That's a freedom worth experiencing, too."

Still another friend, who had left her career as an editor to stay home with her three children, warned me, "Think very carefully about this decision, Liz. It's difficult enough to be a mom when it's what you really want to do. Don't even go near child rearing until you're absolutely sure."

Another woman, though, who has managed to keep her vibrant career thriving even with three kids, and who sometimes takes her children with her on overseas business trips, said, "Just go for it. It's not that hard. You just have to push against all the forces that tell you what you can't do anymore now that you're a mom."

But I was also deeply touched when I met a renowned photographer, now in her sixties, who made this simple comment to me on the topic of children: "I never had 'em, honey. And I never missed 'em."

Do you see a pattern here?

I didn't.

Because there wasn't a pattern. There was just a whole bunch of smart women trying to work things out on their own terms, trying to navigate somehow by their own instincts. Whether I myself should ever be a mother was clearly not a question that any of these women were going to be able to answer for me. I would need to make that choice myself. And the stakes of my choice were personally titanic. Declaring that I did not want to have children effectively meant the end of my marriage. There were other reasons I left that marriage (there were aspects of our relationship that were frankly preposterous), but the question of children was the final blow. There is no compromise position on this question after all.

So, he fumed; I cried; we divorced.

But that's another book.

Given all that history, it should not be surprising to anyone that, after a few years alone, I met and fell in love with Felipe — an older man with a pair of beautiful, adult children, who had not one smidgen of interest whatsoever in repeating the experience of fatherhood. It is also no accident that Felipe fell in love with me — a childless woman in the waning years of her fertility who adored his kids but who had not one smidgen of interest whatsoever in becoming a mother herself.

That relief — the great thrumming relief that we both felt when we discovered that neither one of us was going to coerce the other into parenthood — still sends a pleasant vibrating hum across our life together. I still can't entirely get over it. For some reason, I had never once considered the possibility that I might be allowed to have a lifelong male companion without also being expected to have children. This is how deeply the incantation of "first-comes-love-then-comes-marriage-then-comes-baby-in-the-baby-carriage" had penetrated my consciousness; I had honestly neglected to notice that you could opt out of the baby carriage business and nobody — not in our country anyhow — would arrest you for it. And the fact that, upon meeting Felipe, I also inherited two wonderful adult stepchildren was a bonus gift. Felipe's kids need my love and they need my support, but they do not need my mothering; they had already been beautifully mothered long before I ever arrived on the scene. Best of all, though, by introducing Felipe's children into my own extended family, I pulled off the ultimate generational magic trick: I provided my parents with an extra set of grandchildren, without ever having to raise babies of my own. Even now, the freedom and abundance of it all feels something close to miraculous.

Being exempted from motherhood has also allowed me to become exactly the person I believe I was meant to be: not merely a writer, not merely a traveler, but also — in a quite marvelous fashion — an aunt. A childless aunt, to be exact — which puts me in extremely good company, because here's an astonishing fact that I discovered in the margins of my research on marriage: If you look across human populations of all varieties, in every culture and on every continent (even among the most enthusiastic breeders in history, like the nineteenth-century Irish, or the contemporary Amish), you will find that there is a consistent 10 percent of women within any population who never have children at all. The percentage never gets any lower than that, in any population whatsoever. In fact, the percentage of women who never reproduce in most societies is usually much *higher* than 10 percent — and that's not just today in the developed Western world, where childless rates among women tend to hover around 50 percent. In the 1920s in America, for instance, a whopping 23 percent of adult women never had any children. (Doesn't that seem shockingly high, for such a conservative era, before the advent of legalized birth control? Yet it was so.) So the number can get pretty high. But it never goes below 10 percent.

All too often, those of us who choose to remain childless are accused of being somehow unwomanly or unnatural or selfish, but history teaches us that there have always been women who went through life without having babies. Many of those women *deliberately* elected to skip motherhood, either through avoiding sex with men altogether or through careful application of what the Victorian ladies once called "the precautionary arts." (The sisterhood has always had its secrets and talents.) Other women, of course, had their childlessness thrust on them unwillingly — because of infertility, or disease, or spinsterhood, or a general shortage of eligible males due to wartime casualties. Whatever the reasons, though, widespread childlessness is not quite so modern a development as we tend to believe.

In any case, the number of women throughout history who never become mothers is so high (so *consistently* high) that I now suspect that a certain degree of female childlessness is an evolutionary adaptation of the human race. Maybe it's not only perfectly legitimate for certain women to never reproduce, but also necessary. It's as though, as a species, we *need* an abundance of responsible, compassionate, childless women on hand to support the wider community in various ways. Childbearing and child rearing consume so much energy that the women who do become mothers can quickly become swallowed up by that daunting task — if not outright killed by it. Thus, maybe we need extra females, women on the sidelines with undepleted energies, who are ready to leap into the mix and keep the tribe supported. Childless women have always been particularly essential in human society because they often take upon themselves the task of nurturing those who are not their official biological responsibility — and no other group does this to such a large degree. Childless women have always run orphanages and schools and hospitals. They are midwives and nuns and providers of charity. They heal the sick and teach the arts and often they become indispensable on the battlefield of life. Literally, in some cases. (Florence Nightingale comes to mind.)

Such childless women — let's call them the "Auntie Brigade" — have never been very well honored by history, I'm afraid. They are called selfish, frigid, pathetic. Here's one particularly nasty bit of conventional wisdom circulating out there about childless women that I need to dispel here, and that is this: that women who have no children may lead liberated and happy and wealthy lives when they are young, but they will ultimately regret that choice when they reach old age, for they shall all die alone and depressed and full of bitterness. Perhaps you've heard this old chestnut? Just to set the record straight: There is *zero* sociological evidence to back this up. In fact, recent studies of American nursing homes comparing happiness levels of elderly childless women against happiness levels of women who did have children show no pattern of special misery or joy in one group or the other. But here's what the researchers did discover that makes elderly women miserable across the board: poverty and poor health. Whether you have children or not, then, the prescription seems clear: Save your money, floss your teeth, wear your seatbelt, and keep fit — and you'll be a perfectly happy old bird someday, I guarantee you.

Just a little free advice there, from your Auntie Liz.

In leaving no descendents, however, childless aunts do tend to vanish from memory after a mere generation, quickly forgotten, their lives as transitory as butterflies. But they are vital as they live, and they can even be heroic. Even in my own family's recent history, there are stories on both sides of truly magnificent aunties who stepped in and saved the day during emergencies. Often able to accrue education and resources precisely because they were childless, these women had enough spare income and compassion to pay for lifesaving operations, or to rescue the family farm, or to take in a child whose mother had fallen gravely ill. I have a friend who calls these sorts of child-rescuing aunties "sparents" — "spare parents" — and the world is filled with them.

Even within my own community, I can see

where I have been vital sometimes as a member of the Auntie Brigade. My job is not merely to spoil and indulge my niece and nephew (though I do take that assignment to heart) but also to be a roving auntie to the world — an ambassador auntie — who is on hand wherever help is needed, in anybody's family whatsoever. There are people I've been able to help, sometimes fully supporting them for years, because I am not obliged, as a mother would be obliged, to put all my energies and resources into the full-time rearing of a child. There are a whole bunch of Little League uniforms and orthodontist's bills and college educations that I will never have to pay for, thereby freeing up resources to spread more widely across the community. In this way, I, too, foster life. There are many, many ways to foster life. And believe me, every single one of them is essential.

Jane Austen once wrote to a relative whose first nephew had just been born: "I have always maintained the importance of Aunts as much as possible. Now that you have become an Aunt, you are a person of some consequence." Jane knew of which she spoke. She herself was a childless auntie, cherished by her nieces and nephews as a marvelous confidante, and remembered always for her "peals of laughter."

Speaking of writers: From an admittedly biased perspective, I feel the need to mention here that Leo Tolstoy and Truman Capote and all the Brontë sisters were raised by their childless aunts after their real mothers had either died or abandoned them. Tolstoy claimed that his Aunt Toinette was the greatest influence of his life, as she taught him "the moral joy of love." The historian Edward Gibbon, having been orphaned young, was raised by his beloved and childless Aunt Kitty. John Lennon was raised by his Aunt Mimi, who convinced the boy that he would be an important artist someday. F. Scott Fitzgerald's loyal Aunt Annabel offered to pay for his college education. Frank Lloyd Wright's first building was commissioned by his Aunts Jane and Nell — two lovely old maids who ran a boarding school in Spring Green, Wisconsin. Coco Chanel, orphaned as a child, was raised by her Aunt Gabrielle, who taught her how to sew — a useful skill for the girl, I think we would all agree. Virginia Woolf was deeply influenced by her Aunt Caroline, a Quaker spinster who devoted her life to charitable works, who heard voices and spoke to spirits, and who seemed, as Woolf recalled years later, "a kind of modern prophetess."

Remember that critical moment in literary history when Marcel Proust bites into his famous madeleine cookie, thereby becoming so overwhelmed by nostalgia that he has no choice but to sit down and write the multivolume epic *Remembrance of Things Past?* That entire tsunami of eloquent nostalgia was set off by the specific memory of Marcel's beloved Aunt Leonie, who, every Sunday after church, used to share her madeleines with the boy when he was a child.

And have you ever wondered what Peter Pan really looked like? His creator, J. M. Barrie, answered that question for us back in 1911. For Barrie, Peter Pan's image and his essence and his marvelous spirit of felicity can be found all over the world, hazily reflected "in the faces of many women who have no children."

That is the Auntie Brigade.

But this decision of mine — the decision to join the Auntie Brigade rather than enlist in the Mommy Corps — does set me off as being quite different from my own mother, and I still felt there was something that needed to be reconciled within that distinction. This is probably why, in the middle of my travels with Felipe, I called my mom one night from Laos, trying to settle some last lingering questions about her own life and her choices and how they related to my life and my choices.

We talked for over an hour. My mom was calm and thoughtful, as ever. She did not seem surprised by my line of questioning — in fact, she responded as though she'd been waiting for me to ask. Waiting, perhaps, for *years*.

First of all, right off the bat, she was quick to remind me: "I don't regret anything I ever did for you kids."

"You don't regret giving up the work you loved?" I asked.

"I refuse to live in regret," she said (which did not exactly answer the question, but felt like an honest start). "There was so much to love about those years I spent at home with you girls. I know you kids in a way that your father will never know you. I was there, witnessing your growth. It was a privilege to see you become adults. I wouldn't have wanted to miss that."

Also, my mother reminded me that she chose to stay married all those years to the same man because she happens to love my father dearly — which is a good point, and one well taken. It is true that my parents connect not only as friends, but also very much on a bodily level. They are physical in every way together — hiking, biking, and farming side by side. I remember phoning home from college late one winter's night and catching the two of them out of breath. "What have you guys been up to?" I asked, and my mom, giddy with laughter, announced, "We've been sledding!" They had absconded with their ten-year-old neighbor's toboggan and had been making midnight runs down the icy hill behind our house — my mom lying on my father's back and shrieking with adrenalized pleasure while he steered the speeding sled through the moonlight. Who still *does* this in middle age?

My parents have always had a certain sexual chemistry, ever since the day they met. "He looked like Paul Newman," my mom recalls of their first encounter, and when my sister once asked my father about his favorite memory of my mom, he did not hesitate to reply, "I have always loved the pleasing nature of your mother's form." He still loves it. My dad is always grabbing at my mom's body as she walks by in the kitchen, always checking her out, admiring her legs, lusting after her. She swats him away with fake shock: "John! Stop it!" But you can tell she relishes the attention. I grew up watching that play out, and I think that's a rare gift — knowing that your parents are physically satisfying to each other. So one big part of my parent's marriage, as my mother was reminding me, has always been lodged somewhere beyond the rational, hidden someplace deep in the sexual body. And that degree of intimacy is something beyond any explanation, beyond any argument.

Then there is the companionship. My parents have been married for over forty years now. By and large they've worked out their deal. They live in a pretty smooth routine, their habits polished by time's current. They orbit each other in the same basic pattern every day: coffee, dog, breakfast, newspaper, garden, bills, chores, radio, lunch, groceries, dog, dinner, reading, dog, bed . . . and repeat.

The poet Jack Gilbert (no relation, sadly for me) wrote that marriage is what happens "between the memorable." He said that we often look back on our marriages years later, perhaps after one spouse has died, and all we can recall are "the vacations, and emergencies" — the high points and low points. The rest of it blends into a blurry sort of daily sameness. But it is that very blurred sameness, the poet argues, that

334

comprises marriage. Marriage *is* those two thousand indistinguishable conversations, chatted over two thousand indistinguishable breakfasts, where intimacy turns like a slow wheel. How do you measure the worth of becoming that familiar to somebody — so utterly well known and so thoroughly ever-present that you become an almost invisible necessity, like air?

Also, my mom had the grace to remind me that night, when I called her from Laos, that she is far from a saint, and that my dad has had to give up parts of himself, too, in order to stay married to her. As my mother generously admitted, she is not always the easiest person to be married to. My father has had to learn how to tolerate and endure the effects of being managed at every turn by a hyperorganized wife. In this regard, the two of them are horribly ill-matched. My father takes life as it comes; my mother makes life happen. An example: My father was out working in the garage one day when he accidentally stirred a small bird from its nest in the rafters. Confused and afraid, the bird settled on the brim of my dad's hat. Not wanting to disturb it any further, my father sat for about an hour on the floor of the garage until the bird decided to fly away. This is a very Dad story. Such a thing would never happen to my mother. She is far too busy to allow dazed little birds to rest on her head while there are chores to be done. Mom waits for no bird.

Also, while it's true that my mother has given up more of her personal ambitions in marriage than my father ever did, she demands far more out of marriage than he ever will. He is far more accepting of her than she is of him. ("She's the best Carole she can be," he often says, while one gets the feeling that my mother believes her husband could be — maybe even should be — a much better man.) She commands him at every turn. She's subtle and graceful enough in her methods of control that you don't always realize that she's doing it, but trust me: Mom is always steering the boat.

She comes by this trait honestly. All the women in her family do this. They take over every single aspect of their husbands' lives and then, as my father loves to point out, *they absolutely refuse to ever die.* No man can outlive an Olson bride. This is simple biological fact. I'm not exaggerating: It has never happened, not in anyone's memory. And no man can escape being completely controlled by an Olson wife. ("I'm warning you," my dad told Felipe at the beginning of our relationship, "if you're going to have any kind of life with Liz, you've got to define your space right now, and then defend it forever.") My father once joked — not really joking — that my mother manages about 95 percent of his life. The wonder of it, he mused, is that she's much more upset about the 5 percent of his life that he won't relinquish than he is about the 95 percent that she utterly dominates.

Robert Frost wrote that "a man must partly give up being a man" in order to enter into marriage — and I cannot fairly deny this point when it comes to my family. I have written many pages already describing marriage as a repressive tool used against women, but it's important to remember that marriage is often used as a repressive tool against men, too. Marriage is a harness of civilization, linking a man to a set of obligations and thereby containing his restless energies. Traditional societies have long recognized that nothing is more useless to a community than a whole bunch of single, childless young men (aside from their admittedly useful role as cannon fodder, of course). For the most part, single young men have a global reputation for squandering their money on whores and drinking and games and laziness: They contribute nothing. You need to contain such beasts, to bind them into account-ability — or so the argument has always gone. You need to convince these young men to put aside their childish things and take up the mantle of adulthood, to build homes and businesses and to cultivate an interest in their surroundings. It's an ancient truism across countless different cultures that there is no better accountability-forging tool for an irresponsible young man than a good, solid wife.

This certainly was the case with my parents. "She whipped me into shape," is my dad's summation of the love story. Mostly he's okay with this, though sometimes — say, in the middle of a family gathering, surrounded by his powerful wife and his equally powerful daughters — my father resembles nothing more than a puzzled old circus bear who cannot seem to figure out how he came to be quite so domesticated, or how he came to be perched quite so high up on this strange unicycle. He reminds me in such moments of Zorba the Greek, who replied when asked if he had ever married, "Am I not a man? Of course I've been married. Wife, house, kids, the full catastrophe!" (Zorba's melodramatic angst, by the way, reminds me of the curious fact that, within the Greek Orthodox Church, marriage is regarded not so much as a sacrament, but as a *holy martyrdom* — the understanding being that successful long-term human partnership requires a certain Death of the Self to those who participate.)

My parents have each certainly felt that restriction, that small sense of self-death, in their own marriage. I know this to be true. But I'm not sure they've always minded having each other in the way either. When I once asked my father what kind of creature he would like to be in his next life, should there be a next life, he replied without hesitation, "A horse."

"What kind of horse?" I asked, imagining him as a stallion galloping wildly across the open plains.

"A nice horse," he said.

I duly adjusted the picture in my mind. Now I imagined a *friendly* stallion galloping wildly across the plains.

"What kind of nice horse?" I probed.

"A gelding," he pronounced.

A *castrated* horse! That was unexpected. The picture in my mind changed completely. Now I envisioned my father as a gentle dray horse, docilely pulling a cart driven by my mother.

"Why a gelding?" I asked.

"I've found that life is just easier that

339

way," he replied. "Trust me."

And so life *has* been easier for him. In exchange for the almost castrating constraints that marriage has clamped on my father's personal freedoms, he has received stability, prosperity, encouragement in his labors, clean and mended shirts that appear as if by magic in his dresser drawers, a reliable meal at the end of a good day's work. In return, he has worked for my mother, he has been faithful to her, and he submits to her will a solid 95 percent of the time — elbowing her away only when she comes a little bit too close to achieving total world domination. The terms of this contract must be acceptable to both of them because — as my mother reminded me when I phoned her from Laos — their marriage now endures into its fifth decade.

The terms of my parents' marriage are probably not for me, of course. Whereas my grandmother was a traditional farmwife and my mother was a feminist cusper, I grew up with completely new ideas about the institutions of marriage and family. The relationship I'm likely to build with Felipe is something my sister and I have termed "Wifeless Marriage" — which is to say that nobody in our household will play (or play *exclusively*) the traditional role of the wife.

The more thankless chores that have always fallen on women's shoulders will be balanced out more evenly. And since there will be no babies, you could also call it "Motherless Marriage" I suppose — a model of marriage that my grandmother and mother obviously never experienced. Similarly, the responsibility of breadwinning will not fall entirely on Felipe's shoulders, as it fell to my father and grandfather; indeed, the bulk of the household earnings will probably always be mine. Perhaps in that regard, then, we will have something like a "Husbandless Marriage" as well. Wifeless, childless, husbandless marriages . . . there haven't been a whole lot of those unions in history, so we don't really have a template to work with here. Felipe and I will have to make up the rules and boundaries of our story as we go along.

I don't know, though. Maybe everyone has to make up the rules and boundaries of their story as they go along.

Anyway, when I asked my mother that night on the phone from Laos whether she has been happy in her marriage over the years, she assured me that she'd had a really nice time of it with my father, far more often than not. When I asked her what the happiest period of her life had been, she replied:

"Right now. Living with your dad, healthy, financially stable, free. Your father and I pass our days doing our own thing and then we meet at the dinner table together every night. Even after all these years, we still sit there for hours talking and laughing. It's really lovely."

"That's wonderful," I said.

There was a pause.

"Can I say something that I hope doesn't offend you?" she ventured.

"Go for it."

"To be perfectly honest, the best part of my life began as soon as you kids grew up and left the house."

I started laughing (*Gee — thanks, Mom!*) but she spoke over my laughter with urgency. "I'm serious, Liz. There's something you have to understand about me: I've been raising children my entire life. I grew up in a big family, and I always had to take care of Rod and Terry and Luana when they were little. How many times did I get up in the middle of the night when I was ten years old to clean up somebody who had wet the bed? That was my whole childhood. I never had time for myself. Then, when I was a teenager, I took care of my older brother's kids, always trying to figure out how to do my homework while I was babysitting. Then

I had my own family to raise, and I had to give so much of myself over to that. When you and your sister finally left for college, that was the first moment in my life I hadn't been responsible for any children. I loved it. I can't tell you how much I love it. Having your father to myself, having my own time to myself — it's been revolutionary for me. I've never been happier."

Okay, then, I thought, with a surge of relief. *So she has made her peace with it all. Good.*

There was another moment of silence.

Then my mother suddenly added, in a tone I'd never heard from her before, "But I do have to tell you something else. There are times when I refuse to even let myself think about the early years of my marriage and all that I had to give up. If I dwell on that too much, honest to God, I become so enraged, I can't even see straight."

Oh.

Therefore, the tidy ultimate conclusion is . . . ???

It was slowly becoming clear to me that perhaps there was never going to be any tidy ultimate conclusion here. My mother herself had probably given up long ago trying to draw tidy ultimate conclusions about her own existence, having abandoned (as so many of us must do, after a certain age) the luxuriously innocent fantasy that one is entitled to have unmixed feelings about one's own life. And if I needed to have unmixed feelings about my mother's life in order to calm down my own anxieties about matrimony, then I'm afraid I was barking up the wrong tree. All I could tell for certain was that my mom had somehow found a way to build a quiet *enough* resting place for herself within intimacy's rocky field of contradictions. There, in a satisfactory-*enough* amount of peace, she dwells.

Leaving me alone, of course, to figure out how I might someday construct such a careful habitat of my own.

CHAPTER SIX: MARRIAGE AND AUTONOMY

MARRIAGE IS A BEAUTIFUL THING.
BUT IT'S ALSO A CONSTANT BATTLE
FOR MORAL SUPREMACY.
— *Marge Simpson*

By October 2006, Felipe and I had already been traveling for six months and morale was flagging. We had left the Laotian holy city of Luang Prabang weeks earlier, having exhausted all its treasures, and had taken to the road again in the same random motion as before, killing time, passing hours and days.

We had hoped to be home by now, but there was still no movement whatsoever on our immigration case. Felipe's future was stalled in a bottomless sort of limbo that we had somewhat irrationally come to believe might never end. Separated from his business inventory in America, unable to make any plans or earn any money, utterly dependent on the United States Department of Homeland Security (and me) to decide his fate, he was feeling more powerless by the day. This was not an ideal situation. For if there is one thing I have learned over the years about men, it is that feelings of powerlessness do not usually bring forth their finest qualities. Felipe was no exception. He was becoming increasingly jittery, quick-tempered, irritable, and ominously tense.

Even under the best of circumstances, Felipe has the bad habit of sometimes snapping impatiently at people he feels are either behaving poorly or interfering somehow with the quality of his life. This happens rarely, but I wish it would happen never. All over the world and in many languages I have watched this man bark his disapproval at bungling flight attendants, inept taxi drivers, unscrupulous merchants, apathetic waiters, and the parents of ill-behaved children. Arm waving and raised voices are sometimes involved in such scenes.

I deplore this.

Having been raised by a self-composed midwestern mother and a taciturn Yankee father, I am genetically and culturally incapable of handling Felipe's more classically Brazilian version of conflict resolution. People in my family wouldn't even speak this way to a *mugger.* Moreover, whenever I see Felipe fly off the handle in public, it messes around with my cherished personal narrative about what a gentle and tender-hearted guy I have chosen to love, and that, frankly, pisses me off more than anything else. If there is one indignity I shall never endure gracefully, it is watching people mess around with my most cherished personal narratives about them.

What's worse, my yearning to have everyone in the world be best friends, combined with my near-pathological empathy for underdogs, often leaves me defending Felipe's victims, which only adds to the tension. While he expresses zero tolerance toward idiots and incompetents, I think that behind every incompetent idiot there lies a really sweet person having a bad day. All this can lead to contention between Felipe and me, and on the rare occasions that we argue, it is generally over such questions. He has never let me forget how I once forced him to walk back into a shoe store in Indonesia and apologize to a young salesclerk whom I felt he had treated rudely. And he did it! He marched back into that little rip-off of a shoe store and offered the bewildered girl a courtly expression of regret for having lost his temper. But he did so only because he found my defense of the salesclerk charming. I did not, however, find anything about the situation charming. I never find it charming.

Blessedly, Felipe's outbursts are fairly uncommon in our normal life. But what we were living through right then was not normal life. Six months of rough travel and small hotel rooms and frustrating bureaucratic holdups were taking their toll on his emotional state, to the point that I felt Felipe's impatience rising to almost epidemic levels (though readers should probably take the word "epidemic" with a large grain of salt, given that my hypersensitivity to even the faintest human conflict makes me a thin-skinned judge of emotional friction). Still, the evidence seemed incontrovertible: He was not merely raising his voice at complete strangers these days, he was also snapping out at me. This really was unprecedented, because somehow Felipe had always seemed immune to me in the past — as though I, alone among everyone else on earth, was somehow preternaturally incapable of irritating him. Now, though, that sweet period of immunity seemed to have ended. He was annoyed at me for taking too long on the rented computers, annoyed at me for dragging us to see "the fucking elephants" at an expensive tourist trap, annoyed at me for planting us on yet another miserable overnight train, annoyed when I either spent money or saved money, annoyed that I always wanted to walk everywhere, annoyed that I kept trying to find healthy food when it was clearly impossible . . .

Felipe seemed increasingly stuck in that awful breed of mood where any glitch or hassle whatsoever becomes almost physically intolerable. This was unfortunate, because traveling — particularly the cheap and dirty traveling we were undertaking — is pretty much nothing but one glitch and hassle after another, interrupted by the occasional stunning sunset, which my companion had evidently lost the ability to enjoy. As I hauled the ever more reluctant Felipe from one Southeast Asian activity to the next (exotic markets! temples! waterfalls!), he became only *less* relaxed, *less* accommodating, *less* comforted. I, in turn, reacted to his befouled humor the way I'd been taught by my mother to react to a man's befouled humor: by becoming only more cheerful, more upbeat, more obnoxiously chipper. I buried my own frustrations and homesickness under a guise of indefatigable optimism, barreling forth with an aggressively sunny demeanor, as though I could somehow force Felipe into a state of lighthearted gladness by the sheer power of my magnetic, tireless merrymaking.

Astonishingly, this did not work.

Over time, I became irritated with him — exasperated by his impatience, grumpiness, lethargy. Moreover, I became irritated with *myself,* annoyed by the false notes in my voice as I tried to engage Felipe in whatever curiosity I'd dragged him to this time. (*Oh, darling — look! They're selling rats for food! Oh, darling — look! The mommy elephant is washing her baby! Oh, darling — look! This hotel room has such an interesting view of the slaughterhouse!*) Meanwhile, Felipe would head off to the bathroom and come back fuming about the filth and stink of the place — whatever place we happened to be in — while simultaneously complaining that the air pollution was making his throat sting and the traffic was giving him a headache.

His tension made me tense, which caused me to become physically careless, which caused me to stub my toe in Hanoi, to cut my finger on his razor in Chiang Mai as I dug through the toiletries bag for toothpaste, and — one really awful night — to put insect repellent in my eyes instead of eyedrops because I hadn't looked carefully at the travel-sized bottle. What I remember most about that last incident is howling in pain and self-recrimination while Felipe held my head over the sink and rinsed out my eyes with one lukewarm bottle of water after another, fixing me up as best he could while raging in a steady, furious tirade about the stupidity of the fact that we were even *in* this godforsaken country to begin with. It is a testament to how bad those weeks had become that I do not now specifically remember which godforsaken country we were in.

All this tension reached a peak (or, rather, hit a nadir) the day I hauled Felipe on a twelve-hour bus ride through the center of Laos to visit what I insisted would be a fascinating archaeological site in the middle of the country. We shared the bus with no small amount of livestock, and our seats were harder than Quaker meetinghouse pews. There was no air-conditioning, of course, and the windows were sealed shut. I can't rightly say that the heat was unbearable, because obviously we bore it, but I will say that it was very, very hot. I couldn't rouse Felipe's interest in the upcoming archaeological site, but I also couldn't get a rise out of him about the conditions of our bus ride — and that really was notable, given that this was probably the most perilous public transportation experience I'd ever endured. The driver operated his ancient vehicle with a manic aggression, several times almost dumping us over some fairly impressive cliffs. But Felipe did not react to any of this, nor did he react to any of our near collisions with oncoming traffic. He just went numb. He shut his eyes in weariness and stopped speaking altogether. He seemed resigned to death. Or perhaps he was merely longing for it.

After several more such life-threatening hours, our bus suddenly rounded a curve and came upon the site of a big road accident: Two buses not at all unlike ours had just crashed head-on. There seemed to be no injuries, but the vehicles were a twisted-up pile of smoking metal. As we slowed to pass, I grabbed Felipe's arm and said, "Look, darling! There's been a collision between two buses!"

Without even opening his eyes, he replied sarcastically, "How on earth could *that* possibly have happened?"

Suddenly I was shot through with anger.

"What is it that you *want?*" I demanded.

He didn't answer, which only made me angrier, so I pushed on: "I'm just trying to make the best out of this situation, okay? If you have any better ideas or any better plans — please, by all means, offer some. And I really hope you can think of something that will make you happy, because I honestly can't take your misery anymore, I really can't."

Now his eyes flew open. "I just want a coffeepot," he said with unexpected passion.

"What do you mean, a coffeepot?"

"I just want to be *home,* living with you in one place safely together. I want *routine.* I want a coffeepot of our own. I want to be able to wake up at the same time every morning and make breakfast for us, in our own house, with our own coffeepot."

In another setting, maybe this confession would have drawn sympathy from me, and perhaps it should have drawn sympathy from me then, but it just made me angrier: *Why was he dwelling on the impossible?*

"We can't have any of that stuff right now," I said.

"My God, Liz — you think I don't *know* that?"

"You think I don't want those things, too?" I shot back.

His voice rose: "You think I'm not *aware* that you want those things? You think I haven't seen you reading real estate ads online? You think I can't tell you're homesick? Do you have any idea how it makes me feel that I cannot provide you with a home right now, that you're stuck in all these beat-up hotel rooms on the other side of the world because of me? Do you have any idea how humiliating that is for me, that I can't afford to offer you a better life right now? Do you have any idea how *fucking helpless* that makes me feel? *As a man?*"

I forget sometimes.

I have to say this, because I think it's such an important point when it comes to marriage: I do forget sometimes how much it means for certain men — for certain people — to be able to provide their loved ones with material comforts and protection at all times. I forget how dangerously reduced some men can feel when that basic ability has been stripped from them. I forget how much that matters to men, what it represents.

I can still remember the anguished look on an old friend's face when he told me, several years ago, that his wife was leaving him. Her complaint, apparently, was that she was overwhelmingly lonely, that he "wasn't there for her" — but he could not begin to understand what this meant. He felt he had been breaking his back to take care of his wife for years. "Okay," he admitted, "so maybe I wasn't there for her *emotionally,* but by God, I provided for that woman! I worked two jobs for her! Doesn't that show that I loved her? She should have known that I would have done *anything* to keep providing for her and protecting her! If a nuclear holocaust ever struck, I would've picked her up and thrown her over my shoulder and carried her across the burning landscape to safety — and she *knew* that about me! How could she say I wasn't there for her?"

I could not bring myself to break the bad news to my devastated friend that most days, unfortunately, there is no nuclear holocaust. Most days, unfortunately, the only thing his wife had really needed was a little more attention.

Similarly, the only thing I needed from Felipe at that moment was for him to calm down, to be nicer, to show me and everyone else around us a little more patience, a little more emotional generosity. I didn't need provision or protection from him. I didn't need his manly pride; it wasn't serving for anything here. I just needed him to relax into the situation as it was. Yes, of course, it would have been much nicer to be back home, near my family, living in a real house — but our rootlessness right now didn't bother me nearly as much as his moodiness.

Trying to defuse the tension, I touched Felipe's leg and said, "I can see that this situation is really frustrating for you."

I had learned that trick from a book called *Ten Lessons to Transform Your Marriage: America's Love Lab Experts Share Their Strategies for Strengthening Your Relationship,* by John M. Gottman and Julie Schwartz-Gottman — two (happily married) researchers from the Relationship Research Institute in Seattle who have received a lot of attention lately for their claim that they can predict with 90 percent accuracy whether a couple will still be married in five years merely by studying a fifteen-minute transcript of typical conversation between the husband and the wife. (For this reason, I imagine that John M. Gottman and Julie Schwartz-Gottman make terrifying dinner guests.) Whatever the breadth of their powers may be, the Gottmans do offer some practical strategies for resolving marital disputes, trying to save couples from what they call the Four Horsemen of the Apocalypse: Stonewalling, Defensiveness, Criticism, and Contempt. The trick I had just used — repeating back to Felipe his own frustration in order to indicate that I was listening to him and that I cared — is something the Gottmans call "Turning Toward Your Partner." It's supposed to defuse arguments.

It doesn't always work.

"You don't know how I feel, Liz!" Felipe snapped. "They *arrested* me. They handcuffed me and marched me through that entire airport with everyone staring — did you know that? They fingerprinted me. They took away my wallet, they even took the ring you gave me. They took everything. They put me in jail and threw me out of your country. Thirty years of traveling, and I've never had a border closed to me before, and now I can't get into the United States of America — of all bloody places to get kicked out of! In the past I would've just said, 'The hell with it,' and moved on, but I *can't* — because America is where you want to live, and I want to be with you. So I have no choice. I have to put up with all this shit, and I have to turn my entire private life over to these bureaucrats and to your police, and it's humiliating. And we can't even get any information about when this is all going to be finished, because we don't even *matter.* We're just numbers on a civil servant's desk. Meanwhile, my business is dying and I'm going broke. So of *course* I'm miserable. And now you're dragging me all over goddamn Southeast Asia on these goddamn buses —"

"All I'm trying to do is keep you happy," I snapped back at him, pulling away my hand, stung and hurt. If there had been a cord on that bus to pull to signal the driver that a passenger wanted to get off, I swear to God I would have pulled it. I would have jumped off right there, left Felipe on that bus, taken my chances in the jungle by myself.

He inhaled sharply, as though he was going to say something hard but stopped himself. I could almost feel the tendons in his neck tightening, and my frustration escalated, too. Our setting didn't exactly help, by the way. The bus lurched along, loud and hot and chancy, whacking low-hanging branches, scattering pigs and chickens and children in the road before us, throwing up a stinking cloud of black exhaust, slamming every vertebra in my neck with each jolt. And there were still seven hours left to go.

We said nothing for a long time. I wanted to cry but held myself together, recognizing that crying might be unhelpful. Still, I was angry at him. Sorry for him, yes, of course — but mostly angry at him. And for what? For bad sportsmanship, maybe? For weakness? For caving in before I did? Yes, our situation was lousy, but it could have been infinitely lousier. At least we were *together.* At least I could afford to stay with him during this period of exile. There were thousands of couples in our exact situation who would have killed for the right to spend even one evening together during such a long period of enforced separation. At least we had *that* comfort. And at least we had the education to read the monstrously confusing immigration documents, and at least we had enough money to enlist a good lawyer to help us through the rest of the process. Anyhow, even if worse came to worst and the United States rejected Felipe from its shores forever, at least we had other options. My God, we could always move to Australia, for heaven's sake. Australia! A wonderful country! A nation of Canada-like sanity and prosperity! It wasn't as if we were going to be sent to exile in northern Afghanistan! Who else in our situation had so many advantages?

And why was I always the one who had to think in such upbeat terms anyhow, while Felipe, frankly, had done little over the last few weeks but sulk over circumstances that were largely out of our control? Why could he never bend to adverse situations with a little more grace? And would it have killed him, by the way, to show a *little* enthusiasm about the upcoming archeological site?

I very nearly said this — every word of it, the whole crapping rant of it — but I refrained. An overflow of emotions like this signifies what John M. Gottman and Julie Schwartz-Gottman call "flooding" — the point at which you get so tired or frustrated that your mind becomes deluged (and deluded) by anger. A surefire indication that flooding is imminent is when you start using the words "always" or "never" in your argument. The Gottmans call this "Going Universal" (as in: "You *always* let me down like this!" or "I can *never* count on you!"). Such language absolutely murders any chance of fair or intelligent discourse. Once you have Flooded, once you have Gone Universal on somebody's ass, all hell breaks loose. It's really best not to let that happen. As an old friend of mine once told me, you can measure the happiness of a marriage by the number of scars that each partner carries on their tongues, earned from years of biting back angry words.

So I didn't speak, and Felipe didn't speak, and this heated silence went on for a long time until he finally reached for my hand and said, in an exhausted voice, "Let's be careful right now, okay?"

I slackened, knowing exactly what he meant. This was an old code of ours. It had come up for the first time on a road trip we'd taken once from Tennessee to Arizona early on in our relationship. I'd been teaching writing at the University of Tennessee, and we were living in that strange hotel room in Knoxville, and Felipe had found a gemstone show that he'd wanted to attend in Tucson. So we'd spontaneously driven out there together, trying to make the distance in one long push. It had been a fun trip for the most part. We had sung, and talked, and laughed. But you can only sing and talk and laugh so much, and there came a moment — about thirty hours into the drive — when both of us reached a point of utter exhaustion. We were running out of gas, literally and figuratively. There were no hotels around and we were hungry and weary. I seem to remember a stark difference of opinion between us about when and where we should stop next. We were still speaking in perfectly civil tones, but tension had begun to encircle the car like a light mist.

"Let's be careful," Felipe had said then, out of the blue.

"Of what?" I'd asked.

"Let's just be careful of what we say to each other for the next few hours," he'd gone on. "These are the times, when people get tired like this, that fights can happen. Let's just choose our words *very carefully* until we find a place to rest."

Nothing had happened yet, but Felipe was floating the idea that there are, perhaps, moments when a couple must practice preemptive conflict resolution, arresting an argument before it can even begin. So this had become a code phrase of ours, a signpost to mind the gap and beware of falling rocks. It was a tool that we pulled out every now and again in particularly tense moments. It had always worked well for us in the past. Then again, in the past we had never gone through anything quite so tense as this indeterminate period of exile in Southeast Asia. On the other hand, maybe the tension of travel only meant that we needed the yellow flag now more than ever.

I always remember a story my friends Julie and Dennis told me about a horrible fight they'd had on a trip to Africa together, early in their marriage. Whatever the original dispute may have been, they can't even remember to this day, but here's how it ended up: One afternoon in Nairobi, the two of them became so enraged at each other that they had to walk on opposite sides of the street toward their mutual destination because they could no longer physically tolerate each other's proximity. After a long while of this ridiculous parallel marching along, with four defensive lanes of Nairobian traffic between them, Dennis finally stopped. He opened his arms and motioned for Julie to cross the street and join him. It seemed to be a gesture of conciliation, so she conceded. She walked over to her husband, softening along the way, fully expecting to receive something like an apology. Instead, once she got within speaking distance, Dennis leaned forward and gently said, "Hey, Jules? Go fuck yourself."

In response, she stomped off to the airport and immediately tried to sell her husband's plane ticket back home to a perfect stranger.

They worked it out in the end, happily. Decades later, this makes for an amusing dinner-party anecdote, but it's a cautionary tale, too: You kind of don't want to let things get to that point. So I gave Felipe's hand a small squeeze and said, *"Quando casar passa,"* which is a sweet Brazilian expression meaning "When you get married, this will pass." This is a phrase Felipe's mother used to say to him as a child whenever he fell down and scraped his knee. It's a small, silly, maternal murmur of comfort. Felipe and I had been saying this phrase to each other a lot lately. In our case, it was largely true: When we finally got married, a lot of these troubles *would* pass.

He put his arm around me and pulled me close. I relaxed into his chest. Or as much as I possibly could relax, given the slamming momentum of the bus.

He was a good man, in the end.

He was *basically* a good man anyhow.

No, he was good. He is good.

"What should we do in the meanwhile?" he asked.

Prior to this conversation, my instinct had been to keep us moving at a fast clip from one new place to another with the hope that fresh vistas would distract us from our legal troubles. This sort of strategy had always worked for me in the past anyhow. Like a fussy baby who can fall asleep only in a moving car, I have always been comforted by the tempo of travel. I'd always assumed that Felipe operated on the same principle, since he is the most widely traveled person I've ever met. But he didn't seem to be enjoying any of this drifting.

For one thing — though I often forget it — the man *is* seventeen years older than I am. So we must excuse him if he was feeling moderately less excited than I was about the notion of living out of a small backpack for an indeterminate period of time, carrying only one change of clothing and sleeping in eighteen-dollar hotel rooms. It was clearly taking a toll on him. Also, he'd already seen the world. He'd already seen great huge swaths of the damn thing and had been traveling through Asia on third-class trains back when I was in the second grade. Why was I making him do it again?

What's more, the last few months had brought to my attention an important incompatibility between us — one that I'd never noticed before. For a pair of lifelong travelers, Felipe and I actually travel very differently. The reality about Felipe, as I was gradually realizing, is that he's both the best traveler I've ever met and by far the worst. He hates strange bathrooms and dirty restaurants and uncomfortable trains and foreign beds — all of which pretty much define the act of traveling. Given a choice, he will always select a lifestyle of routine, familiarity, and reassuringly boring everyday practices. All of which might make you assume the man is not fit to be a traveler at all. But you would be wrong to assume that, for here is Felipe's traveling gift, his super-power, the secret weapon that renders him peerless: He can create a familiar habitat of reassuringly boring everyday practices for himself *anyplace,* if you just let him stay in one spot. He can assimilate absolutely anywhere on the planet in the space of about three days, and then he's capable of staying put in that place for the next decade or so without complaint.

This is why Felipe has been able to live all over the world. Not merely travel, but *live*. Over the years, he has folded himself into societies from South America to Europe, from the Middle East to the South Pacific. He arrives somewhere utterly new, decides he likes the place, moves right in, learns the language, and instantly becomes a local. It had taken Felipe less than a week of living with me in Knoxville, for instance, to locate his favorite breakfast café, his favorite bartender, and his favorite place for lunch. ("Darling!" he'd said one day, terribly excited after a solo foray into downtown Knoxville. "Did you know that they have the most wonderful and inexpensive fish restaurant here called John Long Slivers?") He would've happily stayed in Knoxville indefinitely if I'd wanted us to. He had no trouble with the idea of living in that hotel room for many years to come — as long as we could just stay in one place.

All of which reminds me of a story that Felipe told me once about his childhood. When he was a small boy in Brazil, he used to get scared sometimes in the middle of the night by some nightmare or imagined monster, and each time he would scamper across the room and climb into the bed of his wonderful sister Lily — who was ten years older, and therefore embodied all human wisdom and security. He would tap on Lily's shoulder and whisper, *"Me da um cantinho"* — "Give me a little corner." Sleepily, never protesting, she would move over and open up a warm spot on the bed for him. It wasn't much to ask for; just one little warm corner. For all the years that I have known this man, I have never heard him ask for much more than that.

I'm not like that, though.

Whereas Felipe can find a corner anywhere in the world and settle down for good, I can't. I'm much more restless than he is. My restlessness makes me a far better day-to-day traveler than he will ever be. I am infinitely curious and almost infinitely patient with mishaps, discomforts, and minor disasters. So I can *go* anywhere on the planet — that's not a problem. The problem is that I just can't *live* anywhere on the planet. I'd realized this only a few weeks earlier, back in northern Laos, when Felipe had woken up one lovely morning in Luang Prabang and said, "Darling, let's stay here."

"Sure," I'd said. "We can stay here for a

few more days if you want."

"No, I mean let's *move* here. Let's forget about me immigrating to America. It's too much trouble! This is a wonderful town. I like the feeling of it. It reminds me of Brazil thirty years ago. It wouldn't take much money or effort for us to run a little hotel or a shop here, rent an apartment, settle in . . ."

In reaction, I had only blanched.

He was serious. He would just *do* that. He would just up and move to northern Laos indefinitely and build a new life there. But I can't. What Felipe was proposing was travel at a level I could not reach — travel that wasn't even really travel anymore, but rather a willingness to be ingested indefinitely by an unfamiliar place. I wasn't up for it. My traveling, as I understood then for the first time, was far more dilettantish than I had ever realized. As much as I love snacking on the world, when it comes time to settle down — to *really* settle down — I wanted to live at home, in my own country, in my own language, near my own family, and in the company of people who think and believe the same things that I think and believe. This basically limits me to a small region of Planet Earth consisting of southern New York State, the more rural sections of central New Jersey, northwestern Connecticut, and bits of eastern Pennsylvania. Quite the scanty habitat for a bird who claims to be migratory. Felipe, on the other hand — my flying fish — has no such domestic limitations. A small bucket of water anywhere in the world will do him just fine.

Realizing all this also helped me put Felipe's recent irritability in better perspective. He was going through all this trouble — all the uncertainty and humiliation of the American immigration process — purely on my behalf, enduring a completely invasive legal proceeding when he'd just as soon be setting up a newer and much easier life in a freshly rented little apartment in Luang Prabang. Moreover, in the meantime, he was tolerating all this jittery traveling from place to place — a process he does not remotely enjoy — because he sensed that I wanted it. Why was I putting him through this? Why would I not let the man rest, *anywhere?*

So I changed the plan.

"Why don't we just go somewhere for a few months and stay there until you get called back to Australia for your immigration interview," I suggested. "Let's just go to Bangkok."

"No," he said. "Not Bangkok. We'll lose our minds living in Bangkok."

"No," I said. "We won't *settle* in Bangkok; we'll just head in that direction because it's a hub. Let's go to Bangkok for a week or so, stay in a nice hotel, rest up, and see if we can find a cheap plane ticket from there to Bali. Once we get back to Bali, let's see if we can rent a little house. Then we'll just stay there in Bali and wait until this whole thing blows over."

I could see by the look on Felipe's face that the idea was working for him.

"You would do that?" he asked.

Suddenly I had another inspiration. "Wait — let's see if we can get your old Bali house back! Maybe we can rent it from the new owner. And then we'll just stay there, in Bali, till we get your visa back to America. How does that sound?"

It took Felipe a moment to respond, but — honest to God — when he finally did, I thought the man might weep with relief.

So that's what we did. We headed back to Bangkok. We found a hotel with a pool and a well-stocked bar. We called the new owner of Felipe's old house to see if it was available to rent. Marvelously, it was, at a comfortable four hundred dollars a month

— a surreal but perfectly fine price to pay for a house that had once been yours. We reserved a flight back to Bali, leaving in a week's time. Instantly, Felipe was happy again. Happy and patient and kindhearted, as I had always known him to be.

But as for me . . .

Something nagged.

Something pulled at me. I could see that Felipe was relaxing, sitting by the nice swimming pool with a detective novel in one hand and a beer in the other, but now I was the agitated one. I am never going to be the person who wants to sit by a hotel pool with a cold beer and a detective novel. My thoughts kept turning to Cambodia, *which was so tantalizingly close,* which was just over the border from Thailand . . . I had always wanted to see the temple ruins at Angkor Wat but had never quite made it there in my past travels. We had a week to kill, and this would be a perfect time to go. But I couldn't imagine dragging Felipe over to Cambodia with me right now. In fact, I couldn't imagine anything Felipe would want to do less than get on a plane to Cambodia to visit crumbling temple ruins in the searing heat.

What if I went to Cambodia alone, then, just for a few days? What if I left Felipe here in Bangkok sitting happily by the pool? For the last five months, we'd spent nearly every single minute of the day in each other's company, and often in challenging surroundings. It was a miracle that our recent spat on the bus had been the only serious conflict so far. Couldn't we each benefit from a short spell of separation?

That said, the tenuousness of our situation made me concerned about leaving him for even a few days. This was no time to be messing around. What if something happened to me while I was in Cambodia? What if something happened to him? What if there was an earthquake, a tsunami, a riot, a plane crash, a bad case of food poisoning, a kidnapping? What if Felipe wandered out one day in Bangkok while I was gone and got hit by a car and suffered a serious head injury and ended up in a mysterious hospital somewhere with nobody knowing who he was, and what if I could never find him again? Our existence in the world was in critical flux right now and everything was so delicate. We'd been floating across the planet for five months in a single lifeboat, bobbing together uncertainly. Our union was our only strength for the time being. Why risk separation at such a precarious moment?

On the other hand, maybe it was time to ease up a bit on the fanatical hovering. There was no sane reason to assume that things would not ultimately work out just fine for Felipe and me. Surely our strange period of exile would eventually pass; surely Felipe would be granted his American visa; surely we would get married; surely we would find a stable home in the United States; surely we would have many years to spend together in the future. That being the case, I should probably take a quick trip alone right now, if only to set a solid precedent for the future. Because here was something I already knew to be true about myself: Just as there are some wives who will occasionally need a break from their husbands in order to visit a spa for the weekend with their girlfriends, I will always be the sort of wife who occasionally needs a break from her husband in order to visit Cambodia.

Just for a few days!

And maybe he could use a break from me, too. Watching as Felipe and I had become more irritable with each other over the last few weeks, and now feeling so strongly that I wanted some space away from him, I started thinking about my parents' garden — which is as good a metaphor as any for how two married people must learn to adapt to each other and to sometimes simply clear out of each other's path in order to avoid conflict.

My mother was originally the family gardener, but my father has become more interested in home agriculture over the years, maneuvering his way deep into this realm of hers. But just as Felipe and I travel differently, my mother and father garden differently, and often this has led to strife. Over the years, then, they have divided their garden in order to keep some civility out there amid the vegetables. In fact, they have divided the garden in such a complicated manner that, by this point in its history, you would practically need a United Nations peacekeeping force to understand my parents' carefully partitioned spheres of horti-cultural influence. The lettuce, broccoli, herbs, beets, and raspberries are all still under my mother's domain, for instance, because my father has not yet figured out a way to wrest control of that produce from her. But the carrots, leeks, and asparagus are completely my father's province. And as for the blueberries? Dad chases Mom out of his blueberry patch as though she were a foraging bird. My mother is not allowed anywhere near the blueberries: not to trim them, not to harvest them, not even to water them. My father has laid claim to the blueberry patch, and he *defends* it.

Where the garden gets really complicated, though, is with the question of tomatoes and corn. Like the West Bank, like Taiwan, like Kashmir, the tomatoes and the corn are still contested territories. My mother plants the tomatoes, but my father is in charge of staking the tomatoes, but then my mother harvests the tomatoes. Don't ask me why! Those are just the rules of engagement. (Or at least they were the rules of engagement last summer. The tomato situation is still evolving.) On the other hand, there is corn. My father plants the corn and my mother harvests the corn, but my father insists on personally mulching the corn once the harvest is done.

And so they toil on, together but separate. Garden without end, amen.

The peculiar truce of my parents' garden brings to mind a book that a friend of mine, a psychologist named Deborah Luepnitz, published several years ago called *Schopenhauer's Porcupines*. The operative metaphor of Deborah's book was a story that the pre-Freudian philosopher Arthur Schopenhauer told about the essential dilemma of modern human intimacy. Schopenhauer believed that humans, in their love relationships, were like porcupines out on a cold winter night. In order to keep from freezing, the animals huddle close together. But as soon as they are near enough to provide critical warmth, they get poked by each other's quills. Reflexively, to stop the pain and irritation of too much closeness, the porcupines separate. But once they separate, they become cold again. The chill sends them back toward each other once more, only to be impaled all over again by each other's quills. So they retreat again. And then approach again. Endlessly.

"And the cycle repeats," Deborah wrote, "as they struggle to find a comfortable distance between entanglement and freezing."

Dividing and subdividing their control over such consequential matters as money and children, but also over such seemingly inconsequential matters as beets and blueberries, my parents weave their own version of the porcupine dance, advancing and retreating on each other's territory, still negotiating, still recalibrating, still working after all these years to find the correct distance between autonomy and cooperation — seeking a subtle and elusive balance that will somehow keep this strange plot of intimacy growing. They compromise a lot in the process — sometimes compromising away precious time and energy that they might have preferred to spend doing different things, separate things, if only the other person wasn't in the way. Felipe and I will have to do the same thing when it comes to our own spheres of cultivation — and certainly we would need to learn our own steps of the porcupine dance around the subject of travel.

Still, when it came time to discuss with Felipe my idea of going off to Cambodia without him for a spell, I broached the topic with a degree of skittishness that surprised me. For a few days, I could not seem to find the right approach. I didn't want to feel as though I were asking his permission to go, since that placed him in the role of a master or a parent — and that wouldn't be fair to me. Nor, though, could I imagine sitting down with this nice, considerate man and bluntly informing him that I was heading off alone whether he liked it or not. This would place me in the role of a willful tyrant, which was obviously unfair to him.

The fact was, I was out of practice for this kind of thing. I had been on my own for a while before I'd met Felipe, and I had grown accustomed to shaping my own agenda without having to take account of somebody else's wishes. What's more, up until this point in our love story, our externally mandated travel restrictions (as well as our lives led on separate continents) had always ensured that the two of us had plenty of time alone. But with marriage, everything would now change. We would be together all the time now, and that togetherness would bring trying new limits, because marriage is a binding thing, a taming thing, by its very nature. Marriage has a bonsai energy: It's a tree in a pot with trimmed roots and clipped limbs. Mind you, bonsai can live for centuries, and their unearthly beauty is a direct result of such constriction, but nobody would ever mistake a bonsai for a free-climbing vine.

The Polish philosopher and sociologist Zygmunt Bauman has written exquisitely about this subject. He believes that modern couples have been sold a bill of goods when they're told that they can and should have it both ways — that we should all have equal parts intimacy and autonomy in our lives. Somehow, Bauman suggests, we have mistakenly come to believe in our culture that if only we manage our emotional lives correctly we should each be able to experience all the reassuring constancy of marriage without ever once feeling remotely confined or limited. The magic word here — the almost fetishized word here — is "balance," and just about everybody I know these days seems to be seeking that balance with a near-desperate urgency. We are all trying, as Bauman writes, to force our marriages to "empower without disempowering, enable without disabling, fulfill without burdening."

But perhaps this is an unrealistic aspiration? Because love *limits,* almost by definition. Love narrows. The great expansion we feel in our hearts when we fall in love is matched only by the great restrictions that will necessarily follow. Felipe and I have one of the most easygoing relationships you could possibly imagine, but please do not be fooled: I have utterly claimed this man as my own, and I have therefore fenced him off from the rest of the herd. His energies (sexual, emotional, creative) belong in large part to me, not to anybody else — not even entirely to himself anymore. He owes me things like information, explanations, fidelity, constancy, and details about the most mundane little aspects of his life. It's not like I keep the man in a radio collar, but make no mistake about it — he belongs to me now. And I belong to him, in exactly the same measure.

Which does not mean that I cannot go to Cambodia by myself. It does mean, however, that I need to discuss my plans with Felipe before I leave — as he would do with me were our situations reversed. If he objects to my desire to travel alone, I can argue my point with him, but I am obliged to at least listen to his objections. If he strenuously objects, I can just as strenuously overrule him, but I must select my battles — as must he. If he protests my wishes too often, our marriage will surely break apart. On the other hand, if I constantly demand to live my life away from him, our marriage will just as surely break apart. It's delicate, then, this operation of mutual, quiet, almost velvety oppression. Out of respect, we must learn how to release and confine each other with the most exquisite care, but we should never — not even for a moment — pretend that we are not confined.

After a good deal of thinking, I finally brought up the subject of Cambodia with Felipe one morning over breakfast in Bangkok. I selected my words with a ridiculous amount of mindfulness, using such abstruse language that for a time the poor man clearly had no idea what I was talking about. With a good dose of stiff formality and a whole lot of preamble, I awkwardly tried to explain that, while I loved him and was hesitant to leave him alone right now at such a tenuous moment in our lives, I really would like to see the temples in Cambodia . . . and maybe, since he finds ancient ruins so tedious, this was a trip I should perhaps consider undertaking by myself? . . . and maybe it wouldn't kill us to spend a few days apart, given how stressful all the traveling had become?

It took Felipe a few moments to catch the drift of what I was saying, but when the penny finally dropped, he put down his toast and stared at me in frank puzzlement.

"My God, darling!" he said. "What are you even asking me for? *Just go!*"

So I went.

And my trip to Cambodia was . . .

How shall I explain this?

Cambodia is not a day at the beach. Cambodia is not even a day at the beach if you happen to be spending a day at an actual beach there. Cambodia is hard. Everything about the place felt hard to me. The landscape is hard, beaten down to within an inch of its life. The history is hard, with genocide lingering in recent memory. The faces of the children are hard. The dogs are hard. The poverty was harder than anything I'd ever seen before. It was like the poverty of rural India, but without the verve of India. It was like the poverty of urban Brazil, but without the flash of Brazil. This was just poverty of the dusty and exhausted variety.

Most of all, though, my guide was hard.

Once I'd secured myself a hotel in Siem Reap, I set out to hire a guide to show me the temples of Angkor Wat, and ended up with a man named Narith — an articulate, knowledgeable, and extremely stern gentleman in his early forties who politely showed me the magnificent ancient ruins, but who, to put it mildly, did not enjoy my company. We did not become friends, Narith and I, though I dearly wished us to. I do not like to meet a new person and not make a new friend, but friendship was never going to grow between Narith and me. Part of the problem was Narith's extraordinarily intimidating demeanor. Everyone has a default emotion, and Narith's was quiet disapproval, which he radiated at every turn. This threw off my composure so much that after two days I barely dared to open my mouth anymore. He made me feel like a foolish child, which was not surprising given that his other job — aside from being a tour guide — was schoolmaster. I'm willing to wager he's terrifyingly effective at it. He admitted to me that he sometimes feels nostalgic for the good old days before the war, when Cambodian families were more intact, and when children were kept well disciplined by regular beatings.

But it wasn't merely Narith's austerity that prohibited us from developing a warm human connection; it was also my fault. I honestly could not figure out how to talk to this man. I was keenly aware of the fact that I was in the presence of a person who had grown up during one of the most brutal spasms of violence the world has ever witnessed. No Cambodian family was left unaffected by the genocide of the 1970s. Anyone who was not tortured or executed in Cambodia during the Pol Pot years merely starved and suffered. You can safely assume, then, that any Cambodian who is forty years old today lived through an absolute inferno of a childhood. Knowing all this, I found it difficult to generate casual conversation with Narith. I could not find any topics that were not freighted with potential references to the not-so-distant past. Traveling through Cambodia with a Cambodian, I decided, must be something like exploring a house that had recently been the scene of a grisly family mass murder, guided along on your tour by the only relative who had managed to escape death. This leaves one rather desperate to avoid asking questions like "So — is this the bedroom where your brother murdered your sisters?" or "Is this the garage where your father tortured your cousins?" Instead, you just follow along politely behind your guide, and when he says, "Here is a particularly nice old feature of our house," you merely nod and murmur, "Yes, the pergola *is* lovely . . ."

And you wonder.

Meanwhile, as Narith and I toured the ancient ruins and avoided discussing modern history, we stumbled everywhere on groups of unattended children, whole tattered gangs of them, openly begging. Some of them were missing limbs. The kids without limbs would sit on the corner of an abandoned old edifice, pointing at their amputated legs and calling out, "Land mine! Land mine! Land mine!" As we walked by, the more able-bodied children would follow us, trying to sell me postcards, bracelets, trinkets. Some were pushy, but others tried more subtle angles. "What state are you from in America?" one little boy demanded of me. "If I tell you the capital, you can give me a dollar!" That particular boy followed me for long stretches of the day, throwing out the names of American states and capitals like a shrill, strange poem: "Illinois, madam! Springfield! New York, madam! Albany!" As the day passed, he became increasingly despondent: "California, madam! SACRAMENTO! Texas, madam! AUSTIN!"

Strangled by grief, I offered these kids money, but Narith would only scold me for my handouts. I was to ignore the children, he lectured. I was only making things worse by giving out cash, he warned. I was encouraging a culture of begging, which would spell the end of Cambodia. There were too many of these wild children to help, anyhow, and my boon would only attract more of them. True enough, more children gathered whenever they saw me pulling out bills and coins, and once my Cambodian currency was gone, they still flocked around me. I felt poisoned by the constant repetition of the word "NO" coming out of my own mouth again and again: an awful incantation. The kids became more insistent until Narith decided he'd had enough and scattered them back across the ruins with a barking dismissal.

One afternoon, walking back to our car

from a tour of another thirteenth-century palace and trying to change the subject from the begging children, I asked about the nearby forest, wondering about its history. Narith replied, in an apparent non sequitur, "When my father was killed by the Khmer Rouge, the soldiers took our house as a trophy."

I could summon no reply for this, so we walked along in silence.

After a spell, he added, "My mother was sent into the forest with us, with all her children, to try to survive."

I waited for the rest of the story, but there was no rest of the story — or at least nothing more that he wanted to share.

"I'm sorry," I said finally. "That must have been terrible."

Narith shot me a dark look of . . . what? Pity? Contempt? Then it passed. "Let us continue with our tour," he said, pointing to a fetid swamp on our left. "This was once a reflecting pool, used by King Jayavarman VII during the twelfth century to study the mirror image of the stars by night . . ."

The next morning, wanting to offer up something to this battered country, I tried to donate blood at the local hospital. I had seen signs all over town announcing a blood shortage and asking tourists for help, but I didn't even have any luck with this venture. The strict Swiss nurse on duty took one look at my low iron levels and refused to accept my blood. She wouldn't even take a half pint from me.

"You are too weak!" she accused me. "You have obviously not been taking care of yourself! You should not be traveling around like this! You should be home, resting!"

That evening — my last evening alone in Cambodia — I wandered around the streets of Siem Reap, trying to relax into the place. But it did not feel safe to be alone in that city. A peculiar feeling of composure and harmony usually settles on me when I'm moving solo through a new landscape (in fact, that very sensation is what I had come to Cambodia to find), but I never reached it on that trip. If anything, I felt like I was in the way, that I was an irritant, an idiot, or even a target. I felt pathetic and bloodless. As I was walking back to my hotel after dinner, a small swarm of children gathered around me, begging again. One boy was missing a foot, and as he hobbled gamely along he stuck out his crutch in front of me, deliberately tripping me. I stumbled, arms flapping clownishly, but did not quite fall.

"Money," said the boy in a flat tone.

"Money."

I tried stepping around him again. Nimbly, he stuck out his crutch once more, and I had to basically leap over the thing to dodge it, which seemed awful and insane. The children laughed, and then more children gathered: now it was a spectacle. I picked up my pace and walked faster toward the hotel. The crowd of kids tagged behind me, around me, in front of me. Some of them were laughing and blocking my way, but one very little girl kept pulling at my sleeve and crying out, "Food! Food! Food!" By the time I neared the hotel, I was running. It was shameful.

Whatever equanimity I'd proudly and stubbornly been holding together over the last few chaotic months caved in Cambodia, and caved fast. All my expert-traveler's composure fell to bits — along with all my patience and basic human compassion, apparently — as I found myself panicked and adrenalized and running full-speed away from small, hungry children who were openly begging me for food. When I reached my hotel, I dived into my room and locked the door behind me and pushed my face into a towel and trembled like a shitty little coward for the rest of the night.

■ ■ ■ ■

So that was my big trip to Cambodia.

One obvious way to read this story, of course, is that perhaps I should never have gone there in the first place — or at least not at that moment. Perhaps my trip had been an excessively willful or even reckless move, given that I was already fatigued from months of travel, and given the strain of Felipe's and my uncertain circumstances. Perhaps this had been no time for me to go proving my independence, or laying down precedents for future freedoms, or testing the boundaries of intimacy. Perhaps I should have just stayed there in Bangkok with Felipe by the swimming pool the whole time, drinking beer and relaxing, and waiting for our next move together.

Except that I don't like beer and I would not have relaxed. Had I reined in my impulses and stuck around in Bangkok that week, drinking beer and watching the two of us getting on each other's nerves, I might have buried something important within me — something that may have ultimately turned fetid, like King Jayavarman's pool, creating contaminating ramifications for the future. I went to Cambodia because I had to go. It may have been a messy and botched experience, but that doesn't mean I shouldn't have gone. Sometimes life is messy and botched. We do our best. We don't always know the right move.

What I do know is that the day after my encounter with the begging children I flew back to Bangkok and reunited with a Felipe who was calm and relaxed, and who had clearly enjoyed a restorative break from my company. He had passed the days of my absence happily learning how to make balloon animals in order to keep himself busy. Upon my return, therefore, he presented me with a giraffe, a dachshund, and a rattlesnake. He was extraordinarily proud of himself. I, on the other hand, was feeling more than a little undone, and was not at all proud of my performance in Cambodia. But I was awfully glad to see this guy. And I was awfully grateful to him for encouraging me to attempt things that are not always entirely safe and that are not always fully explainable and that do not always work out quite as perfectly as I may have dreamed. I am more grateful for that than I can ever say — because, truth be told, I am certain to do this kind of thing again.

So I praised Felipe for his marvelous balloon menagerie, and he listened carefully to my sad stories about Cambodia, and when we were both good and tired we climbed into bed with each other and lashed our lifeboat together once more and continued on with our story.

Chapter Seven: Marriage and Subversion

OF ALL THE ACTIONS OF A MAN'S LIFE, HIS
MARRIAGE DOES LEAST CONCERN OTHER
PEOPLE; YET OF ALL THE ACTIONS OF OUR
LIFE, 'TIS THE MOST MEDDLED WITH BY
OTHER PEOPLE.
— *John Selden, 1689*

By late October 2006, we had returned to Bali and settled back into Felipe's old house in the rice fields. There, we planned to wait out the rest of his immigration process quietly, with our heads down, inciting no more stress or conflict. It felt good to be in a more familiar place, good to stop moving. This was the house where, almost three years earlier, we had first fallen in love. This was the house that Felipe had given up only one year earlier in order to move in with me "permanently" in Philadelphia. This house was the closest thing to a real home that we could find right now, and man, were we happy to see it.

I watched Felipe melt with relief as he wandered around the old place, touching and smelling every familiar object with an almost canine pleasure. Everything was the same as he had left it. There was the open terrace upstairs with the rattan couch where

Felipe had, as he likes to say, *seduced* me. There was the comfortable bed where we had made love for the first time. There was the dinky kitchen filled with plates and dishes that I had bought for Felipe right after we met because his bachelor accoutrements depressed me. There was the quiet desk in the corner where I had worked on my last book. There was Raja, the neighbor's friendly old orange dog (whom Felipe had always called "Roger"), limping about happily, growling at his own shadow. There were the ducks in the rice field, wandering about and muttering among themselves about some recent poultry scandal.

There was even a coffeepot.

Just like that, Felipe became himself again: kind, attentive, nice. He had his little corner and his routines. I had my books. We both had a familiar bed to share. We relaxed as much as possible into a period of waiting for the Department of Homeland Security to decide Felipe's fate. We fell into an almost narcotic pause during the next two months — something like our friend Keo's meditating frogs. I read, Felipe cooked, sometimes we took a slow walk around the village and visited old friends. But what I remember most about that spell of time in Bali were the nights.

Here's something you wouldn't necessarily expect of Bali: The place is bloody *loud.* I once lived in a Manhattan apartment facing 14th Street, and that place was not nearly as loud as this rural Balinese village. There were nights in Bali when the two of us would be simultaneously awakened by the sound of dogs fighting, or roosters arguing, or an enthusiastic ceremonial procession. Other times, we were pulled out of sleep by the weather, which could behave with startling drama. We always slept with the windows open, and there were nights when the wind blew so hard that we would wake to find ourselves all twisted up in the fabric of our mosquito netting, like seaweed trapped in a sailboat's rigging. Then we would untangle each other and lie in the hot darkness, talking.

One of my favorite passages in literature is from Italo Calvino's *Invisible Cities.* In it, Calvino described an imaginary town called Eufemia, where the merchants of all nations gather at every solstice and every equinox to exchange goods. But these merchants do not come together merely to trade spices or jewels or livestock or textiles. Rather, they come to this town to exchange *stories* with each other — to literally trade in personal intimacies. The way it works, Calvino wrote, is that the men gather around the desert bonfires at night, and each man offers up a word, like "sister," or "wolf," or "buried treasure." Then all the other men take turns telling their own personal stories of sisters, of wolves, of buried treasures. And in the months to come, long after the merchants leave Eufemia, when they ride their camels alone across the desert or sail the long route to China, each man combats his boredom by dredging through his old memories. And that's when the men discover that their memories really *have* been traded — that, as Calvino wrote, "their sister had been exchanged for another's sister, their wolf for another's wolf."

This is what intimacy does to us over time. That's what a long marriage can do: It causes us to inherit and trade each other's stories. This, in part, is how we become annexes of each other, trellises on which each other's biography can grow. Felipe's private history becomes a piece of my memory; my life gets woven into the material of his. Recalling that imaginary story-trading town of Eufemia, and thinking of the tiny narrative stitches that comprise human intimacy, I would sometimes — at three o'clock in the morning on a sleepless night in Bali — feed Felipe a specific word, just to see what memories I could summon out of him. At my cue, at the word I had offered up to him, Felipe would lie there beside me in the dark telling me his scattered stories of sisters, of buried treasures, of wolves, and also more — of beaches, birds, feet, princes, competitions . . .

I remember one hot, damp night when I woke up after a motorcycle without a muffler had blasted past our window, and I sensed that Felipe was also awake. Once more, I selected a word at random.

"Please tell me a story about fish," I requested.

Felipe thought for a long while.

Then he took his time in the moonlit room to recount a memory of going fishing with his father on overnight trips when he was just a little kid back in Brazil. They would head off to some wild river together, just the child and the man, and they would camp there for days — barefoot and shirtless the whole time, living on what they caught. Felipe wasn't as smart as his older brother Gildo (everyone agreed on this), and he wasn't as charming as his big sister Lily (everyone agreed on that, too), but he was known in the family to be the best helper and so he was the only one who ever got to go on the fishing trips alone with his father, even though he was very small.

Felipe's main job on those expeditions was to help his dad set the nets across the river. It was all about strategy. His dad wouldn't talk to him much during the day (too busy focusing on the fishing), but every night over the open fire, he would lay out his plan — man to man — for the next day about where they would fish. Felipe's father would ask his six-year-old son, "Did you see that tree about a mile up the river that's halfway submerged? What do you think about us going there tomorrow, to investigate?" and Felipe would squat there by the fire, all alert and serious, listening manfully, focusing on the plan, nodding his approval.

Felipe's father was not an ambitious guy, not a great thinker, not a captain of industry. Truthfully, he was not very industrious at all. But he was a fearless swimmer. He would clench his big hunting knife in his teeth and swim across those wide rivers, checking his nets and traps while he left his little boy alone back on the bank. It was both terrifying and thrilling for Felipe to watch his father strip down to his shorts, bite that knife, and fight his way across the swift current — knowing all the while that if his father was swept away, he himself would be abandoned there in the middle of nowhere.

But his father was never swept away. He was too strong. In the nighttime heat of our bedroom in Bali, under our damp and billowing mosquito nets, Felipe showed me what a strong swimmer his dad had been. He imitated his father's beautiful stroke, lying there on his back in the humid night air, *swimming,* his arms faint and ghostly. Across all these lost decades, Felipe could still replicate the exact *sound* that his father's arms made as they sliced through the fast dark waters: *"Shush-a, shush-a, shush-a . . ."*

And now that memory — that sound — swam through me, too. I even felt as though I could remember it, despite having never met Felipe's father, who died years ago. In fact, there are probably only about four people alive in the whole world who remember Felipe's father at all anymore, and only one of them — until the moment Felipe shared this story with me — recalled exactly how that man had looked and sounded when he used to swim across wide Brazilian rivers in the middle years of the last century. But now I felt that I could remember it, too, in a strange and personal way.

This is intimacy: the trading of stories in the dark.

This act, the act of quiet nighttime talking, illustrates for me more than anything else the curious alchemy of companionship. Because when Felipe described his father's swimming stroke, I took that watery image and I stitched it carefully into the hem of my own life, and now I will carry that around with me forever. As long as I live, and even long after Felipe has gone, his childhood memory, his father, his river, his Brazil — all of this, too, has somehow become me.

A few weeks into our sojourn in Bali, there was finally a breakthrough in the immigration case.

According to our lawyer back in Philadelphia, the FBI had cleared my criminal background report. I'd passed cleanly. I was now considered a safe risk for marrying a foreigner, which meant that the Department of Homeland Security could finally begin processing Felipe's immigration application. If all went well — if they granted him the elusive golden ticket of a fiancé visa — he might be allowed to return to America within the space of three months. The end was now in sight. Our marriage had now become imminent. The immigration documents, assuming Felipe secured them, would stipulate quite clearly that this man was allowed to enter America again, but for only and exactly thirty days, during which time he had to marry a particular citizen named Elizabeth Gilbert, and *only* a particular citizen named Elizabeth Gilbert, or he would face permanent deportation. The government would not be issuing an actual shotgun along with all the paperwork, but it did sort of have that feeling.

As this news filtered back to all our family members and friends around the world, we started getting questions from people about what kind of wedding ceremony we were planning. When would the wedding be? Where would it be? Who would be invited? I dodged everyone's questions. Truthfully, I hadn't planned anything special around a wedding ceremony simply because I found the whole idea of a public wedding entirely agitating.

I had stumbled in my studies on a letter that Anton Chekhov wrote to his fiancée, Olga Knipper, on April 26, 1901, a letter that perfectly expressed the sum of all my fears. Chekhov wrote, "If you give me your word that not a soul in Moscow will know about our wedding until after it has taken place, I am ready to marry you on the very day of my arrival. For some reason I am horribly afraid of the wedding ceremony and the congratulations and the Champagne that you must hold in your hand while you smile vaguely. I wish we could go straight from the church to Zvenigorod. Or perhaps we could get married in Zvenigorod. Think, think, darling! You are clever, they say."

Yes! Think!

I, too, wanted to skip all the fuss and go straight to Zvenigorod — and I'd never even *heard* of Zvenigorod! I just wanted to get married as furtively and privately as possible, perhaps without even telling anyone. Weren't there judges and mayors out there who could execute such a job painlessly enough? When I confided these thoughts in an e-mail to my sister Catherine, she replied, "You make marriage sound like a colonoscopy." But I can attest that after months of intrusive questions from the Homeland Security Department, a colonoscopy was exactly what our upcoming wedding was beginning to feel like.

Still, as it turned out, there were some people in our lives who felt this event should be honored with a proper ceremony, and my sister was foremost among them. She sent me gentle but frequent e-mails from Philadelphia concerning the possibility of throwing a wedding party for us at her house when we returned home. It wouldn't have to be anything fancy, she promised, but still . . .

My palms dampened at the very thought of it. I protested that this really was not necessary, that Felipe and I didn't really roll that way. Catherine wrote in her next message, "What if I just happened to throw a big birthday party for myself, and you and Felipe happened to come? Would I be allowed to at least make a toast to your marriage?"

I committed to no such thing.

She tried again: "What if I just happened to throw a big party while you guys were at my house, but you and Felipe wouldn't even have to come *downstairs?* You could just lock yourselves upstairs with the lights off. And when I made the wedding toast, I would casually wave my champagne glass in the general direction of the attic door? Is even *that* too threatening?"

Oddly, indefensibly, perversely: *yes.*

When I tried to sort out my resistance to a public wedding ceremony, I had to admit that part of the issue was simple embarrassment. How very awkward to stand in front of one's family and friends (many of whom had been guests at one's first wedding) and swear solemn vows for life all over again.

Hadn't they all seen this film already? One's credibility does begin to tarnish after too much of this sort of thing. And Felipe, too, had once before sworn lifetime vows only to leave the marriage after seventeen years. What a pair we made! To paraphrase Oscar Wilde: One divorce may be regarded as a misfortune, but two begins to smack of carelessness.

Furthermore, I could never forget what the etiquette columnist Miss Manners has to say on this very subject. While expressing her conviction that people should be allowed to marry as many times as they like, she does believe that each of us is entitled to only one big fanfare wedding ceremony per lifetime. (This may seem a bit overly Protestant and repressive, I know — but curiously enough, the Hmong feel the same way. When I'd asked that grandmother back in Vietnam about the traditional Hmong procedure for second marriages, she had replied, "Second weddings are exactly the same as first weddings — except with not as many pigs.")

Moreover, a second or third big wedding puts family members and friends in the awkward position of wondering if they must shower repeat brides with gifts and abundant attention all over again. The answer, apparently, is no. As Miss Manners once coolly explained to a reader, the proper technique for congratulating a serial bride-to-be is to eschew all the gifts and galas and simply write the lady a note expressing how very delighted you are for her happiness, wishing her all the luck in the world, and being very careful to avoid using the words "this time."

My God, how those two indicting little words — *this time* — make me cringe. Yet it was true. The recollections of *last time* felt all too recent for me, all too painful. Also, I didn't like the idea that guests at a bride's second wedding are just as likely to be thinking about her first spouse as they are to be thinking about her new spouse — and that the bride, too, will probably be remembering her ex-husband on that day. First spouses, I have learned, don't ever really go away — even if you aren't speaking to them anymore. They are phantoms who dwell in the corners of our new love stories, never entirely vanishing from sight, materializing in our minds whenever they please, offering up unwelcome comments or bits of painfully accurate criticism. "We know you better than you know yourselves" is what the ghosts of our ex-spouses like to remind us, and what they know about us, unfortunately, is often not pretty.

"There are four minds in the bed of a divorced man who marries a divorced woman," says a fourth-century Talmudic document — and indeed, our former spouses do often haunt our beds. I still dream about my ex-husband, for instance, far more than I would ever have imagined back when I left him. Usually these dreams are agitating and confusing. On rare occasions, they are warm or conciliatory. It doesn't really matter, though: I can neither control the dreams nor stop them. He shows up in my subconscious whenever he pleases, entering without knocking. He still has the keys to that house. Felipe dreams about his ex-wife, too. *I* dream about Felipe's ex-wife, for heaven's sake. I sometimes even dream about my ex-husband's new wife, whom I have never met, whose photograph I have never even seen — yet she appears in my dreams sometimes, and we converse there. (In fact, we hold summit meetings.) And I wouldn't be surprised if somewhere in this world my ex-husband's second wife is intermittently dreaming about me — trying in her subconscious to work out the strange folds and seams of our connection.

My friend Ann — divorced twenty years ago and happily remarried since to a wonderful, older man — assures me that this will all go away over time. She swears that the ghosts do recede, that there will come a time when I never think about my ex-husband again. I don't know, though. I find that hard to picture. I can imagine it *easing,* but I can't imagine it ever going away completely, especially because my first marriage ended so sloppily, with so much left unresolved. My ex-husband and I never once agreed on what had gone wrong with our relationship. It was shocking, our total absence of consensus. Such completely different worldviews are probably also an indication of why we should never have been together in the first place; we were the only two eyewitnesses to the death of our marriage, and we each walked away with a completely different testimony as to what had happened.

Thus, perhaps, the dim sense of haunting. So we lead separate lives now, my ex-husband and I, yet he still visits my dreams in the form of an avatar who probes and debates and reconsiders from a thousand different angles an eternal docket of unfinished business. It's awkward. It's eerie. It's ghostly, and I didn't want to provoke that ghost with a big loud ceremony or celebration.

Maybe another reason Felipe and I were so resistant to exchanging ceremonial vows was that we felt we'd already done it. We'd already exchanged vows in an utterly private ceremony of our own devising. This had happened back in Knoxville, in April 2005 — back when Felipe first came to live with me in that odd decaying hotel on the square. We had gone out one day and bought ourselves a pair of simple gold rings. Then we'd written out our promises to each other and read them aloud. We put the rings on each other's fingers, sealed our commitment with a kiss and tears, and that was it. Both of us had felt like that was enough. In all the ways that mattered, then, we believed that we were already married.

Nobody saw this happen except the two of us (and — one hopes — God). And needless to say, nobody respected those vows of ours in any way whatsoever (except the two of us and — again, one hopes — God). I invite you to imagine how the deputies of the Homeland Security Department, for instance, might have responded back at the Dallas/Fort Worth Airport if I had tried to convince them that a private commitment ceremony held in a Knoxville hotel room had somehow rendered Felipe and me as good as legally married.

Truth be told, it seemed mostly irritating to people — even to people who loved us — that Felipe and I were walking around wearing wedding rings without having had an official and legal marriage ceremony. The consensus was that our actions were confusing at best, pathetic at worst. "No!" declared my old friend Brian in an e-mail from North Carolina when I told him that Felipe and I had recently exchanged private vows. "No, you *cannot* just do it that way!" he insisted. "That's *not* enough! You *must* have some kind of real wedding!"

Brian and I argued over this subject for weeks, and I was surprised to discover his adamancy on the topic. I thought that he, of all people, would understand why Felipe and I shouldn't need to marry publicly or legally just to satisfy other people's conventions. Brian is one of the happiest married men I know (his devotion to Linda makes him the living definition of the marvelous word *uxorious,* or "wife-worshiping"), but he's also quite possibly my most naturally nonconformist friend. He bends comfortably to no socially accepted norm whatsoever. He's basically a pagan with a Ph.D. who lives in a cabin in the woods with a composting toilet; this was hardly Miss Manners. But Brian was uncompromising in his insistence that private vows spoken only before God do not count as marriage.

"MARRIAGE IS NOT PRAYER!" he insisted (italics and capitals his). "That's why you *have* to do it in front of others, even in front of your aunt who smells like cat litter. It's a paradox, but marriage actually reconciles a lot of paradoxes: freedom with commitment, strength with subordination, wisdom with utter nincompoopery, etc. And you're missing the main point — it's not just to 'satisfy' other people. Rather, you have to hold your wedding guests to *their* end of the deal. They have to *help* you with your marriage; they have to support you or Felipe, if one of you falters."

The only person who seemed more annoyed than Brian about our private commitment ceremony was my niece Mimi, age seven. First of all, Mimi felt prodigiously ripped off that I hadn't thrown a real wedding, because she really wanted to be a flower girl at least once in her life and had never yet been given the chance. Meanwhile, her best friend and rival Moriya had already been a flower girl *twice* — and Mimi wasn't getting any younger here, people.

Moreover, our actions in Tennessee offended my niece on an almost semantic level. It had been suggested to Mimi that she could now, after that exchange of private vows in Knoxville, refer to Felipe as her uncle — but she wasn't having it. Nor did her older brother Nick buy it. It wasn't that my sister's kids didn't like Felipe. It's just that an uncle, as Nick (age ten) instructed me sternly, is either the brother of your father or mother, or he is the man who is *legally* married to your aunt. Felipe, therefore, was not officially Nick and Mimi's uncle any more than he was officially my husband, and there was nothing I could do to convince them otherwise. Children at that age are nothing if not sticklers for convention. Hell, they're practically census takers. To punish me for my civil disobedience, Mimi took to calling Felipe her "uncle" using the sarcastic air quotes every time. Sometimes she even referred to him as my "husband" — again with the air quotes and the hint of irritated disdain.

One night back in 2005, when Felipe and I were having dinner at Catherine's house, I had asked Mimi what it would take for her to consider my commitment to Felipe a valid one. She was unyielding in her certainty. "You need to have a *real* wedding," she said.

"But what makes something a real wedding?" I asked.

"You need to have a *person* there." Now she was frankly exasperated. "You can't just make promises with nobody seeing it. There has to be a *person* who watches when you make promises."

Curiously enough, Mimi was making a strong intellectual and historical point there. As the philosopher David Hume explained, witnesses are necessary in all societies when it comes to important vows. The reason is that it's not possible to tell whether a person is telling the truth or lying when he speaks a promise. The speaker may have, as Hume called it, "a secret direction of thought" hidden behind the noble and high-flown words. The presence of the witness, though, negates any concealed intentions. It doesn't matter anymore whether you *meant* what you said; it matters merely that you *said* what you said, and that a third party witnessed you saying it. It is the witness, then, who becomes the living seal of the promise, notarizing the vow with real weight. Even in the early European Middle Ages, before the times of official church or government weddings, the expression of a vow before a single witness was all it took to seal a couple together forever in a state of legal matrimony. Even then, you couldn't do it entirely on your own. Even then, somebody had to watch.

"Would it satisfy you," I asked Mimi, "if Felipe and I promised wedding vows to each other, right here in your kitchen, in front of you?"

"Yeah, but who would be the *person?*" she asked.

"Why don't you be the person?" I suggested. "That way you can be sure it's done properly."

This was a brilliant plan. Making sure that things are done properly is Mimi's specialty. This is a girl who was veritably born to be *the person.* And I'm proud to report that she rose to the occasion. Right there in the kitchen, while her mother cooked dinner, Mimi asked Felipe and me if we would please rise and face her. She asked us to please hand her the gold "wedding" rings (again with the air quotes) that we had already been wearing for months. These rings she promised to hold safely until the ceremony was over.

Then she improvised a matrimonial ritual, cobbled together, I supposed, from various movies she had seen in her seven long years of life.

"Do you promise to love each other all the time?" she asked.

We promised.

"Do you promise to love each other through sick and not sick?"

We promised.

"Do you promise to love each other through mad and not mad?"

We promised.

"Do you promise to love each other through rich and not so rich?" (The idea of flat-out poor, apparently, was not something Mimi cared to wish upon us; thus "not so rich" would have to suffice.)

We promised.

We all stood there for a moment in silence. It was evident that Mimi would have liked to remain in the authoritative position of *the person* for a bit longer, but she couldn't come up with anything else that needed promising. So she gave us back our rings and instructed us to place them on each other's fingers.

"You may now kiss the bride," she pronounced.

Felipe kissed me. Catherine gave a small cheer and went back to stirring the clam sauce. Thus concluded, right there in my sister's kitchen, the second non-legally-binding commitment ceremony of Liz and Felipe. This time with an actual witness.

I hugged Mimi. "Satisfied?"

She nodded.

But plainly — you could read it all over her face — she was not.

What *is* it about a public, legal wedding ceremony that means so much to everybody anyhow? And why was I so stubbornly — almost belligerently — resistant to it? My aversion made even less sense, considering that I happen to be somebody who loves ritual and ceremony to an inordinate degree. Look, I've studied my Joseph Campbell, I've read *The Golden Bough,* and I get it. I thoroughly recognize that ceremony is essential to humans: It's a circle that we draw around important events to separate the momentous from the ordinary. And ritual is a sort of magical safety harness that guides us from one stage of our lives into the next, making sure we don't stumble or lose ourselves along the way. Ceremony and ritual march us carefully right through the center of our deepest fears about change, much the same way that a stable boy can lead a blindfolded horse right through the center of a fire, whispering, "Don't overthink this, buddy, okay? Just put one hoof in front of the other and you'll come out on the other side *just fine.*"

I even understand why people feel it's so important to witness each other's ritualistic ceremonies. My father — not an especially conventional man by any means — was always adamant that we must attend the wakes and funerals of anyone in our hometown who ever died. The point, he explained, was not necessarily to honor the dead or to comfort the living. Instead, you went to these ceremonies so that you could be *seen* — specifically seen, for instance, by the wife of the deceased. You needed to make sure that she catalogued your face and registered the fact that you had attended her husband's funeral. This was not so you could earn social points or get extra credit for being a nice person, but rather so that the next time you ran into the widow at the supermarket she would be spared the awful uncertainty of wondering whether you had heard her sad news. Having seen you at her husband's funeral, she would already know that you *knew.* She would therefore not have to repeat the story of her loss to you all over again, and you would be saved the awkward necessity of expressing your condolences right there in the middle of the produce aisle because you had already expressed them at the church, where such words are appropriate. This public ceremony of death, therefore, somehow squared you and the widow with each other — and also somehow *spared* the two of you social discomfort and uncertainty. Your business with each other was settled. You were safe.

This is what my friends and family wanted, I realized, when they were asking for a public wedding ceremony between Felipe and me. It wasn't that they wanted to dress in fine clothing, dance in uncomfortable shoes, or dine on the chicken or the fish. What my friends and family really wanted was to be able to move on with their lives knowing with certainty where everybody stood in relationship to everybody else. This was what Mimi wanted — to be squared and spared. She wanted the clear assurance that she could now take the words "uncle" and "husband" out of air quotes and continue her life without awkwardly wondering whether she was now required to honor Felipe as a family member or not. And it was quite clear that the only way she was ever going to offer up her full loyalty to this union was if she could personally witness the exchange of legal vows.

I knew all this, and I understood it. Still, I resisted. The main problem was that — even after several months spent reading about marriage and thinking about marriage and talking about marriage — I was still not yet entirely *convinced* about marriage. I was not yet sure that I bought the package of goods that matrimony was selling. Truthfully, I was still feeling resentful that Felipe and I had to marry at all merely because the government demanded it of us. And probably the reason this all bothered me so deeply and at such a fundamental level, I finally realized, is that I am Greek.

Please understand, I do not mean that I am *literally* Greek, as in: from the country of Greece, or a member of a collegiate fraternity, or enamored of the sexual passion that bonds two men in love. Instead, I mean that I am Greek in the way I think. Because here's the thing: It has long been understood by philosophers that the entire bedrock of Western culture is based on two rival worldviews — the Greek and the Hebrew — and whichever side you embrace more strongly determines to a large extent how you see life.

From the Greeks — specifically from the glory days of ancient Athens — we have inherited our ideas about secular humanism and the sanctity of the individual. The Greeks gave us all our notions about democracy and equality and personal liberty and scientific reason and intellectual freedom and open-mindedness and what we might call today "multiculturalism." The Greek

take on life, therefore, is urban, sophisticated, and exploratory, always leaving plenty
of room for doubt and debate.

On the other hand, there is the Hebrew
way of seeing the world. When I say "Hebrew" here, I'm not specifically referring to
the tenets of Judaism. (In fact, most of the
contemporary American Jews I know are
very Greek in their thinking, while it's the
American fundamentalist Christians these
days who are profoundly Hebrew.) "Hebrew," in the sense that philosophers use it
here, is shorthand for an ancient worldview
that is all about tribalism, faith, obedience,
and respect. The Hebrew credo is clannish,
patriarchal, authoritarian, moralistic, ritualistic, and instinctively suspicious of outsiders. Hebrew thinkers see the world as a clear
play between good and evil, with God
always firmly on "our" side. Human actions
are either right or wrong. There is no gray
area. The collective is more important than
the individual, morality is more important
than happiness, and vows are inviolable.

The problem is that modern Western
culture has somehow inherited both these
ancient worldviews — though we have never
entirely reconciled them because they aren't
reconcilable. (Have you *followed* an American election cycle recently?) American

society is therefore a funny amalgam of both Greek and Hebrew thinking. Our legal code is mostly Greek; our moral code is mostly Hebrew. We have no way of thinking about independence and intellect and the sanctity of the individual that is not Greek. We have no way of thinking about righteousness and God's will that is not Hebrew. Our sense of fairness is Greek; our sense of justice is Hebrew.

And when it comes to our ideas about love — well, we are a tangled mess of both. In survey after survey, Americans express their belief in two completely contradictory ideas about marriage. On one hand (the Hebrew hand), we overwhelmingly believe as a nation that marriage should be a lifetime vow, never broken. On the other, Greek, hand, we equally believe that an individual should always have the right to get divorced, for his or her own personal reasons.

How can both these ideas be simultaneously true? No wonder we're so confused. No wonder Americans get married more often, and get divorced more often, than any other people in any other nation on earth. We keep ping-ponging back and forth between two rival views of love. Our Hebrew (or biblical/moral) view of love is based on devotion to God — which is all about submission before a sacrosanct creed, and we absolutely believe in that. Our Greek (or philosophical/ethical) view of love is based on devotion to nature — which is all about exploration, beauty, and a deep reverence for self-expression. And we absolutely believe in that, too.

The perfect Greek lover is erotic; the perfect Hebrew lover is faithful.

Passion is Greek; fidelity is Hebrew.

This idea came to haunt me because, on the Greek-Hebrew spectrum, I fall much closer to the Greek end. Did this make me an especially poor candidate for matrimony? I worried that it did. We Greeks don't feel comfortable sacrificing the Self upon the altar of tradition; it just feels oppressive and scary to us. I worried about all this even more after I stumbled on one tiny but critical piece of information from that massive Rutgers study on matrimony. Apparently the researchers found evidence to support the notion that marriages in which both husband and wife wholeheartedly respect the sanctity of matrimony itself are more likely to endure than marriages where couples are perhaps a bit more suspicious of the institution. It seems, then, that respecting marriage is a precondition for staying married.

Though I suppose that makes sense, right? You need to believe in what you're pledging, don't you, for a promise to have any weight? Because marriage is not merely a vow made to another individual; that's the easy part. Marriage is also a vow made to a *vow*. I know for certain that there are people who stay married forever not necessarily because they love their spouses, but because they love their *principles*. They will go to their graves still bound in loyal matrimony to somebody they may actively loathe just because they promised something before God to that person, and they would no longer recognize themselves if they dishonored such a promise.

Clearly, I am not such a being. In the past, I was given the clear choice between honoring my vow and honoring my own life, and I chose myself over the promise. I refuse to say that this *necessarily* makes me an unethical person (one could argue that choosing liberation over misery is a way of honoring life's miracle), but it did bring up a dilemma when it came to getting married to Felipe. While I was just Hebrew enough to dearly wish that I would stay married forever this time (yes, let's just go ahead and use those shaming words: *this time*), I had not yet found a way to respect wholeheartedly the institution of matrimony itself. I had not yet found a place for myself within the history of marriage where I felt that I belonged, where I felt that I could recognize myself. This absence of respect and self-recognition caused me to fear that not even I would believe my own sworn vows on my own wedding day.

Trying to sort this out, I brought up the question with Felipe. Now I should say here that Felipe was considerably more relaxed about all this than I was. While he didn't hold any more affection for the institution of marriage than I did, he kept telling me, "At this point, darling, it's all just a game. The government has set the rules and now we have to play their game in order to get what we want. Personally, I'm willing to play any game whatsoever, as long as it means that I ultimately can live my life with you in peace."

That mode of thinking worked for him, but gamesmanship wasn't what I was looking for here; I needed a certain level of earnestness and authenticity. Still, Felipe could see my agitation on this subject, and — God bless the man — he was kind enough to listen to me muse for quite a long while on the rival philosophies of Western civilization and how they were affecting my views on matrimony. But when I asked Felipe whether he felt himself to be more Greek or more Hebrew in his thinking, he replied, "Darling — none of this really applies to me."

"Why not?" I asked.

"I'm not Greek *or* Hebrew."

"What are you then?"

"I'm Brazilian."

"But what does that even mean?"

Felipe laughed. "Nobody knows! That's the wonderful thing about being Brazilian. It doesn't mean anything! So you can use your Brazilianness as an excuse to live your life any way you want. It's a brilliant strategy, actually. It's taken me far."

"So how does that help me?"

"Perhaps it can help you to relax! You're about to marry a Brazilian. Why don't you start thinking like a Brazilian?"

"How?"

"By choosing what you want! That's the Brazilian way, isn't it? We borrow everyone's ideas, mix it all up, and then we create something new out of it. Listen — what is it that you like so much about the Greeks?"

"Their sense of humanity," I said.

"And what is it that you like — if anything — about the Hebrews?"

"Their sense of honor," I said.

"Okay, so that's settled — we'll take them both. Humanity and honor. We'll make a marriage out of that combination. We'll call it a Brazilian blend. We'll shape this thing to our own code."

"Can we just do that?"

"Darling!" Felipe said, and he took my face between his hands with a sudden, frustrated urgency. "When are you going to understand? As soon as we secure this bloody visa and get ourselves safely married back in America, *we can do whatever the hell we want.*"

Can we, though?

I prayed that Felipe was right, but I wasn't sure. My deepest fear about marriage, when I dug right down to the very bottom of it, was that matrimony would end up shaping us far more than we could ever possibly shape it. All my months of studying marriage had only caused me to fear this potentiality more than ever. I had come to believe that matrimony as an institution was impressively powerful. It was certainly far bigger and older and deeper and more complicated than Felipe or I could ever possibly be. No matter how modern and sophisticated Felipe and I might feel, I feared we would step onto the assembly line of marriage and soon enough find ourselves molded into *spouses* — crammed into some deeply conventional shape that benefited society, even if it did not entirely benefit us.

All this was disquieting because, as annoying as it may sound, I do like to think of myself as vaguely bohemian. I'm not an anarchist or anything, but it does comfort me to regard my life in terms of a certain instinctive resistance to conformity. Felipe, to be honest, likes to think of himself in much the same way. Okay, let's all be truthful here and admit that *most* of us probably like to think of ourselves in these terms, right? It's charming, after all, to imagine oneself as an eccentric nonconformist, even when one has just purchased a coffeepot. So maybe the whole idea of bending under the convention of marriage stung a bit for me — stung at that stubborn old level of anti-authoritarian Greek pride. Honestly, I wasn't sure I would ever get around that issue.

That is, until I discovered Ferdinand Mount.

Pawing through the Web one day for further clues on marriage, I stumbled on a curious-looking academic work titled *The Subversive Family* by a British author named Ferdinand

Mount. I promptly ordered the book and had my sister ship it to me in Bali. I loved the title and was certain this text would relay inspiring stories of couples who had somehow figured out ways to beat the system and undermine social authority, keeping true to their rebel roots, all within the institution of marriage. Perhaps I would find my role models here!

Indeed, subversion was the topic of this book, but not at all in the manner I'd expected. This was hardly a seditious manifesto, which shouldn't have been surprising given that it turns out Ferdinand Mount (beg pardon — make that Sir William Robert Ferdinand Mount, 3rd Baronet) is a conservative columnist for the London *Sunday Times.* I can honestly say that I never would have ordered this book had I known that fact in advance. But I'm happy that I did find it, because sometimes salvation comes to us in the most unlikely of forms, and Sir Mount (*surmount?*) did provide me with a sort of rescue, offering up an idea about matrimony that was radically different from anything I'd unearthed before.

Mount — I'll eschew his title from here on out — suggests that all marriages are automatic acts of subversion against authority. (All nonarranged marriages, that is.

Which is to say all nontribal, nonclannish, non-property-based marriages. Which is to say Western marriage.) The families that grow out of such willful and personal unions are subversive units, too. As Mount puts it: "The family *is* a subversive organization. In fact, it is the ultimate and only consistently subversive organization. Only the family has continued throughout history, and still continues, to undermine the State. The family is the enduring permanent enemy of all hierarchies, churches and ideologies. Not only dictators, bishops and commissars but also humble parish priests and café intellectuals find themselves repeatedly coming up against the stony hostility of the family and its determination to resist interference to the last."

Now that is some seriously strong language, but Mount builds a compelling case. He suggests that because couples in nonarranged marriages join together for such deeply private reasons, and because those couples create such secret lives for themselves within their union, they are innately threatening to anybody who wants to rule the world. The first goal of any given authoritarian body is to inflict control on any given population, through coercion, indoctrination, intimidation, or propaganda. But authority figures, much to their frustration, have never been able to entirely control, or even monitor, the most secret intimacies that pass between two people who sleep together on a regular basis.

Even the Stasi of communist East Germany — the most effective totalitarian police force the world has ever known — could not listen in on every single private conversation in every single private household at three o'clock in the morning. Nobody has ever been able to do this. No matter how modest or trivial or serious the pillow talk, such hushed hours belong exclusively to the two people who are sharing them with each other. What passes between a couple alone in the dark is the very definition of the word "privacy." And I'm talking not just about sex here but about its far more subversive aspect: *intimacy.* Every couple in the world has the potential over time to become a small and isolated nation of two — creating their own culture, their own language, and their own moral code, to which nobody else can be privy.

Emily Dickinson wrote, "Of all the Souls that stand create — / I have elected — One." That right there — the idea that, for our own private reasons, many of us do end up electing one person to love and defend above all others — is a situation that has exasperated family, friends, religious institutions, political movements, immigration officials, and military bodies forever. That selection, that narrowness of intimacy is maddening to anyone who longs to control you. Why do you think American slaves were never legally permitted to marry? Because it was far too dangerous for slave owners to even consider allowing a person held in captivity to experience the wide range of emotional freedom and innate secrecy that marriage can cultivate. Marriage represented a kind of liberty of the heart, and none of that business could be tolerated within an enslaved population.

For this reason, as Mount argues, powerful entities across the ages have always tried to undercut natural human bonds in order to increase their own power. Whenever a new revolutionary movement or cult or religion comes to town, the game always begins the same way: with an effort to separate you — the individual — from your preexisting loyalties. You must swear a blood oath of utter allegiance to your new overlords, masters, dogma, godhead, or nation. As Mount writes, "You are to renounce all other worldly goods and attachments and follow the Flag or the Cross or the Crescent or the Hammer and Sickle." In short, you must disown your real family and swear that *we are your family now.* In addition, you must embrace the new, externally mandated, family-like arrangements that have been imposed on you (like the monastery, the kibbutz, the party cadre, the commune, the platoon, the gang, etc.). And if you choose to honor your wife or husband or lover above the collective, you have somehow failed and betrayed the movement, and you shall be denounced as selfish, backwards, or even treasonous.

But people keep doing it anyhow. They keep on resisting the collective and electing one person among the masses to love. We saw this happen in the early days of Christianity — remember? The early church fathers instructed quite clearly that people were now to choose celibacy over marriage. That was to be the new social construct. While it's true that some early converts did become celibate, most decidedly did not. Eventually the Christian leadership had to cave and accept that marriage was not going away. The Marxists encountered the same problem when they tried to create a new world order in which children would be raised in communal nurseries, and where there would be no particular attachments whatsoever between couples. But the communists didn't have any more luck enforcing that idea than the early Christians had. The fascists didn't have any luck with it either. They *influenced* the shape of marriage, but they couldn't *eliminate* marriage.

Nor could the feminists, I must admit in all fairness. Early on in the feminist revolution, some of the more radical activists shared a utopian dream in which, given the choice, liberated women would forever select bonds of sisterhood and solidarity over the repressive institution of marriage. Some of those activists, like the feminist separatist Barbara Lipschutz, went so far as to suggest that women should quit having sex altogether — not only with men, but also with other women — because sex was always going to be a demeaning and oppressive act. Celibacy and friendship, therefore, would be the new models for female relationships. "Nobody Needs to Get Fucked" was the title of Lipschutz's infamous essay — which is not exactly how Saint Paul might have phrased it, but essentially came down to the exact same principles: that carnal encounters are always tarnishing, and that romantic partners, at the very least, distract us from our loftier and more honorable destinies. But Lipschutz and her followers didn't have any more luck eradicating the desire for private sexual intimacy than the early Christians, or the communists or the fascists. A lot of women — even very smart and liberated women — ended up choosing private partnerships with men anyhow. And what are today's most activist feminist lesbians fighting for? *The right to get married.* The right to become parents, to create families, to have access to legally binding unions. They want to be *inside* matrimony, shaping its history from within, not standing outside the thing throwing stones at its grotty old façade.

Even Gloria Steinem, the very face of the American feminist movement, decided to get married for the first time in the year 2000. She was sixty-six years old on her wedding day and just as brilliant as ever; one has to assume she knew exactly what she was doing. To some of her followers, though, it felt like a betrayal, as though a saint had fallen from grace. But it's important to note that Steinem herself saw her marriage as a celebration of feminism's victories. As she explained, had she gotten married back in the 1950s, back when she was "supposed to," she would have effectively become her husband's chattel —

or at the very most his clever helpmeet, like Phyllis the math whiz. By the year 2000, though, thanks in no small part to her own tireless efforts, marriage in America had evolved to the point where a woman could be both a wife and a human being, with all her civil rights and liberties intact. But Steinem's decision still disappointed a lot of passionate feminists, who could not get over the stinging insult that their fearless leader had chosen a man over the collective sisterhood. Of all the souls in creation, even Gloria had elected *one* — and that decision left everybody else out.

But you cannot stop people from wanting what they want, and a lot of people, as it turns out, want intimacy with one special person. And since there is no such thing as intimacy without privacy, people tend to push back very hard against anybody or anything that interferes with the simple desire to be left alone with a loved one. Although authoritarian figures throughout history have tried to curb this desire, they can't get us to quit it. We just keep insisting on the right to link ourselves up to another soul legally, emotionally, physically, materially. We just keep on trying, again and again, no matter how ill-advised it may be, to re-create Aristophanes' two-headed, eight-limbed figure of seamless human union.

I see this urge playing out everywhere around me, and sometimes in the most surprising forms. Some of the most unconventional, heavily tattooed, antiestablishmentarian, and socially rebellious people I know get married. Some of the most sexually promiscuous people I know get married (often to disastrous effect — but still, they do try). Some of the most misanthropic people I know get married, despite what appears to be their equal-opportunity distaste for humanity. In fact, I know of very few people who haven't *attempted* a long-term monogamous partnership at least once in their lives, in one form or another — even if they never legally or officially sealed those vows inside a church or a judge's chambers. In fact, most people I know have experimented with long-term monogamous partnerships several times over — even if their hearts may have been utterly destroyed by this effort before.

Even Felipe and I — two dodgy survivors of divorce who prided ourselves on a certain degree of bohemian autonomy — had started creating a little world for ourselves that looked suspiciously like marriage long before the immigration authorities ever got involved. Before we'd ever heard of Officer

Tom, we had been living together, making plans together, sleeping together, sharing resources, building lives around each other, excluding other people from our relationship — and what do you call that, if not marriage? We'd even had a ceremony to seal our fidelity. (Hell, we'd had *two!*) We were shaping our lives in that particular form of partnership because we yearned for something. As so many of us do. We yearn for private intimacy even though it's emotionally risky. We yearn for private intimacy even when we suck at it. We yearn for private intimacy even when it's illegal for us to love the person we love. We yearn for private intimacy even when we are told that we should yearn for something else, something finer, something nobler. *We just keep on yearning for private intimacy,* and for our own deeply personal set of reasons. Nobody has ever been able to completely sort out that mystery, and nobody has ever been able to stop us from wanting it.

As Ferdinand Mount writes, "Despite all official efforts to downgrade the family, to reduce its role and even to stamp it out, men and women obstinately continue not merely to mate and produce children but to insist on living in pairs together." (And I would add to this thought, by the way, that men and men also keep insisting on living in pairs together. And that women and women also keep insisting on living in pairs together. All of which just drives the authorities crazier still.)

Faced with this reality, repressive authorities always eventually surrender in the end, bowing at last to the inevitability of human partnership. But they don't go down without a fight, those pesky powers-that-be. There is a pattern to their surrender, a pattern that Mount suggests is consistent across Western history. First, the authorities slowly glean that they are unable to stop people from choosing loyalty to a partner over allegiance to some higher cause, and that marriage is therefore not going away. But once they have given up trying to *eliminate* marriage, the authorities now attempt to *control* it by establishing all sorts of restrictive laws and limits around the custom. When the church fathers finally surrendered to matrimony's existence in the Middle Ages, for instance, they immediately heaped on the institution a giant pile of tough new conditions: There would be no divorce; marriage would now be an inviolable holy sacrament; nobody would be allowed to marry outside of a priest's purview; women must bow to the laws of coverture; etc. And then the church went a little crazy, trying to enforce all this control over marriage, right down to the most intimate level of private marital sexuality.

In Florence during the 1600s, for instance, a monk (ergo celibate) named Brother Cherubino was entrusted with the extraordinary task of writing a handbook for Christian husbands and wives that would clarify rules for what was considered acceptable sexual intercourse within Christian marriage and what was not. "Sexual activity," Brother Cherubino instructed, "should not involve the eyes, nose, ears, tongue, or any other part of the body that is in no way necessary for procreation." The wife could look at her husband's private parts, but only if he was sick, and not because it was exciting, and "never allow yourself, woman, to be seen in the nude by your husband." And while it was permissible for Christians to bathe every now and again, it was, of course, terribly wicked to try to make yourself smell good in order to be sexually attractive to your spouse. Also, you must never kiss your spouse using your tongue. Not *anywhere!* "The devil knows how to do so much between husband and wife," Brother Cherubino lamented. "He makes them touch and kiss not only the honest parts but the dishonest ones as well. Even just to think about it, I am overwhelmed by horror, fright and bewilderment . . .”

Of course, as far as the church was concerned, the most horrible, frightening, and bewildering thing of all was that the matrimonial bed was so private and therefore so ultimately uncontrollable. Not even the most vigilant of Florentine monks could stop the explorations of two private tongues in one private bedroom in the middle of the night. Nor could any one monk control what all those tongues were talking about once the lovemaking was over — and this was perhaps the most threatening reality of all. Even in that most repressive age, once the doors were closed and the people could make their own choices, each couple defined its own terms of intimate expression.

In the end, the couples tend to win.

Once the authorities have failed at *eliminating* marriage, and once they have failed at *controlling* marriage, they give up and embrace the matrimonial tradition completely. (Amusingly, Ferdinand Mount calls this the signing of a “one-sided peace treaty.”) But then comes an even more curious stage: Like clockwork, the powers-that-be will now try to co-opt the notion of matrimony, going so far as to pretend that they invented marriage in the first place. This is what conservative Christian leadership has been doing in the Western world for several centuries now — acting as though they personally *created* the whole tradition of marriage and family values when in fact their religion began with a quite serious attack on marriage and family values.

This is the pattern that happened with the Soviets and with the twentieth-century Chinese, too. First, the communists tried to eliminate marriage; then they tried to control marriage; then they fabricated an entirely new mythology claiming that "the family" had always been the backbone of good communistic society anyhow, don't you know.

Meanwhile, throughout all this contorted history, throughout all the thrashing and frothing of dictators and despots and priests and bullies, people just keep on getting married — or whatever you want to call it at any given time. Dysfunctional and disruptive and ill-advised though their unions may be — or even secret, illegal, unnamed, and renamed — people continue to insist on merging with each other on their own terms. They cope with all the changing laws and work around all the limiting restrictions of the day in order to get what they want.

Or they flat-out *ignore* all the limiting restrictions of the day! As one Anglican minister in the American colony of Maryland complained in 1750, if he had been forced to recognize as "married" only those couples who had legally sealed their vows in a church, he would have had to "bastardize nine-tenths of the People in this County."

People don't wait for permission; they go ahead and create what they need. Even African slaves in early America invented a profoundly subversive form of marriage called the "besom wedding," in which a couple jumped over a broomstick stuck aslant in a doorway and called themselves married. And nobody could stop those slaves from making this hidden commitment in a moment of stolen invisibility.

Seen in this light, then, the whole notion of Western marriage changes for me — changes to a degree that feels quietly and personally revolutionary. It's as if the entire historical picture shifts one delicate inch, and suddenly everything aligns itself into a different shape. Suddenly, legal matrimony starts to look less like an *institution* (a strict, immovable, hidebound, and dehumanizing system imposed by powerful authorities on helpless individuals) and starts to look more like a rather desperate *concession* (a scramble by helpless authorities to monitor the unmanageable behavior of two awfully powerful individuals).

It is not we as individuals, then, who must bend uncomfortably around the institution of marriage; rather, it is the institution of marriage that has to bend uncomfortably around *us.* Because "they" (the powers-that-be) have never been entirely able to stop "us" (two people) from connecting our lives together and creating a secret world of our own. And so "they" eventually have no choice but to legally permit "us" to marry, in some shape or form, no matter how restrictive their ordinances may appear. The government hops along behind its people, struggling to keep up, desperately and belatedly (and often ineffectually and even comically) creating rules and mores around something we were always going to do anyhow, like it or not.

So perhaps I've had this story deliciously backwards the whole time. To somehow suggest that society invented marriage, and then forced human beings to bond with each other, is perhaps absurd. It's like suggesting that society invented dentists, and then forced people to grow teeth. *We* invented marriage. Couples invented marriage. We also invented divorce, mind you.

446

And we invented infidelity, too, as well as romantic misery. In fact, we invented the whole damn sloppy mess of love and intimacy and aversion and euphoria and failure. But most importantly of all, most subversively of all, most stubbornly of all, we invented *privacy.*

To a certain extent, then, Felipe was right: Marriage is a game. They (the anxious and powerful) set the rules. We (the ordinary and subversive) bow obediently before those rules. *And then we go home and do whatever the hell we want anyhow.*

Do I sound like I'm trying to talk myself into something here?

People, I *am* trying to talk myself into something here.

This entire book — every single page of it — has been an effort to search through the complex history of Western marriage until I could find some small place of comfort in there for myself. Such comfort is not necessarily always an easy thing to find. On my friend Jean's wedding day over thirty years ago, she asked her mother, "Do all brides feel this terrified when they're about to get married?" and her mother replied, even as she calmly buttoned up her daughter's white dress, "No, dear. Only the ones who are actually thinking."

Well, I have been thinking very hard about all this. The leap into marriage has not come easily for me, but perhaps it shouldn't be easy. Perhaps it's fitting that I needed to be persuaded into marriage — even vigorously persuaded — especially because I am a woman, and because matrimony has not always treated women kindly.

Some cultures seem to understand the need for feminine marital persuasion better than others. In some cultures, the task of vigorously enticing a woman to accept a marriage proposal has evolved into a ceremony, or even an art form, in its own right. In Rome, in the working-class neighborhood of Trastevere, a powerful tradition still dictates that a young man who wants to marry a young woman must publicly serenade his lover outside her home. He must beg for her hand in song, right out there in the open where everyone can witness it. Of course, a lot of Mediterranean cultures have this kind of tradition, but in Trastevere, they really go all out with it.

The scene always begins the same way. The young man comes to his beloved's house with a group of male friends and any number of guitars. They gather under the young woman's window and belt out — in loud, rough, local dialect — a song with the decidedly unromantic title *"Roma, nun fa'la stupida stasera!"* ("Rome, don't be an idiot tonight!") Because the young man is not, in fact, singing directly to his beloved; he doesn't dare to. What he wants from her (her hand, her life, her body, her soul, her devotion) is so monumental that it's too terrifying to speak the request directly. Instead, he directs his song to the entire city of Rome, shouting at Rome with an emotional urgency that is raw, crass, and insistent. With all his heart, he begs the city itself to please help him tonight in beguiling this woman into marriage.

"Rome, don't be an idiot tonight!" the young man sings beneath the girl's window. "Give me some help! Take the clouds away from the face of the moon, just for us! Shine forth your most brilliant stars! Blow, you son-of-a-bitch Western wind! Blow your perfumed air! Make it feel like spring!"

When the first strains of this familiar song start wafting through the neighborhood, everyone comes to their windows, and thus commences the amazing audience-participation portion of the evening's entertainment. All the men within earshot lean out of their apartments and shake their fists at the sky, scolding the city of Rome for not assisting the boy more actively with his marriage plea. All the men belt out in unison, "Rome, don't be an idiot tonight! Give him some help!"

Then the young woman herself — the object of desire — comes to her window. She has a verse of the song to sing, too, but her words are critically different. When her chorus comes around, she also begs Rome not to be an idiot tonight. She also begs the city to help her. But what she is begging for is something else altogether. She is begging for the strength to refuse the offer of marriage.

"Rome, don't be an idiot tonight!" she implores in song. "Please put those clouds back across the moon! Hide your most brilliant stars! Stop blowing, you son-of-a-bitch Western wind! Hide the perfumed air of spring! Help me to resist!"

All the women in the neighborhood lean out *their* apartment windows and sing along loudly with the girl, "Please, Rome — give her some help!"

It becomes a desperate duel between the men's voices and the women's voices. The scene becomes so pitched that it honestly starts to feel as though all the women of Trastevere are begging for their lives. Strangely, though, it feels like all the men of

Trastevere are begging for their lives, too.

In the fervor of the exchange, it's easy to lose sight of the fact that, in the end, this is just a game. From the first moment of the serenade, after all, everyone knows how the story will conclude. If the young woman has come to her window at all, if she has even glanced down at her suitor in the street, it means she has already accepted his wedding proposal. By merely engaging in her half of the spectacle, the girl has demonstrated her love. But out of some sense of pride (or perhaps out of some very justifiable sense of fear), the young woman must stall — if only to give voice to her doubts and hesitations. She must make it perfectly clear that it will take all the mighty powers of this young man's love, combined with all the epic beauty of Rome, and all the brilliance of the starlight, and all the seduction of the full moon, and all the perfume of that son-of-a-bitch Western wind before she concedes her *yes.*

Given what she is agreeing to, one might argue that all this spectacle and all this resistance is necessary.

In any case, that is what I've needed, too — a clamorous song of self-persuasion about marriage, belted out in my own street, underneath my own window, until I could

451

finally relax into my own acceptance. That has been the purpose of this effort all along. Forgive me, then, if, at the end of my story, I seem to be grasping at straws in order to reach comforting conclusions about matrimony. I need those straws; I need that comfort. Certainly I have needed Ferdinand Mount's reassuring theory that, if you look at marriage in a certain light, you can make a case for the institution being intrinsically subversive. I received that theory as a great and soothing balm. Now, maybe that theory doesn't work for you personally. Maybe you don't need it the way I needed it. Maybe Mount's thesis isn't even entirely historically accurate. Nonetheless, *I will take it.* Like a good almost-Brazilian, I will take this one verse of the persuasion song and make it my own — not only because it heartens me, but because it actually also excites me.

In so doing, I have finally found my own little corner within matrimony's long and curious history. So that is where I will park myself — right there in this place of quiet subversion, in full remembrance of all the other stubbornly loving couples across time who also endured all manner of irritating and invasive bullshit in order to get what they ultimately wanted: a little bit of privacy in which to practice love.

Alone in that corner with my sweetheart at last, all shall be well, and all shall be well, and all manner of thing shall be well.

CHAPTER EIGHT: MARRIAGE AND CEREMONY

NOTHING NEW HERE EXCEPT
MY MARRYING, WHICH TO ME IS A
MATTER OF PROFOUND WONDER.
*— Abraham Lincoln,
in an 1842 letter to Samuel Marshall*

Things moved very quickly after that.

By December 2006, Felipe still hadn't secured his immigration papers, but we sensed that victory was coming. Actually, we *decided* that victory was coming and so we went ahead and did the one specific thing the Department of Homeland Security expressly tells you not to do if you are waiting for a partner's immigration visa to be cleared: We made plans.

The first priority? We needed a place to settle permanently once we were married. Enough renting, enough wandering. We needed a house of our own. So while I was still there in Bali with Felipe, I started seriously and openly searching for homes on the Internet, looking for something rural and quiet located within a comfortable driving distance of my sister in Philadelphia. It's a crazy thing to look at houses when you can't, in fact, *look* at any of the houses, but I had a clear vision of what we needed — a home inspired by a poem my friend Kate Light once wrote about her version of perfect domesticity: "A house in the country to find out what's true / a few linen shirts, some good art / and you."

I knew I would recognize the place when I found it. And then I did find it, hidden in a small mill town in New Jersey. Or rather, it wasn't really a house, but a church — a tiny, square Presbyterian chapel, built in 1802, that somebody had cleverly converted into a living space. Two bedrooms, a compact kitchen, and one big open sanctuary where the congregation used to gather. Fifteen-foot-tall wavy glass windows. A big maple tree in the front yard. This was it. From the other side of the planet, I put down a bid without ever having seen the property in person. A few days later, over there in distant New Jersey, the owners accepted my offer.

"We have a house!" I announced triumphantly to Felipe.

"That's marvelous, darling," he said. "Now all we need is a country."

So I set forth to secure us a country, damn it. I went back to the States alone, right before Christmas, and took care of all our business. I signed the closing papers on our new house, got our belongings out of storage, leased a car, bought a mattress. I found warehouse space in a nearby village where we could relocate Felipe's gemstones and goods. I registered his business as a New Jersey corporation. All this before we even knew for sure if he would be allowed back into the country. I settled us in, in other words, before we were even officially an "us."

Meanwhile, back in Bali, Felipe plunged into the last frantic preparations for his upcoming interview at the American Consulate in Sydney. As the date for his interview approached (it was alleged to be sometime in January), our long-distance conversations became almost entirely administrative. We lost all sense of romance — there was no time for it — as I studied the bureaucratic checklists a dozen times over, making sure he had assembled every single piece of paper that he would eventually need to turn over to the American authorities. Instead of sending him messages of love, I was now sending e-mails that read, "Darling, the lawyer says that I need to drive to Philly and pick up the forms from him in person, since they have a special barcode and cannot be faxed. Once I mail these to you, the first thing you need to do is sign/date Form

DS-230 Part I and send it to the consulate with the addendum. You will need to bring the original DS-156 document and all the other immigration documents to the interview — but remember: Until you are right there in the presence of the American interviewing officer, DO NOT SIGN FORM DS-156!!!!"

At the next-to-last minute, though, only a few days before the scheduled interview, we realized we had fumbled. We were missing a copy of Felipe's police record from Brazil. Or, rather, we were missing a document that would prove that Felipe did not *have* a police record in Brazil. Somehow this critical piece of the dossier had escaped our attention. What followed was a horrible flurry of panic. Would this delay the whole process? Was it even possible to secure a Brazilian police report without Felipe's having to fly to Brazil to pick it up in person?

After a few days of incredibly complicated transglobal phone calls, Felipe managed to convince our Brazilian friend Armenia — a woman of celebrated charisma and resourcefulness — to stand in line all day at a Rio de Janeiro police station and sweet-talk an official there into releasing Felipe's clean Brazilian police records over to her. (There was a certain poetic symmetry to the fact that she rescued us in the end, given that she was the person who had introduced us to each other three years before at a dinner party in Bali.) Then Armenia overnighted those documents from Brazil to Felipe in Bali — just in time for him to fly to Jakarta during a monsoon in order to find an authorized translator who could render all his Brazilian paperwork into the necessary English in the presence of the only American-government-authorized Portuguese-speaking legal notary in the entire nation of Indonesia.

"It's all very straightforward," Felipe assured me, calling me in the middle of the night from a bicycle rickshaw in the pouring Javanese rain. "We can do this. We can do this. We can do this."

On the morning of January 18, 2007, Felipe was the first person in line at the U.S. Consulate in Sydney. He hadn't slept in days but he was ready, carrying a terrifyingly complex stack of papers: government records, medical exams, birth certificates, and masses of other sundry evidence. He hadn't gotten a haircut in a long while and he was still wearing his travel sandals. But it was fine. They didn't care how he looked, only that he was legitimate. And despite a few testy questions from the immigration official about what exactly Felipe had been doing in the Sinai Peninsula in 1975 (the answer? falling in love with a beautiful seventeen-year-old Israeli girl, naturally), the interview went well. At the end of it all, finally — with that satisfying, librarian-like *thunk* in his passport — they gave him the visa.

"Good luck on your marriage," said the American official to my Brazilian fiancé, and Felipe was free.

He caught a Chinese Airlines flight the next morning from Sydney, which took him through Taipei and then over to Alaska. In Anchorage, he successfully passed through American customs and immigration and boarded a plane for JFK. A few hours later, I drove through an icy-cold winter's night to meet him.

And while I would like to think that I had held myself together with a modicum of stoicism during the previous ten months, I must confess that I now absolutely fell apart as soon as I arrived at the airport. All the fears that I had been suppressing since Felipe's arrest came spilling out in the open now that he was so close to being safely home. I became dizzy and shaky, and I was suddenly afraid of everything. I was afraid that I was in the wrong airport, at the wrong hour, on the wrong day. (I must have looked at the itinerary seventy-five times, but I still worried.) I was afraid that Felipe's plane had crashed. I was retroactively and quite insanely afraid that he would fail his immigration interview back in Australia — when he had, in fact, just *passed* his immigration interview back in Australia only a day earlier.

And even now, even though the Arrivals board clearly announced that his flight had landed, I was perversely afraid that his flight had *not* landed, and that it would never land. *What if he didn't get off the plane? What if he got off the plane and they arrested him again? Why was it taking him so long to get off the plane?* I scanned the faces of every passenger who came down that Arrivals corridor, searching for Felipe in the most preposterous of forms. Irrationally, I had to look twice at every single old Chinese lady with a cane and every single toddling child, just to make doubly sure that it wasn't him. I was having trouble breathing. Like a lost kid, I almost ran over to a policeman and asked for help — but help with *what?*

Then, suddenly, it was him.

I would know him anywhere. The most familiar face in the world to me. He was running down the Arrivals corridor, looking for me with the same anxious expression that I was surely sporting myself. He had on the same clothes he'd been wearing the day he'd been arrested back in Dallas ten months earlier — the same clothes he'd been wearing pretty much every day of this whole year, all over the world. He was a bit tattered around the edges, yes, but somehow he seemed mighty to me nonetheless, his eyes burning with the effort to spot me in the crowd. He was not an old Chinese lady, he was not a toddling child, he was not anybody else. He was Felipe — my Felipe, my human, my cannonball — and then he saw me and he barreled down on me and almost knocked me over with the sheer force of his impact.

"We have circled and circled till we have arrived home again, we two," wrote Walt Whitman. "We have voided all but freedom and all but our own joy."

And now we could not let go of each other, and for some reason I simply could not stop sobbing.

Within a handful of days, we were married.

We got married in our new home — in that odd, old church — on a cold Sunday afternoon in February. It's very convenient, it turns out, to own a church when one has to get married.

The marriage license cost us twenty-eight dollars and a photocopy of one utility bill. The guests were: my parents (married forty years); my Uncle Terry and Aunt Deborah (married twenty years); my sister and her husband (married fifteen years); my friend Jim Smith (divorced for twenty-five years); and Toby the family dog (never married, bi-curious). We all wished that Felipe's children (unmarried) could have joined us, too, but the wedding happened on such short notice that there was no way to get them over in time from Australia. We had to make do with a few excited phone calls, but could not risk a delay. We needed to seal this deal immediately to protect Felipe's place on American soil with an inviolable legal bond.

In the end, we had decided that we wanted a few witnesses at our wedding after all. My friend Brian was right: Marriage is not an act of private prayer. Instead, it is both a public and a private concern, with real-world consequences. While the intimate terms of our relationship would always belong solely to Felipe and me, it was important to remember that a small share of our marriage would always belong to our families as well — to all those people who would be most seriously affected by our success or our failure. They needed to be present on that day, then, in order to emphasize this point. I also had to admit that another small share of our vows, like it or not, would always belong to the State. That's what made this a legal wedding in the first place after all.

But the smallest and most curiously shaped share of our vows belonged to history — at whose impressively large feet we all must kneel eventually. Wherever you have landed in history determines to a large extent what your marriage vows will look like and sound like. Since Felipe and I happened to have landed right there, in that little Garden State mill town, in the year 2007, we decided not to write our own idiosyncratic personal promises (we had done that back in Knoxville anyhow), but to acknowledge our place in history by repeating the basic, secular vows of the State of New Jersey. It just felt like an appropriate nod to reality.

Of course, my niece and nephew attended the wedding, too. Nick, the theatrical genius, was on hand to read a commemorative poem. And Mimi? She had cornered me a week earlier and asked, "Is this going to be a *real* wedding or not?"

"That all depends," I'd said. "What do

you think constitutes a real wedding?"

"A real wedding means there will be a flower girl," Mimi replied. "And the flower girl will be wearing a pink dress. And the flower girl will be carrying flowers. Not a *bouquet* of flowers, but a *basket* of rose petals. And not pink rose petals, either, but *yellow* rose petals. And the flower girl will walk in front of the bride, and she will throw the yellow rose petals on the ground. Will you be having anything like that?"

"I'm not sure," I said. "I guess it just depends on whether we can find a girl somewhere who might be capable of doing that job. Can you think of anyone?"

"I suppose *I* could do it," she replied slowly, looking away with a terrific show of false indifference. "I mean, if you can't find anyone else . . ."

So it turned out that we did have a real wedding, even by Mimi's exacting standards. Aside from our extremely decked-out flower girl, though, it was a pretty casual affair. I wore my favorite red sweater. The groom wore his blue shirt (the clean one). Jim Smith played his guitar, and my Aunt Deborah — a trained opera singer — sang "La Vie en Rose" just for Felipe's benefit. Nobody seemed to mind that the house was still unpacked and largely unfurnished. The only room that was fully usable thus far was the kitchen, and that was only so that Felipe could prepare a wedding lunch for everyone. He'd been cooking for two days, and we had to remind him to take off his apron when it came time to actually get married. ("A very good sign," my mother noted.)

Our wedding vows were administered by a nice man named Harry Furstenberger, the mayor of this small New Jersey township. When Mayor Harry first walked in the door, my father asked him directly, "Are you a Democrat or a Republican?" because he knew that this would matter to me.

"I'm a Republican," said Mayor Harry.

There followed a moment of tense silence. Then my sister whispered, "Actually, Liz, for this kind of thing, you sort of *want* a Republican. Just to make sure the marriage really sticks with Homeland Security, you know?"

So we proceeded.

You all know the gist of the standard American wedding vows, so I need not repeat them here. Suffice it to say, we repeated them there. Without irony or hesitation, we exchanged our vows in the presence of my family, in the presence of our friendly Republican mayor, in the presence of an actual flower girl, and in the presence of Toby the dog. In fact, Toby — sensing an important moment here — curled up on the floor right between Felipe and me just as we were sealing these promises. We had to lean over the dog in order to kiss each other. This felt auspicious; in medieval wedding portraits, you will often see the image of a dog painted between the figures of a newly wed couple — the ultimate symbol of *fidelity*.

By the end of it all — and it really doesn't take very much time, considering the magnitude of the event — Felipe and I were finally legally married. Then we all sat down for a long lunch together — the mayor and my friend Jim and my family and the kids and my new husband. I did not have any way of knowing with certainty on that afternoon what peace and contentment were awaiting me in this marriage (reader: *I know it now*), but I did feel calm and grateful all the same. It was a lovely day. There was much wine and there were many toasts. The balloons that Nick and Mimi had brought with them drifted slowly up to the dusty old church ceiling and bobbed there above us all. People might have lingered even longer, but by dusk it had begun to sleet, so our guests gathered together their coats and belongings, eager to get on the road while the getting was still good.

Soon enough, everyone was gone.

And Felipe and I were left alone together at last, to clean up the lunch dishes and begin unpacking our home.

ACKNOWLEDGMENTS

This book is a work of nonfiction. I have re-created all conversations and incidents to the best of my ability, but sometimes — for the sake of narrative coherence — I have edited down events or discussions that may have taken place over several days into one passage. Moreover, I have changed some — but not all — of the names of the characters in this story in order to protect the privacy of certain people who may not have intended, when their paths accidentally crossed mine, to show up later in a book. I thank Chris Langford for helping me track down appropriate aliases for these good people.

I am not a professional academic, nor a sociologist, nor a psychologist, nor an expert on marriage. I have done my best in this book to discuss the history of matrimony as accurately as possible, but in order to do so, I had to rely a great deal on the work of scholars and writers who have dedicated their entire professional lives to this topic. I won't list a full bibliography here, but I must offer special gratitude to a few specific authors:

The work of the historian Stephanie Coontz has been a shining beacon for me over these last three years of study, and I cannot recommend highly enough her fascinating and extremely readable book *Marriage: A History.* I also owe an enormous debt to Nancy Cott, Eileen Powers, William Jordan, Erika Uitz, Rudolph M. Bell, Deborah Luepnitz, Zygmunt Bauman, Leonard Shlain, Helen Fisher, John Gottman and Julie Schwartz-Gottman, Evan Wolfson, Shirley Glass, Andrew J. Cherkin, Ferdinand Mount, Anne Fadiman (for her extraordinary writing on the Hmong), Allan Bloom (for his contemplations on the Greek-Hebrew philosophical divide), the many authors of the Rutgers University study on marriage, and — most delightfully and unexpectedly of all — Honoré de Balzac.

Aside from these authors, the single most influential person in the shaping of this book has been my friend Anne Connell, who copyedited, fact-checked, and corrected this manuscript to within an inch of its life, using her bionic eyes, her magical golden pencil, and her unparalleled expertise with "the Web nets." Nobody — and I mean nobody — rivals the Scrutatrix for such editorial thoroughness. I have Anne to thank for the fact that this book is divided into chapters, that the word "actually" does not appear four times in every paragraph, and that every frog within these pages has been correctly identified as an amphibian and not a reptile.

I thank my sister Catherine Gilbert Murdock, who is not only a gifted writer of young adult fiction (her wonderful book *Dairy Queen* is a must-read for any thinking girl between the ages of ten and sixteen), but who is also my dearly beloved friend and the greatest intellectual role model of my life. She, too, read this book with time-consuming care, saving me from many errors of thought and sequence. That said, it is not so much Catherine's comprehensive grasp of Western history that amazes me but her uncanny talent for somehow knowing when her homesick sister needs to be airmailed a new pair of pajamas, even when that sister is all the way over in Bangkok and feeling very lonely. In return for all Catherine's kindness and generosity, I have offered her one lovingly crafted footnote.

I thank all the other early readers of this book for their insights and encouragement: Darcey, Cat, Ann (the word "pachyderm" is for her), Cree, Brian (this book will always be known as *Weddings and Evictions* just between us), Mom, Dad, Sheryl, Iva, Bernadette, Terry, Deborah (who gently suggested that I might want to mention the word "feminism" in a book about marriage), Uncle Nick (my most loyal supporter since forever), Susan, Shea (who listened to hours and hours and hours of my early ideas on this subject), Margaret, Sarah, Jonny, and John.

I thank Michael Knight for offering me a job and a room in Knoxville in 2005, and for knowing me well enough to realize that I would much prefer living in a crazy old residency hotel than anywhere else in town.

I thank Peter and Marianne Blythe for sharing their couch and their encouragement with Felipe when he landed in Australia desperate and fresh out of jail. With two new babies, a dog, a bird, and the wonderful young Tayla all living under one roof, the Blythes' house was already overflowing, but somehow Peter and Marianne made room for one more needy refugee. I also thank Rick and Clare Hinton in Canberra, for guiding the Australian end of Felipe's immigration process, and for watching diligently over the mail. Even from half a world away, they are perfect neighbors.

On the subject of great Australians, I thank Erica, Zo, and Tara — my amazing stepkids and daughter-in-law — for welcoming me so warmly into their lives. I must especially credit Erica for giving me the sweetest compliment of my life: "Thank you, Liz, for not being a bimbo." (My pleasure, sweetheart. And right back at you.)

I thank Ernie Sesskin and Brian Foster and Eileen Marolla for guiding — purely out of the real estate–loving goodness of their hearts — the entire complicated transaction of helping Felipe and me buy a house in New Jersey from the other side of the world. There's nothing like receiving a hand-drawn floor plan at three o'clock in the morning to know that somebody's got your back.

I thank Armenia de Oliveira for leaping into action in Rio de Janeiro to save Felipe's immigration process on that end. Also holding up the Brazilian front, as always, have been the wonderful Claucia and Fernando Chevarria — who were just as relentless in their pursuit of antique military records as they were in their encouragement and love.

I thank Brian Getson, our immigration

lawyer, for his thoroughness and patience, and I thank Andrew Brenner for helping us find Brian in the first place.

I thank Tanya Hughes (for offering me a room of my own at the beginning of this process) and Rayya Elias (for offering me a room of my own at the end).

I thank Roger LaPhoque and Dr. Charles Henn for their hospitality and elegance at the budget oasis of the Atlanta Hotel in Bangkok. The Atlanta is a wonder that must be seen to be believed, and even then it cannot really be believed.

I thank Sarah Chalfant for her endless confidence in me, and for her years of constant encircling protection. I thank Kassie Evashevski, Ernie Marshall, Miriam Feuerle, and Julie Mancini for completing that circle.

I thank Paul Slovak, Clare Ferraro, Kathryn Court, and everyone else at Viking Penguin for their patience as I wrote this book. There are not many people left in the world of publishing who would have said "Take as much time as you need" to a writer who had just missed a major deadline. Throughout this entire process, nobody (except myself) has put any pressure on me whatsoever, and that has been a rare gift. Their care hearkens back to an earlier and more gracious way of doing business, and I am grateful to have been the recipient of such decency.

I thank my family — especially my parents and my grandmother, Maude Olson — for not hesitating to allow me to explore in print my very personal feelings about some of their most complicated life decisions.

I thank Officer Tom of the United States Department of Homeland Security for treating Felipe with such an unexpected degree of kindness during his arrest and detention. And that is the most surreal sentence I have ever written in my life, but there it is. (We're not really sure that your name was actually "Tom," sir, but that's how we both remembered it, and I hope that at least you know who you are: a most unlikely agent of destiny who made a bad experience far less bad than it might have been.)

I thank Frenchtown for bringing us home.

Lastly, I offer my greatest gratitude to the man who is now my husband. He is a private person by nature, but unfortunately his privacy ended the day he met me. (He is now known to an awful lot of strangers around the world as "that Brazilian guy from *Eat, Pray, Love*.") In my defense, I have to say that I did give him an early chance to dodge all this exposure. Back when we were first courting, there came an awkward moment when I had to confess that I was a writer, and what that meant for him. If he stayed with me, I warned, he would eventually end up revealed in my books and in my stories. There was no way of getting around it; that's simply how it goes. His best chance, I made clear, would be to leave right then, while there was still time to escape with dignity and discretion intact.

Despite all my warnings, though, he stayed. And he stays with me still. I believe this has been a great act of love and compassion on his part. Somewhere along the line, this wonderful man seems to have recognized that my life would not have a coherent story line anymore without him at the center of it.

ABOUT THE AUTHOR

Elizabeth Gilbert is the author of a story collection, *Pilgrims* (a finalist for the PEN/ Hemingway Prize), a novel, *Stern Men*, the nonfiction book *The Last American Man* (a finalist for the National Book Award and the National Book Critics Circle Award), and most recently the bestseller *Eat, Pray, Love*, which was a *New York Times* hardcover bestseller for three weeks and has been on the trade paperback bestseller list for 133 weeks to date, 57 of those weeks at #1. *Eat, Pray, Love* has been published in more than 30 languages and the film of the book will be released by Columbia Pictures in the summer of 2010, starring Julia Roberts. For five years Gilbert worked as a journalist at *GQ* where her feature writing earned her three National Magazine Award nominations. *Time Magazine* named her one of the People of the Year for 2007.